# FOUNDATIONS

# OF

# MUSIC TECHNOLOGY

V. J. MANZO
*Worcester Polytechnic Institute*

New York     Oxford
OXFORD UNIVERSITY PRESS

Oxford University Press is a department of the University of Oxford.
It furthers the University's objective of excellence in research,
scholarship, and education by publishing worldwide.

Oxford   New York
Auckland   Cape Town   Dar es Salaam   Hong Kong   Karachi
Kuala Lumpur   Madrid   Melbourne   Mexico City   Nairobi
New Delhi   Shanghai   Taipei   Toronto

With offices in
Argentina   Austria   Brazil   Chile   Czech Republic   France   Greece
Guatemala   Hungary   Italy   Japan Poland   Portugal   Singapore
South Korea   Switzerland   Thailand   Turkey   Ukraine   Vietnam

For titles covered by Section 112 of the US Higher Education
Opportunity Act, please visit www.oup.com/us/he for the
latest information about pricing and alternate formats.

Published by Oxford University Press
198 Madison Avenue, New York, New York 10016
http://www.oup.com

Oxford is a registered trademark of Oxford University Press

**Library of Congress Cataloging-in-Publication Data**
Manzo, V. J.
   Foundations of music technology / V. J. Manzo.
      pages cm
   ISBN 978-0-19-936829-7 (alk. paper)
   1. Music--Computer programs. 2. Music--Acoustics and physics. 3. Computer
music--Instruction and study. 4. Electronic music--Instruction and study.
5. Music--Instruction and study--Technological innovations. I. Title.
   ML74.M34 2016
   786.7--dc23
                                                          2015007685

# FOUNDATIONS OF MUSIC TECHNOLOGY

# CONTENTS

# FOREWORD

## David Cope

*Composer, author, and Dickerson Emeriti Professor*
*at the University of California Santa Cruz*

Music technology is an emerging concentration within the field of music. It has influenced every music discipline in some way and has been most notably associated with the creation and use of electronic musical instruments, recording systems, and live sound production, to name just a few implementations. In this regard, the overarching term "music technology" may refer specifically to a composer building an interactive multimedia exhibit, a performer producing an album in which he or she performs all of the parts, an educator designing a computer lab with self-directed instructional software, or something completely different. In short, the scope of what we call "music technology" seemingly has no limits.

When V. J. contacted me to write a foreword for his new book, I was delighted to accept; the fact that he was including material on algorithmic music composition delighted me even more, given that so many books on the subject of computer music do not include a chapter, section, or even a paragraph on that unique aspect of what computers do so well—computational composition—in lieu of algorithms based exclusively on producing new digital sounds, as if computers are solely capable of being sophisticated musical instruments rather than giving us a powerful process to create whole musical compositions.

Digital computer music—I make the distinction "digital" here because a number of composers still use analog computers to do it—is clearly the *lingua franca* of much of today's contemporary and experimental music. For example, it is almost a given in popular music as well as much of today's contemporary classical music. Thus, a book like the one you are reading at this moment is worth its weight in gold, and not only for those who wish to create it but for those who want to appreciate it as well. V. J. has produced a valuable tool for everyone, not just a relatively small percentage of those participating in its production.

It is my pleasure to ignite your journey into the extraordinarily diverse and multifaceted world of music technology, a journey here both beautifully written and wonderfully captivating. So enjoy your reading and then appreciate more fully your experience in creating and listening to the joys of what our digital age has made possible.

Music has been and will continue to be enriched by a wonderful breadth of possibilities, limited only by our willingness to accept the new wonders of a world we've just begun to mine.

# INTRODUCTION

Welcome to this exploration of the *Foundations of Music Technology*. Whether you are a musician with zero technology skills beyond taking selfies, a technology wizard who reads binary code, but not music notation, or someone in between, this textbook will explain concepts of music technology in a straightforward manner and give examples of how the information can be used in a practical sense. Whatever your experiences are with both music and technology, we will tie theoretical concepts into real-life implementations that result in unique, creative, musical activities.

Many people believe that technology alone can transform them into creative musicians. This myth is spread through advertisements for the latest gadgets, software, and gear. The strange reality is that we probably have more music technology, music software, and music controllers and instruments than we need, and certainly more than we realistically know what to do with. Honestly, technology makes it really easy for anyone to create uninteresting music. However, music technology can offer accessibility with regard to music-making activities that traditional acoustic instruments and methods cannot. Coupled with an education in traditional aspects of music theory, counterpoint, and ear-training, an understanding of the functions and inner workings of various technologies can help facilitate a multitude of creative musical objectives.

In this book we will discuss technology and its uses as a mechanism to facilitate musicianship as well as a muse to spark creativity. Whether you are approaching this text with a background in music and limited technology skills or vice versa, I encourage you to think about what is discussed in a very practical way: how can I use this information to facilitate my creative ideas, be they performance, composition, education, or research? In our everyday lives, we encounter machines. from ATMs to coffeemakers, performing all sorts of tasks that make our lives easier, so why should our musical lives be any different? In this book, we'll most often use the word "technology" to refer to electronic devices like computers or software, but "technology" is really some mechanism to help reach some conclusion or solve some problem. For some, the path to incorporating technology into their music-making begins with a commitment to test the waters. As you begin or continue to pursue your musical goals by using different technologies, be patient: don't give up the first time you encounter a roadblock. Instead, think about your musical objectives and let that drive your use of technology.

## BOOK DESIGN

This book is divided into 14 chapters that address foundational concepts of music technology. Chapters 1 to 3 introduce the basic concepts of sound, audio recording, and playback devices, incorporating how computers can be used to make and record new sounds and works. We then introduce the concepts of digital synthesis and the related hardware and software in Chapter 4. There are several hands-on chapters that address issues related to digital notation, recording, and sequencing audio and MIDI (Chapters 5–7). Chapters 8–10 follow with a discussion of the principles of acoustics and digital audio effects. The book continues with Chapter 11–13, which describe specific uses of technology in music performance, music education, and music composition. Finally, an introduction to programming music software is offered in Chapter 14. Hands-on elements are included throughout the chapters that use the included Fundamentals of Music Technology (FMT) software.

This book assumes no previous knowledge of music technology. It is different from other books because it is not tied to a specific piece of software that will change in a few months. Instead, it introduces and demonstrates technology concepts that are universally shared by many applications through the use of small, intuitive, customized software-based lessons that address a single concept. When learning to record, for example, readers experience the concept by using a simple application with a minimal amount of labeled controls. Once the concepts are introduced and demonstrated, readers are referred to some of the popular software applications used by professionals. Having learned the basic concept and techniques using the included software, the skills should transfer to the reader's, or the instructor's, professional software application of choice.

As you proceed through this book, consider the ways in which the content relates to and help support your creative endeavors writing, performing, and, in general, being musical. Consider the audience that is going to be experiencing these creative endeavors of yours and the type of experience that is going to speak to them and then direct your projects toward that end. If your audience is going to enjoy something light and comical, write, perform, engineer, demonstrate, program, etc., along those lines. If the audience is going to enjoy something emotional and dramatic, then work along those lines. In general, consider the audience you want to reach, think about the experience that is going to reach them, and then design that experience; use music, words, and technology as necessary to reach your goals.

You took somewhat of a risk buying this book. Perhaps it was required for a class, but, then, you took a risk getting an education. Really, you're taking a bet on yourself that this education is going to some how reward you and be worth the time and money you put into it. I thank you for involving this book in that decision, and encourage you to consider and determine the ways in which the information will help you reach your musical goals.

## FOR INSTRUCTORS

The notion of a single, all-encompassing music technology textbook as the sole classroom resource is somewhat misleading; even when music technology texts are assigned, instructors vary with regard to the specific software they use. It's entirely common for an instructor to use one book to explain concepts of digital audio and another book for the particular software they're using—or no book at all. This textbook gives the instructor a resource to explain concepts and their historical development, demonstrate the concepts with the included hands-on software, make assignments, describe prominent projects and applications used in the music profession, and, yet, provide enough flexibility for the reader/instructor to take any direction regarding the professional software products they pursue.

The online Instructor Manual provides class lecture outlines for a 14-week semester using this textbook. It also provides specific illustrations to help explain various topics and suggestions for expanding upon the topics in the textbook. Each lecture outline concludes with suggested assignments that relate to and reinforce concepts introduced in the textbook. The Instructor Manual also contains homework and classwork assignments for each chapter

The book uses the companion Mac and PC software FMT to demonstrate concepts in a step-by-step guide. There is also a companion website with further resources for students. Additionally, the source code for FMT has been made available for the instructor or student to use.

## THE FMT SOFTWARE

### Downloading and Installation

The FMT software was developed for use as a companion to the *Foundations of Music Technology* book. There are many different music technology software applications in use by professionals; each professional may prefer a particular piece of software over another. In this book, concepts are explained using a single application, FMT, that simulates a variety of music technology concepts including operating a mixer, recording in a DAW, automating effects, creating synthesized sounds, and many more. As concepts are introduced in the book, the reader may demonstrate them using FMT, where each control, parameter, and function is labeled and described. As the concepts are learned, the acquired skills may transfer to the use of standard music technology software applications that facilitate these same concepts in a similar way, both operationally and graphically. This allows the reader to work through this book using any software application that they have available to them instead of being tied to what software they can afford buy or what their computer can run.

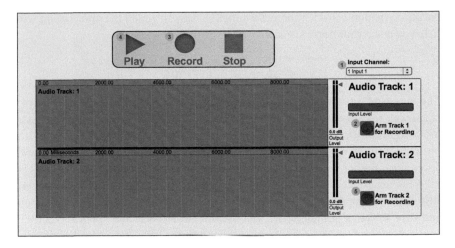

FIGURE I.1: Basic DAW recording concepts as presented in FMT

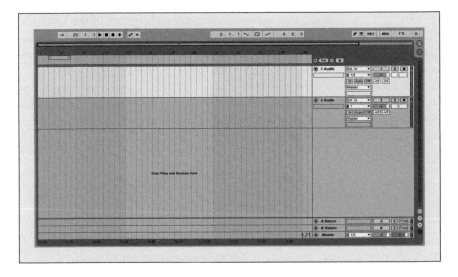

FIGURE I.2: DAW recording as presented in Ableton Live 9

The software may be downloaded from the Oxford University Press Companion website at www.oup.com/us/manzo or from the author's website at http://vjmanzo.com/oup/fmt.

- Download the FMT software for your Mac or Windows computers.
- Unzip the software by double clicking it once it has finished downloading.

On Windows, it is recommended that you do a COMPLETE install of Quick-Time (http://www.quicktime.com) prior to running the FMT software.

- Launch the software by clicking on the FMT icon.

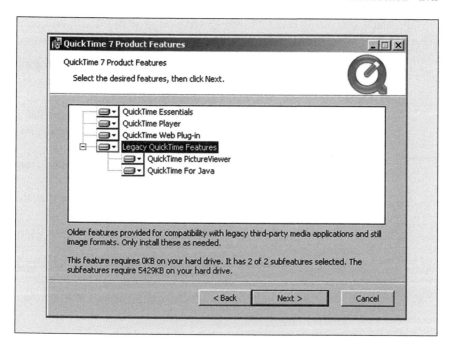

FIGURE I.3: Downloading and installing all additional QuickTime components on a Windows computer

## Open Source

The *FMT* source code is also available from the companion website. If you are stuck getting the program to load on your computer, you may download the *Max Runtime* application from http://www.cycling74.com and run the *FMT* application from the source code.

- Visit http://www.cycling74.com and download the latest *Max Runtime* application; you do not need to download the full *Max/MSP/Jitter* application.
- Download the *FMT* source code from the companion website or vjmanzo .com/oup/fmt.
- Unzip the source code and open the file *FMT.maxproj* with the *Max Runtime* application:
  - Open the *Runtime* application and select open from the file menu, then browse to the *FMT.maxproj* file.
  - On a Mac, you may also drag the *FMT.maxproj* file directly onto the *Runtime* application.

## Testing the App

Within the application, you will need to ensure that three components are working.

- Test that your playback *output* device is working.
- Test that your recording/microphone *input* device is working.
- Test that your MIDI *output* is working. (Note: Testing MIDI input is optional.)

By default, everything in the software should work as intended with your computer. However, complicated computer setups may affect the presets in the software.

- From within the FMT software, look at the main page window to get a sense of where the program controls for the *Master Volume, Audio Settings, Lesson Menu,* and *MIDI Keyboard & Settings* are located.
  - Read through the instructions in the main window and ensure that:
    - Your speaker output works by clicking the *Test Audio* button and listening for two *click* sounds to come from your speakers.
      - If not, choose the appropriate selection for your computer from the *Driver* and *Output* pull-down menus.
    - Your microphone input works by speaking and observing that the LED indicator illuminates in the main window.
      - If not, choose the appropriate selection for your computer from the *Input* pull-down menu.
    - Your MIDI output works by clicking on the graphical on-screen keyboard.
      - If not, choose the appropriate selection for your computer from the MIDI *Output* pull-down menu.

Note that not all lessons in FMT will require MIDI input and output (IO) or audio IO. The input and output methods for all lessons will be indicated in the text.

If you continue to experience difficulties, try using the software on a different computer and see if you experience the same issues. Additionally, you may access the error log on the front page.

## Basic Troubleshooting

The activities provided in this book have been tested, and you should not encounter any problems. However, if you give technology the chance, it will stab you in the back!

A few basic steps will help to make sure that you don't run into problems:

- Make sure you have downloaded **the latest companion files** for this book from the OUP website.
- **Save your work** frequently and keep your saved files organized. Don't accidentally overwrite files with the same name unless instructed to do so.
- **Follow the instructions** exactly as written.
- If you are still running into problems, save your work, **restart the program** completely, and reopen your work.
- **If your computer is being unresponsive, restart it.** Shut it down, wait for a minute or so, and turn it back on (don't forget to turn it back on as this is considered to be an important step).
- If for some reason you still encounter an error, you should try to **recreate the error** on a different computer to identify problems with your machine. It's always possible that your computer's volume is turned down, speakers unplugged, keyboard not working, etc.

- Apple computers tend to run audio applications more stably and with less delay, or *latency*, than Windows-based computers. However, either type of computer will work for the purpose of reading through this text.

Some concepts are a little tricky to understand, and you may have to reread something a few times before the concept sinks in. Consult the online companion resources if and when you get stuck. All in all, the concepts introduced in this book are not hard to learn, but they do require patience. Soon you'll get the hang of it and will be using technology to facilitate your creative ideas in no time. Enjoy!

# ACKNOWLEDGMENTS

I would like to thank all of my colleagues at Worcester Polytechnic Institute for their support and encouragement. To my colleagues in music technology, Frederick Bianchi and Scott Barton: thank you for your commitment to making music technology studies at WPI the most unique program I've seen. Thank you to Dean Karen Oates and my department head Kristen Boudreau for allowing and supporting our vision to make WPI an innovative place where books like this one can be written. Thank you to all of the students at WPI who have helped to test-drive this book—especially, Erica Bowden. Thanks!

To my colleagues in the Kean University Conservatory of Music: thank you for helping to shape my views about how technology can facilitate musicianship. To Matthew Halper: thank you for your friendship through the years and for supporting the notion that all this machinery making modern music can still be openhearted. To my colleagues at the New Jersey Institute of Technology and Montclair State University: thank you for your support and insight throughout my time there. Thank you to Michael Halper and Scott Skeebo for your continued standard of excellence doing good work in that area. To my colleagues in the Boyer College of Music and Dance at Temple University: thank you for your openness to spending time talking about my research ideas involving technology for music education during my doctoral years. To Alex Ruthman, David Elliot, and the music faculty at *NYU*: thank you for demonstrating the vast implications for technology in music. Thank you also to David Cope for writing the forward. To my colleagues in the Technology Institute for Music Educators (TI:ME) and the Association for Technology in Music Instruction (ATMI): thank you for your continued support and input about my work. Thank you Will Kuhn, my co-author for *Interactive Composition* (2015). Thank you Rick Dammers, Bill Bauer, and Dave Williams for your excitement and enthusiasm about using technology to reach the 80% of students that aren't part of their school's band, choir, or orchestra.

Thank you to Ableton, Cycling '74, the many members of the Ableton and Cycling '74 forums, and the numerous developers and artists throughout the world that contribute to this very unique community. Thank you, also, to all users of the Modal Object Library and the EAMIR SDK.

To Queen and Roy Thomas Baker—what could be better than *Queen II*, except, possibly, Queen? Your music from 1973 to 1978 is unparalleled by anything else happening at the time.

To Richard Carlin and Norm Hirschy at Oxford University Press: my continued thanks to you and the rest of the team for your professionalism and expertise during this process.

Of course, I would be lost without the continued support of my wife, Raquel. You should have escaped while you had the chance 'cause now you're stuck with me. Thanks also to my family and friends, and all of my pets. Thank you!

# CHAPTER 1

# PROPERTIES OF SOUND

## OVERVIEW

In this chapter we will discuss the basic properties of sound. This will include terms and concepts commonly associated with the field of physics such as waves, frequencies, and vibration. The discussion may seem more like a science lesson than a music one, but keep in mind that learning these concepts will allow you to better understand how music technology works and how it can be used to facilitate your musical objectives.

## WHAT IS SOUND?

We all have some internal definition of what a *sound* is: "It's something you hear with your ears"; "It has something to do with frequencies"; "It's a wave of pressure traveling from an instrument through the air to your ears bumping into all of the molecules along the way." In fact, sound is all of those things. A sound is a collection of waves that travel through some medium, most notably air. The term **wave** (or **sound wave**), for our purposes as musicians, refers to air pressure that moves through a room and is heard by the audience.

## FREQUENCIES

Waves move in a pattern that goes up and down; this movement is known as a **cycle**. We use the term **frequency** to describe the number of cycles a wave completes in one second.

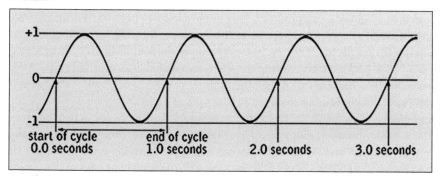

FIGURE 1.1: A sine wave completing one cycle each second

1

The wave shown in Figure 1.1 completes only one cycle per second. A wave traveling at twice that speed would complete two cycles in one second, or 2 **hertz** (abbreviated Hz). Using this terminology, a wave that completes 440 cycles in one second is said to move at 440 Hz.

## ☝ GO TO THE SOFTWARE LESSON: *SINE WAVE*

In the FMT companion software, choose the lesson *Sine Wave* from the pull-down menu. If necessary, slowly increase the main level slider at the top left of the software to hear the sound of this sine wave. Notice that this wave, called a **sine wave** or **sinusoid**, is moving, or **oscillating**, at 440 Hz.

- Locate the orange circle *1,* and change the frequency of this sine wave by clicking on the number 440 and typing in a new value, or by clicking and sliding the value up or down.

Notice that the number of waves shown in the window changes as you change the frequency value. Changing the knob on the left side of the wave window at the orange circle *2* will also change the size and strength of the wave; this is a property known as **amplitude**.

The frequency 440 has special significance to musicians since, as you may already know, it is the pitch *A* located above middle C and is commonly used as a reference pitch while tuning. However, you may belong to an orchestra that prefers to tune their A to 438 Hz or at 442 Hz, in both cases still referring to that pitch as A. The letter names we use in notation are meant to reference a frequency. If we wanted to be precise, we would say to a musician, "Play the notes based on the frequency 261.623 Hz, followed by 293.66 Hz, then 329.62 Hz," but it's easier to say, "Play the notes C, D, and E." Within the software, a graphical on-screen keyboard has been given that will play the frequency corresponding to the keys you click.

- Click the *A* and *C* arrows above the keyboard to play major scales ascending and descending.

The **oscillator** in this software creates a sine wave that repeats a cycle at the specified frequency. Suppose that you were able to swing your backpack over your head 440 times in one second. In this regard, you are the oscillator since you control the frequency of the cycle. In addition to the sounds of everything flying out of your backpack and hitting the walls, you would hear your backpack itself emit the pitch that we call A 440, the A above middle C. Suppose then that you got tired and could only swing your backpack at half that speed: 220 times per second. Your backpack's pitch would now sound like the *A* one octave below— the A below middle C. Suppose, then, that you then ate a candy bar and got the energy to speed back up to 440 times per second, back to the A above middle C, and then had so much energy that you were able to swing your backpack at twice that speed: 880 times per second! The pitch would no longer sound like the A above middle C, but the A two octaves above middle C.

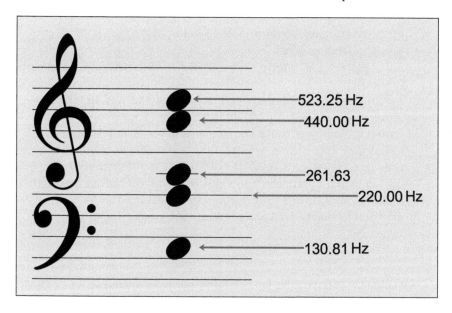

FIGURE 1.2: A few notes on the grand staff showing their frequency equivalent

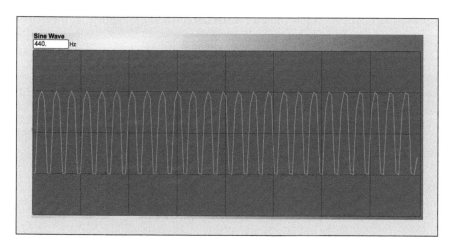

FIGURE 1.3: A 440 Hz sine wave generated within the companion software

## DID YOU KNOW?

### Tuning Systems

All cultures that produce music have some way of referencing the **octave**, typically as being twice the value of some pitch; for example, A 440 Hz and A 880 Hz. The way that the notes within that octave are realized is another concept related to the various tuning systems that exist. In most Western tuning systems, the octave is divided into 12 pitches or notes. In the most common tuning system used today, **equal temperament**, these 12 pitches are spaced equally in the octave.

In the past, tuning systems influenced the way in which music was composed for certain instruments. For example, early Baroque composers could not compose suites in unrelated keys unless they were willing to wait for the performers to retune their instruments. Today, many of the difficulties and shortcomings of implementing a particular non-equal temperament tuning system in traditional acoustic instruments can be alleviated with the use of digital tuning systems and software-based musical instruments in general.

Of course, it is impossible (and certainly not recommended!) for you to actually swing a backpack over your head as fast as 440 (or even 220) times per second. However, we do experience some form of this phenomenon every day. For example, when you step on the gas pedal of your car, your engine revs at a certain speed. The more gas you give it, the faster the engine spins and the higher the pitch goes.

## DID YOU KNOW?

### Singing Cars?

Visit the companion website for this book (www.oup.com/us/manzo or http://vjmanzo.com/oup/fmt) or simply search online for links to videos of people using their car engines to "sing" by programming computers to make the car engine rev at a sequence of different speeds.

In many ways, this is the basis of the ways that synthesizers work. There are similarities in the mechanics of many instruments, from a guitar string vibrating, to a car engine spinning, to your backpack swinging over your head. The real difference is in the particular characteristic of each instrument—the characteristic that lets you distinguish a middle C played on the piano from a middle C played on the trumpet. That characteristic is called timbre.

## TIMBRE

**Timbre** is the property of a sound that we, as musicians, refer to as **tone** or **tone color**. As you have probably noticed from playing with the software oscillator, the sine wave it produces hardly resembles a traditional acoustic instrument like a piano or a violin. The reason is because when a note is played on one of these acoustic instruments, it's not a single sine wave that is sounded but, actually, a large number of waves that are sounded simultaneously at different levels.

If you partially cover your mouth while you speak, you might describe your vocal tone as sounding a little "muddy," "dark," or "covered." In essence, you are blocking or "filtering" certain frequencies from coming through like they normally would, and as a result, the timbre of your voice is changed. A violinist will read in a score the instruction *sul ponticello* and play near the bridge to "brighten" the sound being produced by emphasizing the higher frequencies of the sound. A number of physical properties of your voice or musical instrument help define its timbre: physical size is certainly one of them, as well as the materials that the sound has to travel through in order to be heard. Did you ever try to sing with a stuffy nose? The air inside of your instrument, your voice, is not allowing you to resonate properly and, as a result, changes the timbre. If you filled your violin with putty, or chose not to change your strings for 3 years, it too would sound much different from other violins. Acoustic instruments have a defined range of pitches that they can produce, yet their timbre is largely a result of the physical design and construction of the instrument itself and how it's played.

## THE HARMONIC SERIES AND TIMBRE

A sound's timbre—the splatter of waves that is sounded simultaneously when a note is played—is related to something known as the **harmonic series**. Perhaps you're now thinking to yourself: I remember hearing about the harmonic series, but I don't quite recall what it is or how it works. Is that sort of like the overtone series?

The answer to the last question is *yes*. The harmonic series is a set of frequencies (**partials**) in which **overtones** (**harmonics**) are built above some base tone (the **fundamental frequency**). The fundamental frequency is the first partial in a given harmonic series. The relative balance of these overtones (other harmonics above the fundamental frequency) built from the fundamental frequency is an important factor in establishing the timbre of an instrument. So how do you build a harmonic series from a fundamental frequency? Let's build one together using the companion software.

## ✋ GO TO SOFTWARE LESSON: *HARMONIC SERIES*

In the FMT companion software, choose the lesson *Harmonic Series*. If necessary, slowly adjust the main output level slider at the top left of the software to hear the sound of this sine wave playing at 440 Hz, the A above middle C, as shown near the orange circle 1. This A will be the *fundamental* of our harmonic series. The first overtone, which is the second harmonic (the first frequency above the fundamental), is an octave above the fundamental. To get the second harmonic of the series, you simply multiply the fundamental frequency by 2. Since the fundamental frequency is 440 Hz, the first overtone is

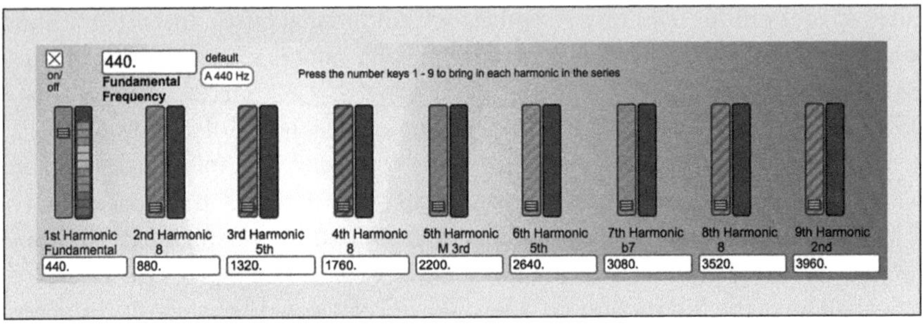

FIGURE 1.4: Level sliders within the companion software to control the nine harmonics

at 880 Hz. You may slowly raise the level slider marked "2nd Harmonic." To get the third harmonic of the series, multiply by 3, and so on. It's actually a really easy concept to grasp.

Instead of manually raising the level slider for each harmonic, you may press the number keys on your computer keyboard (1–9) to bring each slider to a moderate level, as indicated at the orange circle 2. Note that changing the level of each overtone will change the overall timbre of your sound.

Now try this:

- Press the number keys 1–9 on your computer keyboard to raise the level of each harmonic.
- Using the on-screen keyboard, click the notes of a scale starting on C and ending on the C one octave above.
- Adjust the level of each "partial" by adjusting the sliders.
- Play the scale again.

Notice that you hear a single pitch even though you know that each sound is composed of several individual sine waves combined together to produce a complex wave. Does it seem odd that you can no longer distinguish the individual sine waves within the timbre?

- Beginning with the number 9, press the keys 9–1 to remove each harmonic from the timbre.

The instrument in this software lesson has its own unique timbre. In actuality, our brains grouped a bunch of different waves together into a single construct we called its timbre. (The ability of our brain to combine multiple waves into a single sound is known as the **gestalt effect**.) With control over enough sine waves, you could, in principle, construct a timbre that sounds like a Stradivarius (though that would take some time). We are synthetically manipulating waves to create new timbres, a process known as **synthesis**. As we will discuss more thoroughly in Chapter 4, the process we just experienced is known as **additive synthesis**: a type of synthesis in which an individual *adds* waves together to create new timbres or emulate the timbres of existing sounds.

## OUR HEARING RANGE

Musical pitches really have no defined "starting point" or "ending point"; if playing descending pitches, at some point a note will become so low and rumbly that you will feel the vibration of it more than you hear it, like the bass rumble you feel on your chest at a rock concert. As notes ascend, they become higher, and at some point they will become so high that it sounds like ringing in your ears—like the day after a rock concert.

The range of hearing for humans is somewhere around 20–20,000 Hz, or 20 Hz to 20 **kilohertz (kHz)**, although most people can't hear the extremes of this range. When a sine wave oscillates with a fast enough frequency, we can hear the frequency as having a definite pitch, such as the reference *A* that we tune to.

### DID YOU KNOW?

#### Definite and Indefinite Pitch

I once told a group of middle school students to mimic the pitches I played on an instrument by singing them. I then played a few notes on the piano and a few on the guitar in different octaves, and the students attempted to sing back the pitches. As you would expect, when I began playing the kick drum, the students had trouble singing those pitches and would start imitating "boomy" noises and what sounded at times like explosions. The difficulty in their task was not only that the frequency was so low that they couldn't physically sing it, but also that it was too low for them to determine the sound as having a **definite pitch.** Some sounds move at such a slow speed that they are not heard as having a definite pitch that one could imitate by singing. We refer to these sounds as having an **indefinite pitch.**

Dog whistles emit sounds that are outside the range of human hearing but within the range of canine hearing. The market is full of products for repelling wildlife, such as bats, by emitting frequencies that broadcast loud high-pitched frequencies that humans are unable to hear but bats find obnoxious. Perhaps you've heard of the Mosquito alarm (and later the ringtone) invented by Howard Stapleton in 2005. The device is used to discourage teens and young adults from loitering by emitting high frequencies at loud levels that is within their range of hearing, but outside the range of hearing for most adults. The basic concept of the device hinges on the statistical data suggesting that most adults suffer some wear and tear on their ears so that by their mid- to late twenties, they cannot hear the same high frequencies they were able to hear when they were in their early teens.

Thus, playing a loud frequency at 18 kHz or so in a crowded mall or street corner would only bother people who were able to physically hear it: young people. The concept was implemented into the "mosquito ringtone," whereby, for the converse purpose, students in a classroom could be notified that they were receiving a phone call or a message by hearing a high frequency played through their phone that their teacher, most likely older, would not be able to hear.

Let's conduct an informal test of your hearing.

## 🖑 GO TO SOFTWARE LESSON: *HEARING TEST*

Using the FMT companion software, choose the lesson *Hearing Test*. If necessary, slowly adjust the main level slider at the top left of the software to hear the sound of this sine wave playing at 8 kHz (8,000 Hz).

- Press the space bar to step through a number of frequencies noting the general age range that should be able to hear that frequency.

Notice that this software shows the level for the sine wave as vertical height with the frequencies being plotted horizontally.

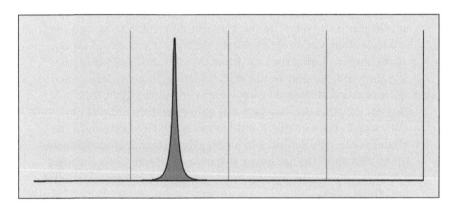

FIGURE 1.5: A wave's level represented vertically within the companion software

Please understand that a proper hearing test would involve an ideal listening environment, headphones, and the expertise of an audiologist. This test is meant to give you a basic sense of the ways in which we perceive sounds as they approach the upper threshold that our ears can handle.

## SPECTROGRAM ANALYSIS

Did you ever mimic the sound of certain instruments? Have you ever heard a capella group or a beatbox artist imitate instrument timbres in a way that was particularly convincing? Humans have the ability to produce some of the same sounds as musical instruments because there is an overlap in the range of frequencies, or **spectrum**, that humans and instruments can produce.

A number of analysis tools can be used to learn about the properties of certain sounds. For example, a **spectrogram** shows the frequency spectrum of a sound on a grid.

## 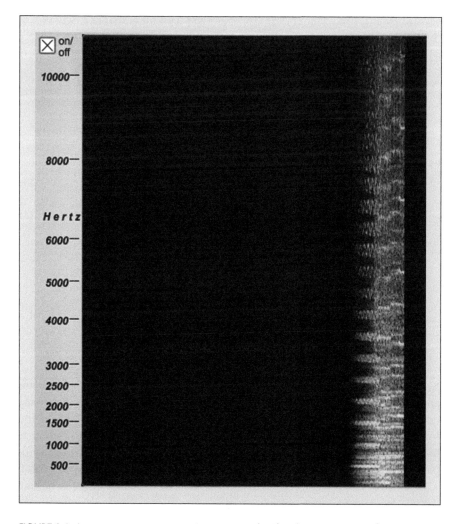 GO TO SOFTWARE LESSON: *SPECTROGRAM*

Using the FMT companion software, choose the lesson *Spectrogram*. If necessary, slowly adjust the main level slider at the top left of the software.

- With the main level at the midway point, select the *Drum* label from the pull-down menu near orange slider *1*.

Notice that the sound is displayed over time horizontally. The vertical values show the frequencies that are present in the sound with respect to the entire

FIGURE 1.6: A spectrogram representation generated within the companion software

audible spectrum; the higher the height of the spectrogram data, the higher the frequency. The variations in color refer to amplitude, which we can think of as the strength of those particular frequencies; yellow and green lines show stronger amplitude levels at those frequencies than frequencies with blue lines.

Learning how to interpret a spectrogram can take some practice, so:

- Choose some of the other sounds from the drop-down menu near the orange circle *1*.
- Replay clips by clicking near the orange circle *2*, and note how instruments like the *String Quartet* visually differ from the *Speech* sample.
- Record your own voice and see it represented by clicking the *Record* button near the orange circle *3*.

If this was your first time recording your voice, congratulations! Take a moment to appreciate how different your voice sounds hearing it in your head versus how it sounds to everyone else. (See Chapter 8 for a further discussion of this concept.)

## DID YOU KNOW?

### Loudness? Volume? Level?

"Loudness" is a subjective term used to refer to things that make sounds like instruments and speakers. Other terms that are used rather loosely include "volume" ("Turn that volume down!") and "level." Professionals measure the strength of sounds with measurements like sound pressure. A common way of expressing the "loudness of a sound" is by referring to its decibel (dB) level. We will discuss these terms in detail in future chapters. In practice, referring to a sound's "level" is an acceptable and common general-use term. When someone is referring to "volume", they are likely referring to the relative level of some sound compared to another.

## COMBINING TIMBRES

Because there is an overlap in the range of frequencies, or spectrum, that humans and instruments can produce, it is possible for certain frequencies that really define a timbre to become lost or obscured in the context of a multiple sound sources. Think about a singer in a jazz band who works meticulously to enunciate the lyrics to a song, only to find that certain words are covered up by the saxophonist in the band who has decided to play the notes of the melody in unison with the singer. Is the reason for the lost, or **masked**, articulation of the lyrics a result of the saxophonist being too loud in general—after all, the drums and bass are loud, too—or is it also that the saxophonist is occupying some of the same frequency space as the vocalist? Numerous factors can contribute to masking, to which, as you probably know, there are numerous solutions.

If you've ever taken an orchestration class, you've probably heard the instructor talk about ways to write for, as an example, the flute section that can "color" the melody played by the violin section. This is possible because violins and flutes have an overlapping frequency range. In rock music, a bass guitar player may play notes on the same downbeats that the drummer is placing the kick drum to make the bass notes seem to have more "punch" than they actually do in isolation. These techniques manipulate our tendency toward grouping similar sounds together into a single timbral construct; as such, the bass player and the drummer collectively create the sonic illusion that the bass guitar has an explosive impact on the downbeat.

If you consider the entire sound spectrum used when an ensemble performs, you can probably group the types of sounds that are heard into categories based on which instruments generally produce low frequencies, which frequencies produce middle, or *mid-range* frequencies, and which instruments produce high frequencies. Whether you're a composer, an ensemble director, or an engineer, part of producing a good ensemble balance lies in knowing how to "carve out" space in the spectrum so that all of the instruments can be heard in the desired manner with the understanding that instruments have frequency ranges that overlap each other to some extent. During a loud, heavy rock song, a guitar solo played in the upper register might "cut through" the mix easier than a guitar solo played in the lowest register of the instrument simply because there aren't as many instruments competing for that upper frequency space in the spectrum. However, if, during the solo, the singer begins singing in the upper register of his or her voice, masking issues may occur between the guitar solo and the singer.

Sometimes, masking can be a good thing. For example, if a singer tends to sing out of tune or generally produces a poor timbre, finding a good balance between his or her voice and the ensemble where the voice sits just on top of the music can help make him or her sound less exposed. Perhaps you've heard a karaoke performance where the sound engineers decided to feature the singer more prominently by making them louder than the backing soundtrack. While it may be a kind gesture to favor the singer's voice over a backing track, poor overall balance like this can be very unflattering for a vocalist and can make even good singers sound bad.

Have you ever heard a synthesized string orchestra sound, such as that from a notation software application, that sounded so fake and unrealistic that it made you laugh? Well, in the context of a mix, the "fake" qualities of the sound that reveal to the listener, "Hey, this is a fake string sound," can be balanced and processed in such a way so that the convincing qualities of their sound support the overall mix while the fake-sounding qualities are masked.

# 🖑 GO TO SOFTWARE LESSON: *MASKING*

Using the FMT companion software, choose the lesson *Masking*. If necessary, slowly adjust the main level slider at the top left of the software. Within the software:

- Click the "Play: strings in the mix" button near the orange circle *1* to hear the ensemble mix which includes a string ensemble.
- Click the "Play: strings isolated with effects" button near the orange circle *2* to hear the synthesized string ensemble part apart from the ensemble mix, but with digital echo effects applied.
- Click the "Play: strings isolated with no effects" button near the orange circle *3* to hear the synthesized string ensemble part apart from the ensemble mix with no effects applied, or "dry."

Obviously, the string ensemble sound is synthetic, but did you feel that in the presence of the guitars, bass, drums, and a singer, the string ensemble sound is "good enough" to be convincing? It's often the initial onset of striking the notes, called the **attack**, more so than the **sustain** of the notes that might reveal to the listener that what they are hearing is synthetic. In fact, one study by Schlegel and Lane (2013) suggests that the attack portion of a note may be a significant indicator to listeners of the expertise level (beginner of professional) of a performer. Now, if you are intending to have your latest string quartet sold to the masses, you should consider hiring some good players and recording them with good microphones. The point of this masking exercise is to point out that, for better or worse, frequencies gang up and change the way we perceive sound. In this example, the phenomenon helped to mask some of the "fakeness" of the string sound. However, as we will discuss in future chapters, multiple instruments, room size, speaker placement, microphone quality, effect processes, and many other factors contribute to the overall spectrum of your music and can make your live performance or recordings sound poor even if the musicians are playing well or great even if the musicianship is not so strong. Part of music-making is creating an experience for the listener. The process of achieving a great sound begins with great musical ideas and posits a number of technical issues related to composition and performance to be addressed along the way. In the chapters ahead we will discuss some of the technologies in place that can help us facilitate our creative objectives.

## SUMMARY

Sounds are all around us; some have simple waveforms, others complex waveforms. The timbre of different sounds is related to the combination of waves within these waveforms, and the various timbral qualities possible can be used for different musical outcomes. Just as sounds occur naturally, we can use technology to expand the possibilities of using those sounds for creative purposes through synthesis, audio manipulation, and other techniques.

# KEY CONCEPTS

- Waves move in a pattern known as a cycle.
- Frequency is the *number* of cycles a wave completes in one second.
- Timbre is a result of the waves present in a complex waveform.
- The harmonic series is the result of multiplying frequencies by the fundamental.
- Our hearing range is roughly 20–20,000 Hz.
- Spectrogram analyses may be performed on a sound to graphically represent the frequencies that make it up.
- Frequency masking refers to the phenomenon in which one sound covers up (or "masks") another one.

# KEY TERMS

additive synthesis
amplitude
attack
cycle
definite pitch/indefinite pitch
equal temperament
frequency
fundamental frequency

gestalt effect
harmonic series
hertz (Hz)
kilohertz (kHz)
masked sound/masking
oscillating/oscillation
oscillator
overtones/harmonics
partials

sine wave or sinusoid
spectrogram
spectrum
sustain
synthesis
timbre
tone or tone color
wave/sound wave

# CHAPTER 2

# AUDIO

## OVERVIEW

In this chapter we will discuss the nature of working with audio in live and re-cording contexts. We will describe the common components used, including input sources like microphones and electric instruments and output systems like PA speaker systems, amplifiers, and computer recording systems. Some discussion of signal types is included to help you better understand the many different kinds of cables and connectors that are used in professional audio situations.

By the end of this chapter you should have a firm understanding of how to set up audio equipment to record or amplify your performance. This understanding will include the types of hardware and cabling you need, how and where to plug in the cables, and some basic recording and microphone positioning techniques.

## BEFORE WE BEGIN

Discussing audio in the abstract may seem again like more of an exercise in science than music making. Working with audio itself is complicated because many different components can be involved in doing this work and there are endless variations in the types of microphones, cables, and other associated equipment that can be used. Additionally, the concept of converting something we hear with our ears into something we observe with a computer can be difficult to grasp. However, at the very least, a basic understanding of the ways in which audio technology works will help you to avoid and troubleshoot common problems when capturing live performances and working with digital audio.

Read this chapter slowly and try to conceptualize what is being described. There are lots of terms introduced here, and the nature of thinking of "what plugs into what" can be confusing. Take breaks and reread sections if necessary. It is encouraged that you consult the resources available on the companion website for this book to help you understand the concepts introduced in this chapter.

You might ask, "What are the right settings to use for the equipment I have," or, "Can you tell me what equipment I should buy in order to record my band or ensemble so it sounds right?" The truth is that different instruments playing different notes produce different sounds in different rooms when captured with different equipment. It's best to develop good listening skills, know what you'd like the music you're working with to sound like, know how the technology you're using works in concept, and then use the technology to facilitate the recording that you want to make. Developing a good set of "listening ears" is probably the most difficult and the most important skill to acquire, and it's certainly one of the most sought-after skills for a producer, engineer, composer, or performer. If you feel comfortable with your skills as a listener, you should be relieved, because learning how the technology works and how to work it is relatively easy once you know what your music *should* sound like.

We'll begin by discussing the basic concept of working with audio and then describe, in some detail, many of the individual components involved.

## THE SIGNAL PATH

Based on our understanding of sound from Chapter 1, we know that *sound* refers to waves traveling through the air. When these waves "hit" a microphone, it converts their oscillations into an electrical signal. This electrical signal is transmitted through a cable that begins at the base of the microphone and travels until it eventually comes out of a speaker. The signal will typically travel to a number of other audio devices along the way in what is commonly referred to as the **signal path**, **signal chain**, or **signal flow**.

One signal path in a live sound situation might be as follows. (First read the numbered elements of the list, and then, once you understand the signal path, read the lettered elements of the list.)

1. Signal source origin: a person is singing.
2. A microphone is placed in front of the person singing.
   a. The acoustic sound of the singer is converted into an electrical signal.
3. A cable connects the microphone to a **mixing board**.
   a. The electrical signal from the microphone travels to a mixing board through the cable.
   b. The mixing board adds some strength to the signal using a built-in **preamplifier**, or **preamp**.
4. The signal from the mixer's preamplifier is sent through a cable to a **power amplifier** to make the signal even stronger.
5. The signal from the power amplifier is sent through cables to one or more **speakers**.
   a. The speakers, by pushing air back and forth, convert the signal back into a sound that we can hear with our ears.
      i. Sometimes the amplifier is even built into the speaker cabinet.

When a signal reaches a device (like a microphone or preamp), it is called the **input**; when it leaves that device, it is called the **output**. The input (original signal) will be changed in some way before it leaves the device as output. For example, as we have noted, the microphone changes the input (sound waves) into a different output (an electrical signal).

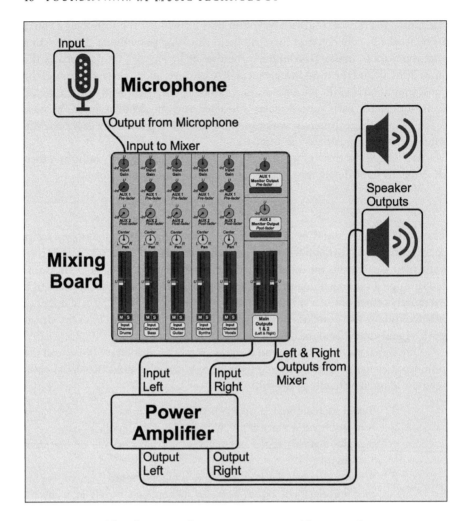

FIGURE 2.1: Signal flow from microphone to mixer to an amplifier to speakers

Numerous variations can be applied to this signal path depending on your application. For example, if you were recording, instead of a mixer, the signal would likely be sent to an audio interface that converts the signal into a digital format so that it can be captured on a computer. However, at some point the signal will ultimately return to its nonelectrical state when it passes through the speakers.

## MICROPHONES

The most important part of a recording is the quality of the performance taking place in front of the microphone. However, we rely on microphones to capture this performance and accurately convert the air pressure waves (sound) to an electrical signal. Think of the microphone as a person who has ears with a really

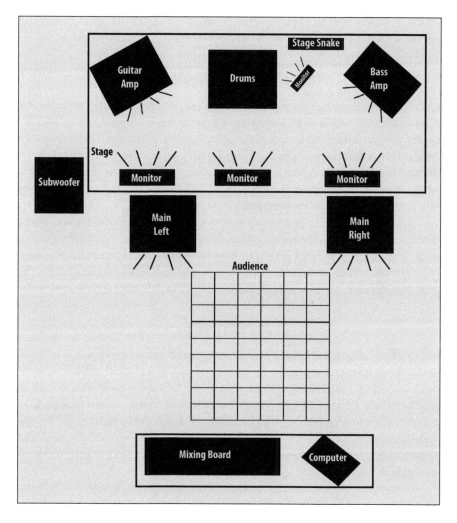

FIGURE 2.2: Some typical components in a signal path on a stage

good hearing range who will listen to the sounds taking place in front of him or her, and then describe them in a very articulate way (by converting them to electrical signals). As the first component in the signal path, if your microphone is not of high quality, the representation, when you listen back to the recording, will not sound the same as what you'd heard with your ears. There are ways to manipulate a poor recording in the studio to make it sound like a more accurate representation of the original sound source, but it's easiest and best to use the proper equipment in the proper way from the start. (We'll discuss the different types of microphones later in this chapter.)

Although quality microphones can be very expensive, as can speakers, both microphones and speakers tend to retain their value through the years and remain mostly unchanged by advancements in technology. Whereas digital devices like effects and recording technologies change rapidly, many of the microphones and speakers used in professional studios today were designed decades ago.

## KEEPING A UNIFORM SIGNAL

Once the sound source has been converted into a signal by a microphone, we want to keep the signal clean and strong wherever it goes. To ensure this, it's necessary to understand what each piece of equipment in the signal chain (reverb unit, mixer, amplifier, stompbox, cable, adapter, etc.) is doing to the signal. Some devices like effects sound better placed at different "stages" in the signal path, while others like amplifiers absolutely need to be placed in the proper order or else your equipment can be damaged.

Knowing "what goes where" can be very confusing but, in most cases, can be determined by reading the manuals that come with each piece of equipment you own. The goal of any signal path is to keep the signal moving smoothly between gear. The manual for each piece of equipment will give you some insight into the type of signal each device receives at the input stage and delivers at the output stage.

## IMPEDANCE

For example, a synthesizer keyboard typically produces a type of signal strength said to be at **line level**. A digital device like a synthesizer contains what is essentially a computer to produce and amplify its synthesized sounds and, as such, is able to output a relatively strong signal; a line level signal is a strong signal. In comparison, there are weaker signals said to be at **microphone level**, or "**Lo-Z**," and **instrument level**, or "**Hi-Z**." With these weaker-level signals, the symbol Z refers to the concept of signal **resistance**, or **impedance** with regard to signal strength and flow.

In layman's terms: the "Hi" in Hi-Z refers to high impedance—the signal flow is "impeded," thus denoting a weak signal flow. Low impedance, or Lo-Z, means low resistance and denotes a stronger output. Electric guitars, basses, and their associated accessories all typically transmit Hi-Z signals, which is why Hi-Z level signals are commonly referred to as instrument level. The term instrument level distinguishes Hi-Z inputs from Lo-Z inputs, such as microphones, which, as you may have guessed, commonly transmit Lo-Z signals. For this reason, Lo-Z signals are commonly referred to as **microphone level**. The amount of resistance, or the "Z," is measured in ohms. Links to more technical resources are available on the companion website for this book.

Microphones and other electronic components are built to different standards and have varying input and output levels of resistance. In modern day audio equipment, the impedance types are, for the most part, clearly spelled out for you. A mixer, for example, may have a number of inputs and outputs labeled "Hi-Z," "Lo-Z," or even "instrument" and "microphone." Sometimes they also have graphic icons representing keyboards, guitars, mics, amps, and so on clearly printed on the device inputs and outputs themselves. The purpose of knowing

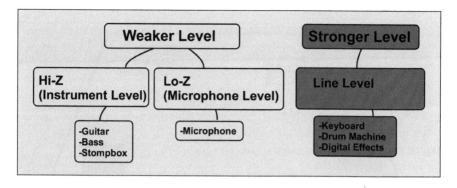

FIGURE 2.3: A few microphone level and line level input and output classifications

about impedance ratings is to ensure that the signal types are matched as they enter each new device in the chain.

This might seem confusing, but it all boils down to ensuring that the signal is strong enough, but not too strong, as it enters each device in the signal path. A mismatch in the impedance type can result in unpleasant **distortion** or very low signal, so it's important to make sure that you have the right signal strength going to each device in the signal path. For example, some mixing boards and audio interfaces only accept either line level input or Lo-Z microphone input. Plugging a Hi-Z instrument like an electric guitar into a device that is expecting a Lo-Z or line level input could produce a very weak signal. As you might suspect, numerous devices exist to convert from one impedance type to another. A device known as a **direct box** or **DI** may be used to take a Hi-Z instrument level signal at its input and convert it into a Lo-Z microphone level.

A direct box can take a Hi-Z instrument level output, like an acoustic-electric guitar, and convert the signal into a Lo-Z microphone level signal that can be connected to a mixing board. Direct boxes typically also have a **Thru output** that allows an additional feed of the unchanged input signal to be sent to other Hi-Z inputs like that of a guitar amplifier (Figure 2.4). In this manner, the acoustic guitar can be sent to both the mixer as a Lo-Z signal and the stage amp as a Hi-Z signal.

## CABLES

One way to visibly note the impedance difference used by each component can be the cable type. Microphones typically use a three-prong **XLR cable**, while instruments typically use a ¼″ **cable**. However, important exceptions may include synthesizer outputs that may use ¼″ **jacks** for signals at the instrument level or microphone level.

### XLR Cables

The three prongs at the end of an XLR cable connect to three wires inside the cable: a "ground" wire (sometimes called "earth"), a positive "hot" signal, and a

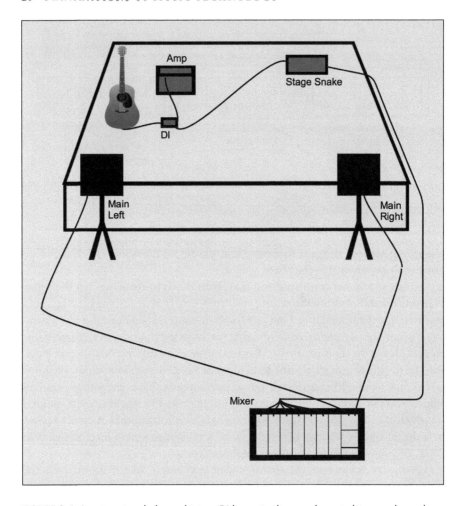

FIGURE 2.4: A guitar signal plugged into a DI box, simultaneously routed to a snake and a stage amp

negative "cold" signal, which is an inverted copy of the hot signal. To put it succinctly, inverting the hot signal (changing its polarity) allows the cold signal to cancel out unwanted hum and noise from the signal while boosting the desirable signal. A cable with three conductors functioning in this manner is said to be balanced. Additionally, the ground wire is useful because it can carry voltage to power certain microphones that require voltage in order to work.

## Balanced and Unbalanced Signals

Balancing a signal is important because it helps reduce external noise from entering or existing in the signal path. All Lo-Z microphones with an XLR output are typically **balanced signals**. Instruments like guitar and bass with their Hi-Z outputs are typically all unbalanced and are susceptible to the same noise and

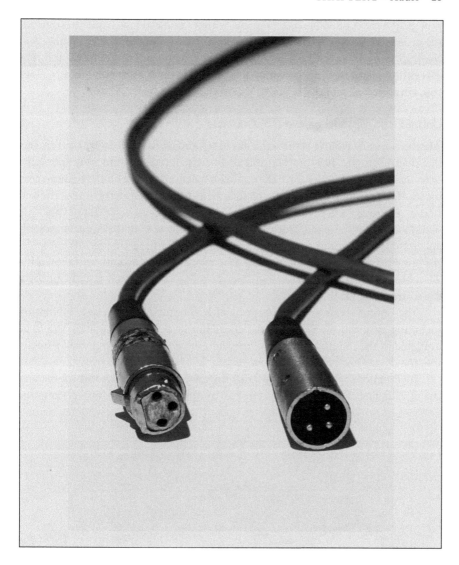

FIGURE 2.5: An XLR cable with the female end on left and the male end on right (Courtesy abzee/iStock)

interference as any **unbalanced signal**. However, a guitar or bass signal coming through a microphone that is placed in front of an amplifier or through the XLR output of a direct box is a balanced Lo-Z output; a microphone signal is balanced, and a direct box balances unbalanced instrument signals.

## Balanced ¼″ Tip, Ring, and Sleeve (TRS) Cables

Like XLR cables, balanced ¼″ cables commonly transmit three things: a ground and two copies of the signal with opposite polarities. Instead of having three prongs like the XLR cable, the ¼" cable with its reduced size is able to transmit the ground and signals using the parts of the cable identified as tip, ring, and sleeve. Shown in Figure 2.6, the sleeve carries the ground, while the tip and ring carry the signals. For this reason, a ¼" cable like this is referred to as a ¼" **TRS (tip, ring, sleeve)** cable. A ¼" TRS cable is also said to be balanced.

## Unbalanced Tip and Sleeve (TS) Cables

Another type of ¼" cable is the unbalanced **tip and sleeve (TS) cable**. Instruments like electric guitars, bass guitars, and keyboards all typically use ¼" output jacks to transmit the signal but don't all produce a balanced signal. Electric guitars and basses, for example, output an unbalanced signal consisting of just a tip and sleeve. As a result, a TS cable—commonly referred to as an **instrument cable**—is used to transmit the signal from a guitar to other devices that also accept unbalanced signals like guitar stomp boxes and guitar amplifiers. Since a TRS cable has the same tip and ring conductors as a TS cable, in many cases it may be used if a TS cable is unavailable, but this will not make the unbalanced signal balanced; use a direct box for that.

The output levels and connections of keyboards may be any combination including balanced ¼", XLR, or unbalanced line level. This information would be available in the manual for the instrument and is sometimes engraved directly into the device itself near the output jacks.

In situations where there is a great distance between the sound source and the mixing board, it's common to use an **audio snake** to route audio from one

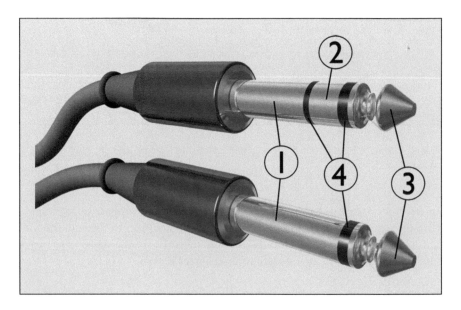

FIGURE 2.6: A balanced ¼" TRS cable above an unbalanced ¼" TS "instrument" cable: 1, sleeve; 2, ring; 3, tip; 4, insulating rings (From Pedersen, 2005)

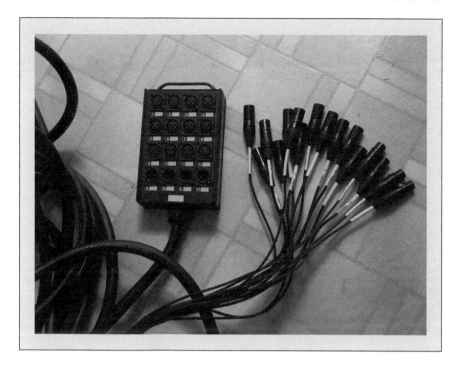

FIGURE 2.7: A "12 × 4" snake with 12 female XLR jacks and 4 male XLR jacks (From VK1LW, 2012)

location to another. "Snakes" are, in layman's terms, a bundle of cables wrapped together. Snakes usually have some combination of XLR and ¼" TRS connections with the "male" pronged end given as a cable and the "female" receiving end given as a jack fixed on top of a metal box. Balanced audio signals can travel greater distances than unbalanced signals without picking up noise and interference along the way. A snake helps to consolidate the number of cables that are run at great distances by essentially wrapping numerous cables into one large cable. A microphone on the stage would connect to the snake, and the snake would run the distance to the back of the venue and connect to the mixing board.

## Other Cables

Many other types of cables exist with varying connectors at the end. For example, computers and portable devices commonly use ⅛" **TRS connections** through headphone jacks. Unlike ¼" TRS cables, ⅛" TRS ones typically send two different audio signals, referred to as **channels**, on the tip and ring wires. Two-channel signals like this are referred to as **stereo**; this can be thought of as two separate audio signals—one for the left speaker and one for the right speaker—simultaneously coming through your stereo sound system at home.

Another cable used in consumer products and some audio products is the **RCA connection**. This cable comes in the "white and red" type for audio devices

FIGURE 2.8: An RCA cable with three wires (Courtesy Krasyuk/iStock)

and in the "white, red, and yellow" type for consumer TVs and video devices, sometimes referred to as a composite cable. In these cases, the white connector carries an audio channel for the left speaker, red carries an audio channel for the right speaker, and yellow carries a video signal.

## MIXERS

A **mixing board**, also known as a **mixer, mixing console**, or **mixing desk**, is a device that can receive multiple channels of audio through XLR or ¼" TRS input. The purpose of a mixer is to allow a sound engineer to create a balanced mix of the different audio signals and send that mixed signal to speakers, recorders, or other output destinations.

FIGURE 2.9: A mixing board (From Ten, 2013)

Audio signals enter the mixer via XLR and TRS jacks on the mixer itself. Most mixers allow engineers to increase or decrease the amplitude, or signal strength, of the incoming signal using a built-in preamplifier, or preamp. The amount of **boost** (strengthening) or **cut** (weakening) is measured in what is called **gain** as soon as the sound signal enters. The goal at this point in the mixer, called the **gain stage**, is to ensure that the incoming signal is strong, but not too strong. A weak signal will make it difficult to use the features of the mixer for that channel, which can include effects, tone shaping, and routing the audio to different speakers. A signal that is too strong will **clip** the signal, resulting in unpleasant and undesired distortion. Gain can be adjusted using the knobs on the mixer commonly labeled "gain" or "trim." Additionally, some mixers have buttons labeled "pad" or "boost" that will decrease or increase, respectively, the incoming signal by some amount.

Past the gain stage, mixers vary in terms of their controls and features. Some mixers will have sound effect processors and "tone-shaping" controls built into the board. All will have at least one volume slider, called a fader, or rotary knob that controls the level of the signal that will be sent to the main speaker outputs facing the audience. Some mixers will have the option to send the signal to additional output destinations, such as smaller monitors on the stage that the performers use to hear the mix, in-ear monitors, recorders, or other places. The knobs on the mixer that allow a signal to be sent to these other locations are generally labeled Aux (Aux 1, Aux 2, etc.), short for "auxillary."

Imagine that a rock band is performing on a stage. The audio engineer will balance the individual instrument levels coming into the soundboard using the volume sliders. Suppose that the singer wants to hear his or her voice louder on the stage but is overpowered by the level of the instruments. Placing a small speaker on stage, referred to as a **stage monitor**, will allow the engineer to send a special mix that is different from the main mix in that only the singer's microphone signal is present. The special mix comes by adjusting the levels of the Aux and routing the Aux output from the mixer to that speaker through a cable. A singer might then ask the sound engineer to add a little bit of the guitar or keyboard signal in the stage monitor/Aux mix.

The overall number of Aux mixes available is determined by the size of the mixers. The available features vary from mixer to mixer and may include the ability to group similar channels together onto a single channel, called "subgroups" or "submixes," add internal effects and processing, route signals to and from "outboard" external effects processors, and more. A mixer that is said to be 16 × 4 refers to 16 input channels and 4 subgroups. If there are four members in the band, each member can have their own mix routed to individual stage monitors, in-ear monitors, and so on using an Aux send or a subgroup.

## DID YOU KNOW?

### Performing Live without Sophisticated Sound Equipment

Imagine playing with your band on stage and not being able to hear the other instruments clearly. This was the case for most bands in the '60s. The screaming fans and the general noise made it difficult for most groups to hear themselves. The Beatles, for example, took to miming their vocals and guitar movements because neither they—nor their fans—could hear what they were doing anyway! Stage amplification was primitive and the sound that the audience heard was far from ideal. Later bands like the Grateful Dead took to carting their own sound equipment and employing their own technicians and engineers in order to ensure the sound quality of their shows was up to their standards.

## 🖑 GO TO THE SOFTWARE LESSON: *MIXER*

In the FMT application, the *Mixer* lesson shows a simulated view of a soundboard. The application allows you to play back 5 independent channels of audio and work with them as you would with a hardware mixer. At the orange circled *1*:

• Choose an output destination.

Remember that the main outputs are what the audience hears, whereas the Aux mixes are what the musicians hear through stage monitors and personal in-ear monitoring systems. The first Aux, Aux 1, is an example of a pre-fader Aux in which the signal sent to the Aux is unaffected by the volume fader on the channel.

At the orange circle *2*:

- Press play to begin playing the 5 tracks.

Each of the individual instrument **tracks**, or **stems**, has been included for this song. Note that not all of the tracks will sound simultaneously. As the music plays:

- Adjust the volume sliders, known as faders, to increase signal strength
- Adjust the Aux knobs on various channels to increase the level of signal strength to the auxes, then change the output destination to observe the balance of the auxes compared to the main mix.

It is recommended that you lower the level of all instruments as they play simultaneously and slowly match the relative balance between each instrument using your ears. It is often preferred to match the levels of the bass and drums first before adding other instruments.

- Adjust the preamp gain, pan, and other elements carefully as not to hurt your ears through loud bursts of sound.

The **U** stands for **unity gain**, the level of gain where no volume is being added or taken away from the signal. The **-inf** stands for **negative infinity decibels**, which means "no sound." These levels can be called by clicking on the letters U and -inf within the software.

If you have access to other multitrack stems, you may use them within this software lesson by dragging and dropping the audio files onto the track header or label beneath each slider where "Input Channel" is specified. Bands and artists will sometimes release songs as stems or multitracks in order to encourage re-mixes to take place. These audio file collections would be ideal for this activity.

## DID YOU KNOW?

### Feedback

It is important to note that if a microphone is placed too closely to a speaker that is outputting that microphone's signal, it will produce a piercing sound known as **feedback**. In essence, the speaker is amplifying its own signal being picked up through the microphone. To prevent feedback, keep sound levels moderate if the microphone is being used within close proximity to a speaker or simply move the main speakers in front of the singers facing the audience. Be aware that stage monitors facing the musicians are also susceptible to feedback and that engineers in the back of the room may be unaware that feedback is starting on stage until it becomes noticeable to the audience.

## AUDIO INTERFACES

Instead of a mixing board, you might just want to record the live signals directly into your computer. To do so, you would use an **audio interface**, also known as a **soundcard** or **recording interface**, to convert the audio signal into a digital format so that a computer can understand it. This conversion is said to be from "analog to digital," or **A to D**. In this sense, the word "analog" refers to the electrical signal captured by the microphone travelling in the signal flow, which is "analogous" to, or a representation of, the sound source originally captured by the microphone. The word "digital" represents the conversion of the signal into numbers that the computer can understand.

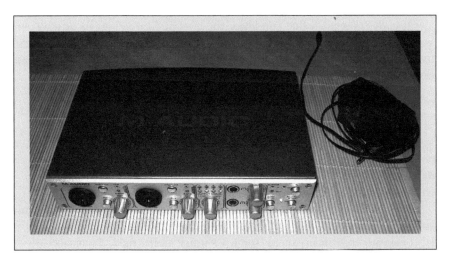

FIGURE 2.10: A USB digital audio interface for recording (From Kamilbaranski, 2010)

In digital recordings, the term **samples** refers to a rate by which an audio signal—for example, a violinist sustaining a note, which is a continuous flow of audio—can be broken down into "discrete" and evenly spaced signals. The conversion of audio we hear with our ears into a series of digits means that each of the discrete signals is given a numerical value to represent the overall continuous signal that was broken down. Each of these values is referred to as a sample.

### DID YOU KNOW?

#### Discrete Signals

Consider a flip-book drawing or an animation in which a series of still images are grouped together and shown sequentially. The number of images used and the rate at which they are shown will influence the way the audience experiences a sense of flow. If there are too few images, the animation will appear choppy. Increasing the number of images will help ensure that there are no gaps in representing the flow of motion in the animation. If there are many images but the rate at which they are shown is too slow—i.e., the person flipping the flip-book is doing a poor job flipping—the animation will, again, feel wrong. Additionally, if the transitions between the motions of the characters in the animation are not gradual, there will be breaks in the flow. To this end, there needs to be a large number of high-quality individual images drawn with gradual transitions within the animated character motions that occur at a rate that feels natural to the way we experience motion in real life. In the same regard, we capture or "sample" audio at a quality or "resolution" that captures as many audio frequencies that we can at a very fast rate—many times a second—so that when we hear the audio played back it sounds as close as possible to the way we hear sounds in real life.

There are different numerical rates by which someone can sample audio. For example, many computer sound cards can record 44,100 samples per second. This means that for a 1-second recording of a violinist sustaining a note, there are 44,100 samples representing that 1 second of continuous audio. Some more advanced sound cards have the ability to use more samples per second in the sampling process.

## Higher Sampling Rates

There is much debate as to whether humans can perceive a noticeable increase in audio quality with higher sample rates. Remember, the human hearing range stops at around 20 kHz. The default sampling rate for many devices is 44.1 kHz, a little more than twice the highest frequency that our ears can hear. According to what is known as the *Nyquist-Shannon theorem*, audio must be sampled at a rate that is at least two times that of the highest frequency that is to be present in the audio source. Sampling at 44.1 kHz accurately captures 22.5 kHz. Compact discs playback audio at 44.1 kHz, so recordings made with a higher sampling rate like 96 or 192 kHz must be downsized to this rate if they are intended to be put on CD. Some feel that recording audio at sample rates higher than 44.1 kHz is recording a lot of information that humans can't perceive. Is this recoding practice producing a waste of hard drive space? Some might contend that audio interface manufacturers use these advanced sampling capabilities as a marketing ploy.

## Compressed Audio

Audio formats like MP3 use methods of **compression** in order to reduce the file size by sacrificing some of the audio quality. If you've ever been to a website like YouTube, you've noticed that higher-quality videos look and sound better but require longer to load. This is also true for compressed and uncompressed audio.

Compression as an audio effect (a different notion altogether) will be discussed in Chapter 9, but in this capacity we can think of it as file compression, a process that reduces the quality of the audio in order to achieve a smaller file size.

A 5-minute uncompressed WAV or AIF audio file may be about 50 megabytes in file size or greater, whereas a compressed MP3 audio file may only be about 5 megabytes in file size with little perceived difference in the quality. Some parts of the audio can be compressed or completely thrown away if they are outside the range of what a human being can actually hear or perceive. The "throwaway" part can be the overall dynamic range of the recording, the full-spectrum range—above the frequency range of what our ears can actually hear—or more. In this manner, MP3 compression is referred to as **lossy compression** because audio content has been removed from or modified within the audio file and cannot be retrieved. File sizes are decreased with, ideally, little or no perceived loss of quality depending on the type of compression used, making them suitable for digital transmission on websites and other means compared to high-quality audio that is larger in file size. By contrast, a zip file is a **lossless** type of compression in which files are identical prior to compression as they are once they are uncompressed.

## DID YOU KNOW?

### Perception of Quality

Vast numbers of perception studies have been conducted seeking to determine if the average person can tell the difference between a high-resolution uncompressed audio file, a CD-quality audio file, and a compressed MP3 audio file of the same piece. You can easily conduct a similar study with your friends. As we will discuss in Chapter 8, the field of psychoacoustics deals with these types of issues directly among other concepts. Being able to detect the difference may seem obvious, but to what extent have online video sites, low-quality speakers in restaurants, and built-in speaker(s) in portable electronic devices conditioned our ears to accept lower-fidelity audio as an acceptable standard of quality? Additionally, would a poor-quality instrument timbre recorded at 44.1k sound noticeably "better" if it was recorded at 192k? Can you notice the difference between a high-quality MP3 and an uncompressed format? an AAC, FLAC, OGG, or other compression format? The discussion continues.

### Bit Depth and Sampling Rate

The **sampling rate** is different from a **bit depth**, which refers to the amount of binary digits, or **bits** for short, that can be used to represent the data being recorded. For example, as you may know, "binary code" refers to a counting system using only the numbers 1 and 0 where 1 represents that something is in the state of being "on" and 0 represents that something is "off." Think about this in terms of your light switch having two states: the switch is on, state one; the switch is off, state zero.

The more 1s and 0s you string together, the longer the number will be and the more states you will be able to represent. For example, the 16-character binary "word" 1011101011110001 represents many more "on/off" states, 65,536 possible combinations of 0 and 1, than the 4-character word 1011 with its 16 possible states, and certainly more than a 1-character word with only two states: 0 or 1. A longer binary word can better represent something than a shorter one simply because it has more numbers to work with.

When a binary word is 16 characters long, it is said to be 16-bit; 32 characters is 32-bit, and so on. A 1-bit word has only one character and two possible states: 0 or 1. A 2-bit word has two characters and 4 possible combinations of 1s and 0s. An 8-bit word has 8 characters and can represent 256 possible values given the combination of 1s and 0s.

Recording something at 24-bit means that you are using more numbers to digitally represent the amplitude fluctuations of the recorded analog signal than if you recorded it at 16-bit. The sampling rate, as described earlier, refers to how frequently you will take "snapshots" (samples) of a continuous audio signal. Audio interfaces are compared to each other according to the quality of their A-to-D converters. In short: if you have the equipment necessary to record at a higher bit depth, do so!

## Audio Interface I/Os

Like mixers, audio interfaces have a number of input channels, commonly with XLR and ¼" connections; some are even shaped like mixers or double as live mixers and audio interfaces. The audio interface will probably also have built-in preamps, but that is where the similarities to the mixing board end. Once the signal is preamped, it is converted to digital and sent to a connected computer via some digital connection (typically USB or FireWire). Given the popularity of the electric guitar, it's not uncommon for one of the input channels on the soundcard to accept a Hi-Z "instrument level" input signal so that a guitarist can connect directly to the audio interface using a standard ¼" instrument cable.

Computers, especially portable computers, typically have built-in (sometimes called "on-board") soundcards that allow ⅛" stereo cables to be plugged into the computer as a line-in recording input in addition to microphones that are also built in. These built-in microphones, though convenient, are of lesser quality than would typically be used on a serious audio recording.

## DIGITAL AUDIO WORKSTATIONS

A computer communicates with audio interface using recording/editing/playback software programs. These programs are referred to as **digital audio**

**workstations**, or **DAWs**. Many DAWs are used for recording, including Pro Tools, Logic, GarageBand, Audacity, Cubase, FL Studio, and Live. Though they differ in terms of their appearance on the screen and some functionality, they are all able to receive digital audio from an audio interface and play it back in some manner through speakers. From within the DAW, the audio interfaces connected to your computer and their input channels will be accessible from the software. Clicking the Record button from within the software will allow signals received at the inputs of the audio interfaces to be imported digitally in real time within the DAW. In Chapter 3 we will examine the common features available when working with audio in a DAW.

## DID YOU KNOW?

### When Should You Convert the Analog Signal to Digital?

Once the signal is digital, the only limit to the amount of processing that can be done to the sound source is determined by what the computer's processing power can handle without crashing and by what the DAW software allows; literally millions of audio effects can be added, analyses can be calculated, and so on, all in real time. For this reason, some recording engineers prefer to convert the signal to digital as early in the signal flow as possible. The idea is to capture the live performance and convert it to the digital domain immediately and then use the computer to handle all of the effects processing. Eventually, the digital signal is converted back to an analog signal when it is sent from the soundcard to the speakers. An engineer following this approach might even use a digital snake, (like the snake described earlier, but uses analog signals converted into digital signals) if necessary, to take multiple inputs from a distant location and route them directly into the recording DAW being used.

Another school of thought is to get the analog signal sounding "just right" and then simply record what is heard into the digital domain at the last stage of the signal flow. Some engineers prefer to record the sound of a choir in a reverberant room, while others prefer to record them in a "dry" room and add digital reverb within a DAW. An engineer may run a vocal track through a dozen external hardware vocal effects processors before the signal ever reaches the recording console. The advantage of the former approach is that, for example, the amount and type of reverb can be changed freely in software, whereas it cannot be removed, only masked, if present on a recording.

# 🖑 GO TO SOFTWARE LESSON: *AUDIO RECORDER*

Using the FMT companion software, choose the lesson *Audio Recorder*. If necessary, slowly adjust the main volume slider at the top left of the software. To begin, let's demonstrate the basic function of all DAW:

- Click the play button near the orange circle *4*, or press the space bar.

Notice that the red playback line scrolls through the track. All DAWs operate in this fashion: a playback line moves forward at some tempo playing back anything in its path. Currently, there's nothing on this track, so let's record something. First:

- Ensure that the microphone input channel from your sound card or audio interface is selected in the menu near the orange circle *1*; for notebook computers, this is probably input channel *1* or *2*.

Next:

- Make sure the track is "armed" by observing the indicator near the orange circle *2*; DAWs use tracking "arming" as a way to distinguish tracks that will be recorded onto from tracks that will just play back.

If the track is armed, you should be able to see activity in the meter above the "arm" button. Make sure that your input is not so loud that it clips. Finally:

- Press the record button near the orange circle *3*.

This will allow you to record on this track for 10 seconds. After 10 seconds, recording will automatically stop. After recording:

- Press the play button again by clicking near orange circle *4* or by pressing the spacebar.

Consider the simplicity of the steps above, and understand that most DAWs are actually no different. What makes an unfamiliar DAW intimidating is the layout of the controls and other elements related to its operation, not understanding basic concepts like setting input channels, arming tracks, and clicking the master record button.

## SPEAKERS AND AMPLIFIERS

When the signal leaves the mixer, it is sent to speakers at the front of the stage, facing the audience. The speakers are the final stop in the signal path. The electrical signal causes the speaker to move, pushing air back and forth, which reproduces the sound. The signal being sent to the speakers must be increased using an amplifier. Powered speakers, also known as active speakers, have amplifiers built into the speaker cabinet, while passive speakers require the signal to first be sent to a dedicated power amplifier before connecting to the speaker.

Speakers have the difficult task of authentically reproducing the frequencies captured by the original sound source at the other end of the signal path. Instead of one single speaker having to represent all of these frequencies, the frequency range is distributed so that certain groups of frequencies, referred to as **bands**, are sent to speakers that are better suited to represent them more accurately.

For example, a subwoofer is a dedicated speaker used to play back low frequencies. When the signal from the mixer hits the amplifier in the speakers, a component, known as a **crossover**, filters the low-frequency content below a certain specified number (in Hz) and sends it to the subwoofer, which is designed to reproduce these low frequencies accurately. Even though speakers might be rated as "full range," meaning that they can accurately reproduce all of the audible frequency content that is sent to them, a subwoofer helps to ease some of this responsibility by handling the lowest frequencies.

In general, a good-sounding speaker setup, be it a PA, an instrument amplifier, or a home theater, will faithfully represent the full frequency range of the audio content that is being sent through it. Poor-quality speakers may have "gaps" or "holes" in the playback where bands of frequencies are attenuated, or lost, by the speakers' inability to accurately reproduce those frequencies.

A typical "House Public Address (PA)," or "Front of House (FOH)," sound system involves at least two main speakers. If the sound system is set up so that each of the main speakers is capable of playing back different audio content, the system is said to be in "**stereo**." If the same audio content comes out of both speakers, the system is said to be in "**mono**." Running a PA in stereo can improve clarity in the overall sound.

Imagine a band with two guitarists. If each guitarist's signal is primarily coming through only one of the two main speakers, the listener will likely experience some sense of spatiality in the mix, whereas if the same audio content comes from each speaker, the individual guitar parts might become hard to distinguish. The downside of using a stereo configuration is that some people seated on the right side of the venue might not be getting the same sound experience as the people on the left side. It's not uncommon for large venues to have multiple stereo pairs of speakers placed in clusters around the hall.

Multi-channel speaker configurations are also popular in theaters. For example, a configuration with three speakers in the front of the audience (left, center, and right), two speakers behind the audience (rear left and rear right), and one subwoofer is known as a "5.1" configuration; the "5" indicates the number of speakers and the "1" indicates the number of subwoofers. A "10.2" configuration would mean 10 speakers and two subs. Note that a subwoofer can typically be placed anywhere in the room since the low-frequency waves it produces are not as easily blocked or absorbed by people in the venue as other frequencies are.

## MICROPHONE TYPES AND BASIC PLACEMENT

Microphones, or **mics**, come in many different varieties. In concept, they are the same; they capture sounds as they travel through the air and convert them into electrical signals. Microphones are labeled as being able to capture sounds within some specified range of frequencies and are designed to have different directional patterns by which they pick up sound. For example, some microphones are said to be **omnidirectional**, meaning that they pick up sound in all directions, which can be useful with choirs or recording sounds in nature. **Unidirectional** microphones record in one pattern and are ideal for use directly in front of a sound source. Some microphones have the ability to switch the directional pattern and will often depict the "polar pattern" in a graphic within the manual. An engineer should consider the sound source being recorded and choose the ideal pattern; for example, if you're recording a vocalist, it's probably not necessary to use an omnidirectional microphone pattern.

**Dynamic microphones** are popular for use in live and studio applications. In practice, these mics are best placed close to the sound source being mic'd so as to prevent other sounds from "bleeding" into the mic. Dynamic microphones are known to increase the volume of the bass frequencies when placed in close proximity to the sound source. For example, a vocalist who puts the microphone very close, even touching, his or her mouth while singing will produce a warmer, bassier tone on the receiving end of the mic line, even if his or her tone in actuality is somewhat thin.

Windscreens are soft foam covers used on mics to filter pops and other unwanted noises from passing through to the mic. This is especially useful for mic'ing singers for whom plosive consonants often cause the signal level to clip in the microphone. For example, words beginning with the letter P tend to cause a pop that can be softened with the use of a windscreen.

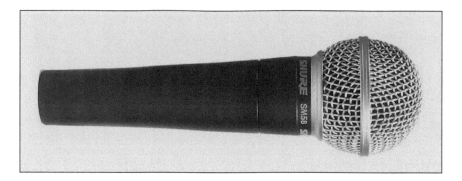

FIGURE 2.11: The popular Shure SM58 dynamic mic (From Fergusson, 2006)

Wireless microphones are typically just dynamic microphones with an additional wireless transmitter component through which the signal is sent via the airwaves to a receiver connected to the mixer. Because of the inherent loss of signal quality during the wireless transmission, wireless microphones are not used in studio situations but are common in live performance situations where such quality loss is less noticeable.

**Condenser microphones** are another type of microphone that are ideal for live and studio situations. Unlike dynamic microphones, condenser mics are much more sensitive to sound and, as a rule of thumb, should not be placed in any location that you wouldn't feel comfortable putting or leaving your ears; for example, not directly on a kick drum or guitar cabinet. Instead, a good starting place for a condenser microphone is some distance away from the sound source where it is agreed the sound is most pleasant to the ears.

Unlike dynamic mics, condenser mics require power in order to operate. For this reason, most mixers and audio interfaces are equipped with a "48-V" switch, referred to as "phantom power," which sends power to the microphone.

FIGURE 2.12: An AKG C414 Condenser microphone

## Microphone Placement

There are numerous techniques for and approaches to achieving great-sounding audio recordings and live mixes, much of which is contextual. Proper microphone placement can be approached scientifically by observing the construction of the room and accounting for the ways in which the room design will change the sound source. However, there is also something to be said for the real-world experimentation with mic placement that tends to happen "on the fly." For example, the balance of the ensemble you're recording may be so poor that it's better to mic each individual instrument, called "spot mic'ing," and rely on the

CHAPTER 2 • Audio 37

engineer to balance the mix using a mixer or from within the computer DAW. On the other hand, the ensemble balance may be so perfect that just two mics are needed to capture the live mix of a performance. Sometimes it's nice to use a combination of both approaches in which an overall balanced mix is mic'ed while additionally spot mic'ing each individual instrument, or groups of instruments, in case they need to be boosted in the mix.

One popular technique for capturing a balanced mix is to use two identical—referred to as "matched"—condenser microphones placed near each other in order to simulate the way our ears capture a single sound source. The mics are usually placed very high in the room using microphone stands and are positioned so that the mics themselves are at angles facing each other, almost touching, in what is known as an XY pattern. In concept, the sound arrives at each of the microphones at the same time from different angles. Typically, on the receiving side (i.e., the mixer or the DAW), each respective mic signal would then be sent to either the left or right speaker to represent the manner in which the audio was captured with a "left" and "right" microphone.

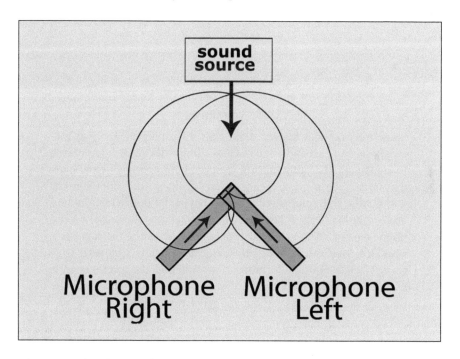

FIGURE 2.13: The X/Y microphone position (From Fergusson, 2007)

## Panning

Adjusting the relative volume that an audio signal has in a particular speaker is called **panning**. An audio track can be "panned" left to make it more present in the left speaker, panned center with an even distribution of the signal in both speakers, or panned right. Panning a signal all the way to the left speaker, for example, with no representation of the signal in the right speaker, is called panning the signal "hard left." Panning "hard left" and "hard right" is common in simple stereo recording situations like the XY pattern recording technique that we just discussed.

## Other Technologies and Techniques

There are various different mic'ing techniques in existence for recording and live situations, many of which are discussed in online forums and professional musician publications. Often times, new techniques come about through experimentation. If you only have one microphone, you might be surprised to learn that there are specialized techniques and approaches to mic'ing drum sets, ensembles, choirs, and more. An engineer recording an electric guitar 4 × 12 cabinet might place two mics against the speaker—one offset from the amp logo, one placed behind it—or more mics 25 feet away, and so on, then mixing these tracks to create a unique sound that is, perhaps, even better than the original. Use your ears as your guide.

### DID YOU KNOW?

#### USB Microphones

Some microphones marketed as "USB microphones" are part microphone and part audio interface in a single device. It is important to remember that although the cost of these hybrid microphones may seem like a great savings over equally priced microphones without the USB connectivity, you are paying for both a microphone and an audio interface. For example, the quality of the actual microphone part of a $600 USB microphone might not be the same as a standard $600 microphone. The same is typically true with anything labeled "portable," "compact," or "mobile"; the convenience of using something that is smaller comes often with a higher price tag than the larger version without an increase in quality.

A **pickup** found in electric guitars and other electroacoustic instruments is a small transducer used to convert the acoustic sound of a host instrument into an electrical signal. The source signal is "picked up" through vibration of the instrument, although the actual mechanism will vary depending on the type of pickup being used. In electric guitars, magnetic pickups are installed inside the body of the guitar, which, depending on the location of the pickup beneath the strings, will produce a different timbre given the way the strings resonate at the location of the pickup. There are also guitar pickups that convert the analog signal to digital just as USB microphones do.

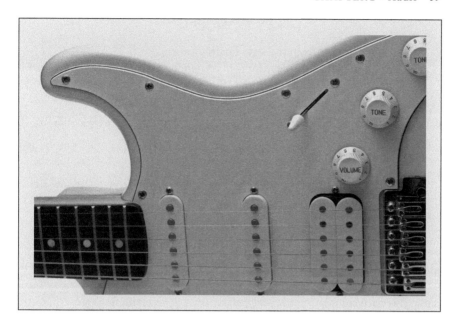

FIGURE 2.14: Electric guitar pickups (Courtesy MarianoR/iStock)

Many types of audio equipment exist, and it is easier to think about each component in terms of "what you need" as opposed to "what is available." A choir ensemble needs a good set of stereo microphones, a small PA or recording system, and likely little else. A 19-piece jazz fusion ensemble with electronic instruments may need much more: direct boxes, microphones, amplifiers, XLR cables, ¼″ cables, stage monitors, in-ear monitors, effects processors, and so on. Consider the music you like and the types of music you intend to record and mix, and determine the types of equipment you may need to obtain. Do you really need to mic every instrument in your drum kit, or will a few mics positioned properly do the trick for your purposes? To what extent does the technology facilitate your live sound? Does it dictate it? Does it make it possible? Does it make it better or worse?

## SUMMARY

This chapter contains a broad spectrum of information regarding the types of equipment used in audio production. In general, the goal in using this equipment is to keep the musical material at the start of the signal chain "pure" right through the entire path until it comes out of the speakers or goes into the computer. In order to preserve the signal's integrity, we need to understand the nature of the signal being transmitted or recorded in terms of balanced and unbalanced signals, and so on; many of the devices and cable types differ with regard to how they can help you preserve the signal without introducing artifacts in a way that would degrade the signal quality. Once you are working with high-quality audio in a "clean" signal path that is free of "hum," "buzzes," "hiss," and other annoying sounds, you are free to mix and record your musical material in any way you see fit.

# KEY CONCEPTS

- It is important to keep the signal path uniform.
- You can make better recordings if you understand the various cable connector types, including XLR and ¼″.
- Dynamic microphones are good for mic'ing loud sounds up close.
- Condenser microphones are sensitive and shouldn't go directly against or near loud sounds.
- Mixers receive multiple channels of audio.
- Audio interfaces allow for analog-to-digital conversion.
- Bit depth and sampling rate relate to the conversion from an analog signal to a digital one and the way the signal is captured.

# KEY TERMS

analog-to-digital (A-to-D) conversion
audio interface/sound card/recording interface
audio snake
band (frequency)
bit
bit depth
boost
channel
clip
compression
condenser microphone
crossover
cut
digital audio workstation (DAW)
direct box/DI
dynamic microphone
feedback
gain
gain stage

Hi-Z (high impedance)
-inf (negative infinity decibels)
input
instrument level signal
line level signal
lossy/lossless compression
Lo-Z (low impedance)
mic (microphone)
microphone level signal
mixing board/mixer/mixing console
mono
omnidirectional microphone
output
panning
pickup
power amplifier
preamplifier/preamp
RCA connection/cable

resistance/impedance
sample
sampling rate
signal
signal path/signal chain/signal flow
speakers
stage monitor
stems
stereo
Thru output
tracks
⅛″ TRS cables
TRS (tip, ring, sleeve)
¼″ cable
TS (tip and sleeve)
¼″ cable/instrument cable
U/unity gain
unidirectional microphone
XLR cable
Z (symbol)

# CHAPTER 3

# AUDIO EDITING SOFTWARE

## OVERVIEW

**D**igital audio workstations, or **DAWs,** allow users to record, edit, and publish audio in some manner. In this chapter we'll do some basic recording and editing using the application Audacity, as well as some loop-based composition using the application GarageBand, for Macintosh users, and Mixcraft, for Windows users.

While the term "DAW" typically implies the use of hardware like a computer in the audio production process, it is common for individuals to refer to the audio editing software as the DAW. All DAWs typically offer some way of working with audio, through recording and sound manipulation, and MIDI, a software-based representation of musical pitches used in synthesis applications (see Chapter 5).

Although many DAWs claim to be "the industry standard," a variety of DAWs are in use by professional musicians and engineers. Among the most popular DAWs are **Pro Tools, Logic, Live, Cubase, FL Studio, and Digital Performer.** While each DAW is different in layout and the organization of tools, they all are fundamentally the same: they all house musical material and play it back over time. Of course, some DAWs have more sophisticated ways of doing this as well as performing additional tasks. Some DAWs can be used to facilitate live performance in some manner (see Chapter 10). A list of popular commercial and free DAWs is available on the companion website for this book.

## BASIC DAW FUNCTIONS

In Chapter 2 we addressed the basic functionality of most DAWs by using the FMT software lesson Audio Recorder. There we discussed arming tracks, selecting the input channels, and so on. One main function of a DAW is to allow you to edit and manipulate what you've recorded. For the demonstration purposes of this chapter, we will use the free software Audacity to record some audio and edit it. Take a moment to download Audacity from http://audacity.sourceforge.net and install it onto your computer. Even if you decide to never use Audacity after this chapter, many of the concepts discussed will transfer to any DAW of your choosing.

## Basic Recording and Editing

- Open Audacity.
- When the application has loaded, take a moment to explore each menu item within the application.

You can expect that some menus will house unfamiliar terms.

We're going to record a new audio track and edit it together. Within Audacity:

- Ensure that your *Input Device* and other soundcard properties are properly selected from the menus beneath the playback transport.

For most computers with built-in microphones, this input source will be selected by default. If you encounter problems with this step, open *FMT* and, within Audacity, select the same audio properties that were used in *FMT*.

FIGURE 3.1: The basic transport menu in Audacity

- Click the Record button from the transport to begin recording onto a new track.
- Read the following narrative from *Hamlet* while recording:
  - What a piece of work is a man! How noble in reason, how infinite in faculty! In form and moving how express and admirable! In action how like an angel, in apprehension how like a god! The beauty of the world. The paragon of animals. And yet, to me, what is this quintessence of dust? Man delights not me. No, nor woman neither, though by your smiling you seem to say so (2.2.13).
- Click the Stop button to end the recording.

Don't worry if you messed up, stuttered, or mispronounced "quintessence." We will edit those mistakes and more.

You should now have a single track of audio resembling that pictured in Figure 3.2. If your recording session was a complete disaster, click the X near the top left of the track to delete it, then repeat these steps until you are happy with the result.

- Press the Play button on the transport to play back what you recorded.

There is likely a small amount of space at the beginning and end of your track that occurred between the times you clicked the Record/Stop button and

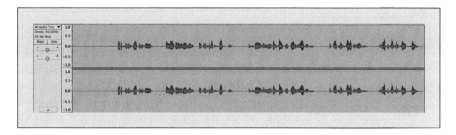

FIGURE 3.2: A track containing recorded audio

began/ended speaking. Perhaps there's even a "click" sound that occurred when your microphone recorded the sound of your finger touching the mouse or track-pad. To trim this out:

- Highlight the space you'd like to delete by clicking within the waveform on the audio track and selecting the region to delete.

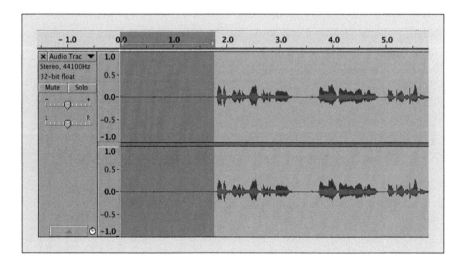

FIGURE 3.3: Highlighted selection for deletion

DAWs like Audacity provide the flexibility to work with recorded audio just as you would the text of a Microsoft Word document; copying, pasting, cutting, deleting, etc. Take a moment and do the following to your recorded audio:

- Highlight some portion of audio on the track, copy it, and paste it elsewhere using the options available from the Edit menu or the equivalent key commands you may already know.
- Adjust the level and panning from the controls on the track.

## Gain Levels

In most DAWs, knobs, sliders, or other controls are used to allow the engineer to reduce or increase the strength of the signal coming into the software at the recording stage and going out of the software during the playback stage. As we have discussed, the measure of increase or decrease of the level is expressed in gain. Increasing the gain controls will ultimately increase the strength of the signal.

The controls in most DAWs are labeled using **decibels (dB)** as the unit of measure for the strength of the signal. As sounds are played, indicators will reflect the decibel level reached. Although it might seem that a decibel level of 0 would result in no sound, the decibel unit is read according to a different scale (see Chapter 8). The decibel level 0 dB on an input recording channel means that there is no increase or decrease in gain being applied to the signal as it's being recorded. Remember, the level where no gain is being added to or taken away from a signal is known as unity gain (see Chapter 2).

If, after playing the sound within the DAW, it is determined that the recorded sound is too loud, the output gain, sometimes labeled Track Volume, Master Volume, or Main Volume, is lowered and the decibel level of the sound is decreased.

## Importing Audio

It is also possible to download audio files from a website or from a portable recorder and import that audio into Audacity and other DAWs. In some DAWs, this is as simple as dragging the audio files from their folder into the DAW timeline. In other cases, such as Audacity, choose File>Import>Audio from the main menu. It can be a great learning experience to import several songs into a DAW and create a "mashup" of different styles.

## OVERDUBBING AND PREVENTING FEEDBACK

Let's record an additional audio track into this session by **overdubbing** a $\frac{4}{4}$ kick drum pattern. If you don't have a kick drum handy, vocalize the sound, tap on the desk, or stomp on the floor.

Before we begin, we need to consider the signal chain we've been working with. As pictured in Figure 3.4, the microphone input comes into the soundcard. The signal is then converted into numbers by the computer through an analog-to-digital (A-to-D) converter, where it is graphically displayed in Audacity. Then, upon playback, the digital signal is converted back into an analog signal through a **digital-to-analog (DAC)** converter, where we hear it with our ears through the speakers. Depending on your setup, your microphone, soundcard, and speakers may be built into the computer you're using.

When we overdub a recording, we're playing back the existing recorded tracks while recording new tracks. However, if your speaker is playing back those prerecorded tracks while you're recording new audio material, the microphone will record what is playing through the speakers while it records the new audio. This concept of **unintentionally recording unwanted external sound sources is**

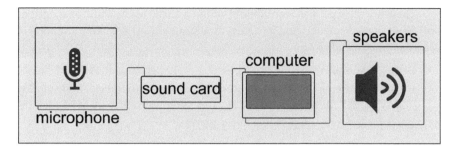

FIGURE 3.4: A typical signal path using a computer and a soundcard

known as **bleed**. To prevent bleed, we have to isolate the audio output from the audio input so they are not interfering with each other.

Wearing headphones is one solution. When you plug headphones into your computer's soundcard, you will or may disable the computer's speakers. This results in audio being sent to the headphones alone and prevents it from being picked up from the microphone when an overdubbed recording begins.

- Plug in a set of headphones.
- Press the Play button on the transport to ensure that audio is playing back through the headphones and not through the speakers. (Note: For some setups, powering off the speakers may be necessary.)
- Click the Record button on the transport and vocalize or play a consistent $\frac{4}{4}$ bass drum sound throughout the duration of the previously recorded track.
- Press the Stop button on the transport when you are done.
- Play back the session, which should now feature two tracks.
- Adjust the level of each track accordingly.

## DID YOU KNOW?

### Preventing Bleed

Imagine trying to record a saxophonist and a drummer simultaneously as isolated tracks. There's no way that bleed won't occur across the tracks if the performers are standing near each other. You need to get creative. Having the talent play in separate rooms while they monitor their performance with headphones is one solution. Another solution is to use recording baffles or other sound-dampening material to block the sound from reaching the microphone. Unidirectional microphone patterns are good at avoiding unwanted sound but need to be positioned away from the other sound sources. This will reduce the amount of bleed on the tracks. If a band records simultaneously, some bleed across the tracks is normal, though, ideally, it is minimal.

These are the basics of overdubbing within a DAW. Many additional options will be discussed in later chapters such as adding effects, adjusting the tone of recorded tracks, and so on.

- Click File>Save to save this session.
- Click File>Export to save this recording as an uncompressed, high-quality WAV or AIF file suitable for a CD, or as a compressed, lossy **MP3** file suitable for the web and portable music players.

## DID YOU KNOW?

### Always Explore the Menu Items

A software application doesn't always have an icon for every useful feature it allows. That's why it's important to check the menu items and submenu items to get a sense of what a particular piece of software has to offer in terms of functionality. For example, you can change the tempo of a song without changing the pitch just by going to the *Effect* menu in Audacity and choosing *Change Tempo*—an incredibly useful feature for learning to play along with fast songs at slower tempos. Consider the implications for composition, performance, and education that this one feature alone contains!

## LOOP-BASED DAWS

As mentioned, there are many different kinds of DAWs in existence. Some DAWs contain large libraries of prerecorded ostinato patterns called **loops**. Using prerecorded looped patterns of drums, bass, guitar, keyboards, and other instruments allows users to compose music through **recombinance**—recombining music ideas to make new musical ideas. Building compositions from loops can allow you to combine a dense background track from looped patterns with newly composed material that you record through a microphone.

Among the most popular looping programs are GarageBand (Mac computers) and Mixcraft (Windows). If you own a Mac, you likely already have Garage-Band in your *Applications* folder. For Windows users, download the free trial of *Mixcraft* from http://www.acoustica.com/mixcraft and install it onto your computer.

- Open GarageBand or Mixcraft and begin a new blank session.
- When the session has loaded, take a moment to explore each menu item within the program.

Take a moment to identify the similarities between this DAW and Audacity. Notice how they are visually different, but their functionality is quite similar.

- Click in the middle of the DAW and press the spacebar to begin playback.

Notice how the playback head, or scrubber, moves through the empty DAW session. This is, essentially, the fundamental task of each DAW: to play back what you put into this timeline. Putting interesting material into that timeline is the task of the user.

• Locate the Loop library within the DAW, often revealed by clicking an icon or by going to the *View* menu.

FIGURE 3.5: The loop library icon in GarageBand

You are given the option to view the loops in the library according to descriptive criteria about its timbre or associated style.

• Drag a few loops into your timeline, noting that tracks are automatically created.

There is a visual distinction in most DAWs between loops that were recorded with a microphone and synthesized MIDI loops. Audio loops and recordings display an audio waveform, while MIDI loops and recordings display a line-based graphic. (See Chapter 5 for a further discussion of MIDI, but for now, MIDI can be thought of as a computerized representation of pitches.)

| Reset ⊗ | Favorites ♥ | Rock/Blues | Electronic |
|---|---|---|---|
| Click to find loops by instrument, genre, and mood. | | | World |
| Beats | Percussion | Jazz | Orchestral |
| Bass | Tambourine | Experimental | Cinematic |
| Synths | Shaker | Country | Other Genre |
| Piano | Conga | Single | Ensemble |
| Elec Piano | Bongo | Clean | Distorted |
| Organ | Mallets | Acoustic | Electric |
| Clavinet | Vibes | Relaxed | Intense |
| Guitars | Strings | Cheerful | Dark |
| Slide Guitar | Woodwind | Dry | Processed |
| Banjo | Horn | Grooving | Arrhythmic |
| Vocals | Saxophone | Melodic | Dissonant |
| Sound Effects | Textures | Part | Fill |

FIGURE 3.6: A loop library menu for auditioning new looped material

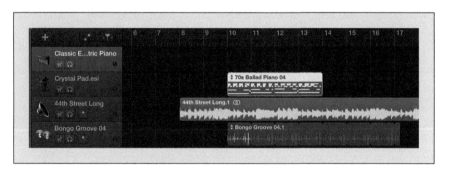

FIGURE 3.7: Loops dragged to the DAW timeline

Every DAW provides the flexibility to add tracks to the session. Both Garage-Band and Mixcraft, along with nearly every DAW, allow users to record and work with audio and MIDI tracks.

• Add a new audio track in your DAW by choosing Track>New Track . . . from the menu.

Recording an audio track can be accomplished using the same general steps we followed in using Audacity. Arm the new track for recording, if necessary, ensuring that the proper input channels are selected, and click the Record button from the transport. Some applications like GarageBand attempt to simplify the recording process and, by default, arm the track for you when it's selected. You

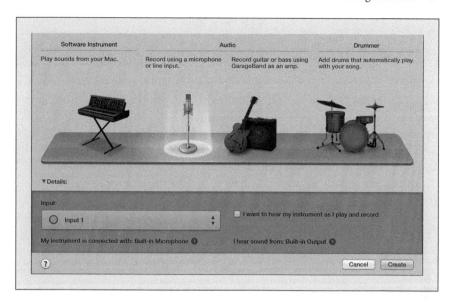

FIGURE 3.8: The "New Track" window in GarageBand prompts you to add MIDI and audio tracks to your session

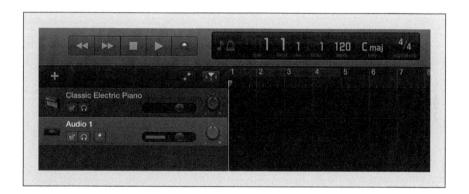

FIGURE 3.9: A new track armed for recording

are then only required to select the track you want to record into and click the Record button from the transport.

Recording MIDI data into a DAW is nearly the same operation with the exception that, instead of using a microphone to capture audio into a track, you use a MIDI device like a keyboard to record "MIDI data" onto a track. This will be discussed further in Chapter 5, but you may explore this option now if you have a MIDI keyboard.

Continue to explore the features available within the DAW and view the helpful tutorial videos and "Getting Started" documents available from the developer's website and popular video website channels.

# SUMMARY

There are many types of music software that allow individuals to record and edit audio. The concepts of obtaining the initial audio are generally the same: record the audio, or import it in some way. Once the audio is in the DAW, the software will allow individuals to edit the recording to their liking. It is important to remember that most DAWs will differ in terms of their on-screen graphical user interface, or GUI, and the quality and number of effects and process they may offer but will generally operate quite similarly. Whether you continue to use the DAW described in this chapter or have already become fond of a particular DAW doesn't matter as long as you know how to use the technology to facilitate your creative ideas.

# KEY CONCEPTS

- Digital Audio Workstations, or DAWs, typically allow audio and MIDI to be sequenced and edited in some sophisticated way.
- Recording is the process of capturing an analog signal and, in the case of computer recording, converting that signal into a digital representation.
- Overdubbing is the process of layering recorded audio on top of previously recorded audio.
- Feedback occurs when a speaker's output signal "bleeds" into the microphone's input.
- Loops are prerecorded patterns and phrases of audio and MIDI used in combinatory methods of composition.

# KEY TERMS

analog-to-digital (A-to-D) conversion

bleed

digital-to-analog (DAC) conversion

digital audio workstation (DAW)

loop

MP3

overdubbing

recombinance

# CHAPTER 4

# SYNTHESIS

## OVERVIEW

In this chapter we will discuss several methods of synthesis and some of the general controls used to create synthesized sounds with keyboards and computers. We will describe the nature of creating new timbres through a variety of synthesis methods including additive synthesis, subtractive synthesis, AM and FM synthesis, and granular synthesis. We will also discuss ways to change qualities of the synthesized sounds over time. By the end of this chapter, you should feel comfortable approaching a software or hardware synthesizer and be able to adjust the controls to create your desired sound.

If there's one chapter in this book that is going to require more of your focus and patience than others, it's probably this chapter. The difficulty here is that thinking about signals and waves is not something musicians often do. Fortunately, it's something that music technologists do or, at least, have done. Thankfully, a lot of the ground has already been broken in the synthesis world. You only need to get a grasp of what types of things you can do with synthesizers and roughly how to do them. In this way, your creative works will benefit from the vast uses of synthesizers.

## WAVEFORMS

Until this point, we have primarily been discussing sine waves, but, as you may know, there are other types of **waveforms**.

## 🖑 GO TO SOFTWARE LESSON: *SINE WAVE*

Using the FMT companion software, choose the lesson *Sine Wave*. If necessary, slowly adjust the main volume slider at the top left of the software. We have previously examined this lesson in Chapter 1 for the purpose of observing sinusoids.

- Click the small *waveform select* icon at the bottom right of the wave display window and select a different waveform icon.
- Set the wave frequency to *100* and observe the shape, sound, and name of each wave as you select them from the *waveform select* icon.

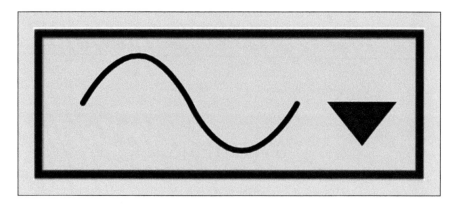

FIGURE 4.1: The *waveform select* icon

The square wave, for example, resembles a square shape. Given their unique shape, these waves produce harmonics above their fundamental frequency that give them distinct timbral properties that differ from sine waves. Notice, for example, that a square wave looks like a sine wave that was too loud and has had its signal "clipped"; in fact, the sound of a square wave seems somewhat clipped or distorted compared to the pure tone of a sine wave. Understanding these sonic differences will help you to synthetically construct new sounds from these basic waveforms.

## ADDITIVE SYNTHESIS

**Additive synthesis** is a type of synthesis in which waves are combined to make new timbres. This is the same technique we discussed when describing *timbre* (see Chapter 1). In that *Harmonic Series* example, we had nine oscillators generating sine waves at different frequencies, and we literally added all those sine waves on top of each other to make a new complex sound.

## ☝ GO TO SOFTWARE LESSON: *HARMONIC SERIES*

Using the FMT companion software, choose the lesson *Harmonic Series*. If necessary, slowly adjust the main volume slider at the top left of the software.

- Press the number keys 1–9 to fade in the overtones for a given fundamental frequency as noted near orange circle 2.
- Adjust the amplitude slider for each overtone to change the overall timbre for notes played using the onscreen keyboard.

This is an example of additive synthesis because we are literally *adding* sine waves together to create a new timbre. Note, however, that "adding" a 100 Hz wave and a 200 Hz wave does not give you a single 300 Hz wave; it's not that type of summation. It simply yields two waves, one at 100 Hz and one at 200 Hz, that, when sounded together, are perceived as a single timbre with a pitch of 100 Hz.

- Click the small *waveform select* icon at the bottom left of the screen and select a different waveform icon.

Notice how simply swapping one waveform for another drastically changes the overall timbre.

---

### DID YOU KNOW?

### Fourier Transform

In additive synthesis, we're building new complex sounds using simple waves as building blocks. When attempting to emulate existing sounds, spectral analysis processes can be used to break a complex sound into smaller parts for the purpose of analyzing its individual, or *discrete*, wave makeup. A special process known as the **Fourier Transform**, named after Jean-Baptiste Fourier, a mathematician and physicist in the late 1700s, is used to convert from the "time domain" to the "frequency domain." The time domain can be thought of as an audio signal represented in units of time like milliseconds and seconds; the frequency domain can be thought of as the representation of the frequencies, in hertz, of that same audio signal. One implementation of this process is the spectrogram in Chapter 1 that plots visual representations of frequencies and amplitudes from an audio file (revisit the *Spectrogram* lesson in the accompanying software if desired). In the *Spectrogram* lesson, for each sound example that is played, tiny slices of the audio file, called **frames**, are analyzed and information about the frequencies in each sample of the frame, called **bins**, are reported.

The Fourier Transform is a complicated process, and, as such, an algorithm called the **Fast Fourier Transform,** or **FFT**, is used instead to quickly perform the calculations of the Fourier Transform. In addition to analysis, there are numerous audio processes that use FFTs, including processes related to pitch-shifting and "autotuning" as well as those that change the playback speed of sounds without changing the pitch.

---

## ENVELOPES AND ADSR CURVES

Consider a vocalist singing a sustained note. Even though the note remains the same in pitch, there are properties about its sound that evolve over time. In fact, even the way in which the singer opened his or her mouth to begin the note had a lot to do with the note's sound. The note doesn't just begin and stay the same volume until it ends. There are tiny fluctuations along the way that give the singer's voice its unique timbre. However, synthesizing a sound by simply combining sine wave results in sounds that don't evolve over time. Therefore, various synthesis techniques have been designed, in part, to allow electronic instruments to be musically expressive, harmonically rich, and timbrally interesting.

Every sound can be described in terms of its **envelope**, the "shape" of the sound's perceived volume as it varies over time. The properties of an envelope are generally divided into four sections: **attack time, decay time, sustain volume,** and **release time**. These four properties are often referred to collectively as an **ADSR envelope,** or simply **ADSR**.

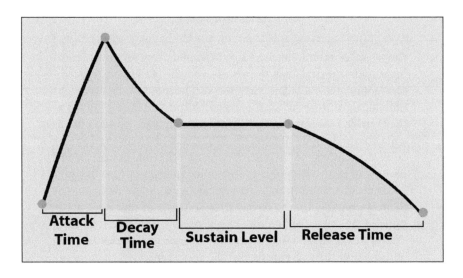

FIGURE 4.2: An ADSR envelope curve

## 🖑 GO TO SOFTWARE LESSON: *ADSR*

Using the FMT companion software, choose the lesson *ADSR*. If necessary, slowly adjust the main volume slider at the top left of the software. Notice the *ADSR* envelope curve shown as a graphic within the software.

- Click and hold a key on the graphic keyboard as shown near the orange circle *1*.

Notice that the sound follows the contour of the graphic curve. The note reaches its peak in level over some amount of time (*attack*), decays to another level over another period of time (*decay*), and sustains at that same level as long as the key is held down (*sustain*). When the key is lifted, the note fades out over some amount of time (*release*).

- Click the preset envelope shapes as shown near orange circle *2*, then audition the timbral change resulting from the envelope shape change by, once again, clicking the keyboard near orange circle *1*.

- Adjust the components of the *ADSR* envelope manually using the controls near orange circles *3–6*.
- The synthesized note is generated by summing the signal from 9 oscillators as we did in the *Harmonic Series* lesson.
- Change the waveform type by clicking the *waveform select* icon near orange circle *7*.

An abundance of sophisticated synthesizers, both hardware and software, exist. Some basic controls found on most synthesizers include the ability to adjust the envelope, quantity, and waveform of its oscillators. Synthesizers may even add audio effects and processes at various points in the signal chain to expand the timbral possibilities.

## PHYSICAL MODELING

In principle, with enough time, the right information, and a powerful computer, one can create a synthesized sound that sounds identical to any existing acoustic sound. In fact, a type of synthesis called **physical modeling** exists in which computers are used to implement a mathematical model of the physics of an acoustic instrument, ideally, capturally all of the aspects of the instrument's sound. One such physical modeling process, known as the **Karplus-Strong string synthesis** algorithm, was developed to synthetically produce the sound of a plucked string using a computer. The process of producing such a model begins by obtaining information about how each component of a plucked string, such as on a guitar, changes over time. For example, a researcher would observe the sound of a plucked string and make note of what happens to the sound over time:

- the initial noise burst when the string is plucked
- the frequencies present in the burst based on the string and note plucked
- how those notes decayed
- the fluctuations in amplitude and pitch as the overall sound decayed

The information is then implemented inside of a computer model to create sounds based on the data that was gathered. Physical models are also used to simulate the extension of an instrument range beyond the pitch range of what it can actually produce. Imagine what a piccolo would sound like in the pitch range of a double bass; a physical model can realize this concept.

As you might imagine, this is a computationally intense data-driven process. It is useful to point out one of the main obstacles of producing any sound you'd like with a computer is computational power, and its limitations. For example, an additive synthesis approach to creating a clarinet sound would involve adding numerous time-varying sine waves together to imitate the instrument. To save time and reduce the computational load, an approach called **wavetable synthesis** is often used. A wavetable simply stores a set of values that represent what a clarinet waveform look likes. Wavetable synthesis uses that wavetable to synthesize the desired timbre instead of computing and adding together multiple sine waves.

Even though conserving computer-processing power is becoming less of a concern as computers become more powerful, many synthesis techniques were developed so that new sounds can be created with a minimal number of oscillators and controls to conserve computer-processing resources. As we begin discussing some of these techniques, you may be surprised to learn how our understanding of engineering and physics has influenced these pursuits.

## COMBINING WAVES

Even with an ADSR curve applied, combining sine waves produces synthesized sounds that lack the evolving timbral color present when playing a harmonically-rich acoustic instrument: the way a piano string changes timbrally over time as it decays, the way that harmonics from an overdriven electric guitar slowly turn into feedback, and so on. To address this problem, synthesis techniques have been developed to give synthetic sounds the characteristic that their timbre is more richly and subtly changing over time.

## 🖐 GO TO SOFTWARE LESSON: *COMBINING WAVES*

Using the FMT companion software, choose the lesson *Combining Waves*. If necessary, slowly adjust the main volume slider at the top left of the software.

In the graphic display, the first section labeled "Wave 1" is added with "Wave 2" to produce "Wave 3." In this example, two waves, one at 440 Hz and one at 441 Hz, are added together. The summed signal is shown in the graphical display near orange circle 3. Slowly increase the amplitude of the second oscillator near orange circle 2 from 0 to 1 (full signal strength) and observe the shape of the combined signal as well as the sound.

If two identical signals are played at the same time—for example, both frequencies at 440 Hz—the overall amplitude of the combined signal will be boosted. However, having one frequency at 440 Hz and one at 441 Hz demonstrates a concept known as **beating** or **beat interference,** commonly experienced by instrumentalists while tuning instruments. If the frequency value of the second oscillator is close to the first oscillator, the amplitude of the combined signals dips and increases slowly over time, an effect referred to as **tremolo.** The perceived notion to the listener is that the first (the lower) frequency is slowly decreasing and increasing in volume. As you increase the frequency of the second oscillator, the rate of the beating will increase. As the degree of separation between the two frequencies increases, the second oscillator will be perceived as having a pitch that is noticeably different from the first oscillator. This noticeable change in pitch is known as **vibrato**.

- Click the preset near orange circle 4 labeled *"Play: 440–450 vibrato"* to demonstrate this concept.

DID YOU KNOW?

## Is It Tremolo or Vibrato?

The tremolo effect refers to a perceived change in amplitude, whereas vibrato refers to a perceived change in pitch. Guitarists beware: the so-called tremolo arm or "whammy bar" on your electric guitar would be more appropriately named the vibrato arm since it is used to noticeably change the pitch.

## Phase

Remember that if two identical signals are played at the same time, the overall amplitude of the combined signal will be boosted. In the previous example, the rates by which each of the two waves cycled from an amplitude of 0 to 1 were slightly out of sync with each other, with one moving at 440 times per second and another moving at 441 times per second. If instead of using two sine waves we had used a sound source with multiple frequencies such as a square wave or even a recorded song, a similar effect called **phase** would occur. If one of the signals is delayed slightly, a slow "sweeping" effect called phase is produced whereby the amplitude of certain frequencies in the signal are varied over time.

- Click the *Phase* preset to demonstrate this effect.

In this preset, two sawtooth waveforms, which contain overtones above their fundamental frequency, are used in place of the sine waves. Notice that the combined mix seems to evolve or "sweep" over time. It is the same concept as the tremolo and vibrato phenomena, but because the example uses a harmonically rich sound source—that is, the sawtooth wave—the phase effect is more pronounced. You may change the waveform type from sawtooth waves to other waves by clicking the small waveform select icon near orange circles 5 and 6.

## Multiplying Waves

In addition to adding waves together to create new sounds, it's also possible to multiply one wave by another. In essence, this concept is a type of **modulation** in which one signal is used to change properties of another signal.

## 🖐 GO TO SOFTWARE LESSON: *MULTIPLYING WAVES*

Using the FMT companion software, choose the lesson *Multiplying Waves*. If necessary, slowly adjust the main volume slider at the top left of the software.

This lesson is similar to the *Combining Waves* lesson with the exception that the waves are now being multiplied. In the graphic display, the first section labeled "Wave 1" is multiplied by "Wave 2" to produce "Wave 3." The result is that the first frequency, referred to as **the carrier signal,** or simply the **carrier,** is changed by the second frequency, referred to as the **modulator signal,** or simply the **modulator.** If the second frequency, the modulator, is low, below 20 Hz or so, the first frequency, the carrier, produces a type of perceived vibrato.

- Click the preset *Play: LFO 440 Vibrato* near the orange circle *4* to demonstrate this concept.

The carrier signal deviates in pitch only slightly from 440 Hz as a result of the low frequencies used to modulate it.

### DID YOU KNOW?

### Low-Frequency Oscillation (LFO)

Traditional instruments—like the voice and violin—allow performers to add gentle vibrato in order to increase expressivity. With synthesizers, we may emulate this process by adjusting the pitch of the carrier signal with a slow-moving (less than 20 times per second) modulator oscillator. The slow rate of the modulator, less than 20 Hz, gives this technique the name **low-frequency oscillation,** or **LFO.** Adding subtle or drastic LFO is a way to make synthesized notes sound more expressive over time. With an LFO, the rate of vibrato is determined by the frequency of the modulator signal. A common implementation of LFO in live performance using a synthesizer is to assign the LFO rate to the "modulation wheel" of a keyboard synth. When LFO vibrato is desired, the performer may simply turn the modulation wheel.

## Ring Modulation

When the modulator frequency remains low, the modulation sounds like vibrato. As the modulator frequency is increased above 20 Hz, the result of multiplying the two waves produces two frequencies that are neither the frequency of the carrier signal nor the modulator signal. In other words, instead of two sine waves being present in the final "combined" mix as they are in typical additive synthesis, the final combined mix will result in two new waves, known as **sidebands,** which have resulted from the multiplication of the two oscillators.

- Click the preset *Ring Modulation.*

This is a type of synthesis referred to as **ring modulation.** The amplitude of the mixed signal is determined by the amplitude of the modulator, which dips up and down at some rate of speed that is the modulator's specified frequency. Ring modulation is a form of amplitude modulation in which we modulate the amplitude of one oscillator by multiplying it by another. The notion of using one signal to change another is an important and commonly implemented concept in synthesis.

## Amplitude Modulation (AM) Synthesis

In ring modulation, the amplitude of the modulator signal causes periodic dips in the amplitude of the carrier signal as the modulator cycles in amplitude from −1 to 1.

• Click the preset *AM Synthesis* near the orange circle 4.

**Amplitude modulation synthesis**, or simply **AM synthesis**, is similar to ring modulation except that the amplitude of the modulator signal is controlled in some way other than the normal wave cycle from −1 to 1; a third oscillator or some other mechanism could control it.

In the software example, the amplitude dial of the second oscillator has been renamed "tremolo depth" to more accurately represent its function. Notice that a component is added called **DC offset,** which compensates for the dip in amplitude caused by the modulator. In AM synthesis, we don't want the amplitude to dip between −1 and 1 like it does in ring modulation. To this extent, the DC offset changes the amplitude of the modulator in the opposite direction from the tremolo and, thus, maintains the amplitude level at 1.

The important thing to remember is that, in AM synthesis, the amplitude of the carrier signal is still controlled by the modulator, just in a different way than in ring modulation synthesis. The resulting timbre of the final mixed signal will differ from ring modulation in that the resulting AM synthesis sound will contain the frequency of the carrier signal.

## Frequency Modulation (FM) Synthesis

A synthesis technique known as **frequency modulation synthesis,** or simply **FM synthesis,** similarly uses a modulator frequency to change properties of the carrier signal. In the case of FM synthesis, it is the frequency of the carrier signal that changes. This produces timbres that are rich in sideband frequencies and great for bell-like and metallic sounds.

## ☝ GO TO SOFTWARE LESSON: *FM SYNTHESIS*

Using the FMT companion software, choose the lesson *FM Synthesis.* If necessary, slowly adjust the main volume slider at the top left of the software.

• Play notes on the onscreen keyboard as you click through each preset in this lesson.

In the first preset a simple sine wave is produced at 440 Hz, as shown near the orange circle 1. Click the "Small deviation" preset near orange circle 2. Notice that the carrier signal deviates 10 Hz, the rate indicated in the Deviation field, at the rate of once per second, the rate of the modulator frequency. The carrier signal will deviate from 440 Hz to both 450 Hz and 430 Hz. The same concept is applied in the preset "Larger deviation" near orange circle 3; there are simply different values plugged in.

- Click a single note on the onscreen keyboard then click on each of the presets between 1 and 4 to demonstrate the vast variety of timbres available through FM synthesis.

The first four presets demonstrate the basic concepts of FM synthesis: a modulator frequency is used to change the frequency of the carrier signal. The remaining presets use a slightly different implementation commonly used in FM synthesizers in which the carrier signal is routed to a third modulation source, still labeled the Deviation, and is used to control aspects of the modulator. During this phase, the modulator signal becomes a sort of controlled feedback loop in which the carrier signal is modulated and fed back into the modulator, producing numerous sidebands. For this reason, the modulator frequency has been renamed as the **carrier/ modulator ratio**. Whole numbers used for the ratio will result in more consonant overtones based on the frequency of the carrier, whereas fractions will produce more dissonance. The modulator is then combined with an untouched version of the original carrier signal. In this regard, the deviation can be thought of as a control over the amount of modulator signal transmitted into the final signal mix.

- Click the preset "More complex modulation" near orange circle 5, and then change the *Deviation* value to 0 to bypass the modulated signal leaving only the untouched carrier signal in the mix.

In practical uses, FM synthesizers use an ADSR curve or some other controls to vary the FM portion of the final mix over time. In the preset "A breakpoint function" near orange circle 6, a multipoint ADSR-type curve called a **breakpoint function** is used so that each time a new note is played, the FM portion of the signal follows a certain contour to vary its sound over time.

- Click the presets near orange circle 8 to vary the shape of the breakpoint function while you play notes on the onscreen keyboard.
- Click in the graphic to draw your own breakpoint function.

## DID YOU KNOW?

### FM Synth History

FM synthesis and synthesizers are widely used in a variety of musical styles from the opening few chords of Michael Jackson's "Beat It" (1983) to the original run of *Les Misérables*. FM synthesis stemmed from the research of John Chowning at Stanford University in the late 1960s. The Yamaha DX-7 was the first commercially successful FM synthesizer and was based on Chowning's work.

Finally, the preset "ADSR" near orange circle 7 applies an ADSR curve to the amplitude of the final mixed signal.

## SUBTRACTIVE SYNTHESIS

**Subtractive synthesis** is a method that can be thought of as the opposite of additive synthesis. In additive synthesis, one makes new sounds by adding waves together, whereas in subtractive synthesis, one begins with a complex waveform or harmonically rich sound source and reduces, or filters, out desired frequencies to make a new timbre. One common way of doing this is by filtering white noise reshaping the sound. **White noise,** for our purposes, is a sound source containing the presence of all frequencies. With all frequencies present in the sound source, we can use certain processes called **filters** to remove or boost certain frequencies to create a new sound.

### DID YOU KNOW?

#### Equalization

Frequencies are normally referred to in groups called bands. For example, your car stereo probably has bass, mid, and treble controls in addition to the master volume knob. Raising the bass knob increases the volume of a group of "low" frequencies on the music coming from your car speakers, lowering the knob reduces the volume of the bass frequency band, and leaving the knob at the middle notch neither increases nor decreases the bass frequency band. The same can be said for the mid and treble knobs. Therefore, a car stereo with three knobs to shape the entire audible range of music playing through the sound system can be referred to as a three-band system, it has three filters to adjust the audio timbre. The lower frequencies are grouped into the bass band knob, the middle frequencies are grouped into the mid band knob, and the higher frequencies are grouped into the treble band knob. The greater the number of knobs your car stereo system has, the greater the number of bands are available; thus, the user has greater control over the timbral balance of the sounds coming through the speakers.

If you feel that the kick drum on the recording you're listening to is just not loud enough, raising the bass knob, or alternately lowering the mid and treble knobs and raising the master volume, will adjust the sound to your liking. This process of "tone-shaping" is known as **equalization,** or simply **EQ.**

In subtractive synthesis, we begin with all frequencies and use filters to remove other frequencies to create different timbres.

## 🖑 GO TO SOFTWARE LESSON: *SUBTRACTIVE SYNTHESIS*

Using the FMT companion software, choose the lesson *Subtractive Synthesis*. If necessary, slowly adjust the main volume slider at the top left of the software.

In this lesson, we may use either *white noise* or the slightly "less hissy" sounding **pink noise** as the sound source, as shown near orange circle *1*. We will use filters to subtract certain frequencies away from the noise source and "shape" a new sound. By default, the noise source passes through the "EQ-styled Filters" section unchanged; notice that the filter type, near orange circle *2*, is set to all pass. Using **all pass filters**, all frequencies in the noise source will be allowed to pass through to our speakers. Notice that **bandpass filters** only let certain specified bands of frequencies through and **highpass filters** only let high frequencies through.

- Select all of the different filter types in the menu near orange circle *2*.

The center frequency for the filter can be changed by typing in a number near orange circle *3* or by playing a note on the onscreen keyboard. The graphic can also be adjusted by clicking on it. The shape of the band, called the **Q,** is also adjustable.

There are many different combinations of filters and noise/sound sources that can be used to shape new sounds.

- Select the "Comb Filter" button near orange circle *4* to apply a different filter type.

A **comb filter** takes an incoming signal, delays it, and feeds it back with the mixed signal.

- Play a note on the onscreen keyboard, and slowly increase the *Feedback* knob near orange circle *5*.

As the feedback signal increases, the frequency specified by the keyboard resonates within the comb filter and spikes up higher than the white noise as shown in the display. The spikes, which resemble a comb, give comb filtering a unique timbre in which certain frequencies are boosted among the others frequencies present in the sound source.

### DID YOU KNOW?

Paul Lansky's composition *Night Traffic* (1990) applies pitched comb filters to recordings of automobile traffic. The loud unpitched approaching sound of typical traffic is, in this context, pitched in a variety of ways by using comb filters.

## SAMPLE-BASED SYNTHESIS

One of the more common forms of synthesis, which isn't actually synthesis in the wave-combining sense we've been discussing, is **sample-based synthesis**. The concept is simple: instead of synthetically combining waves together to emulate existing timbres, like a note on the piano, one simply plays a recording of that note on the piano whenever that key is pressed. The recordings themselves are known as samples. Since the sounds in sample-based playback are actual recordings of real instruments and not the result of combining waves in any synthetic manner, the realism of the timbres is unmatched. (See Chapter 5 for a further discussion of sample-based playback.)

### DID YOU KNOW?

#### Sample-Based Speech?

In the 1950s, researchers began using computers to synthesize speech, notably at Bell Labs. Today, we hear both synthesized and sample-based approaches to speech synthesis in our daily routines. Have you ever heard a funny-sounding robotic voice through a PA announce the arrival of the train? Perhaps you've recently listened to an automated voice while leaving someone a voicemail message. Visit the companion website for this book to hear two audio files of Speech Synthesis and Speech Sampling.

## GRANULAR SYNTHESIS

Like sample-based synthesis, **granular synthesis** is a type of synthesis that involves playing back prerecorded sounds. However, instead of playing back the samples as they were recorded, small sections of a sample, commonly less than 150 milliseconds of the sample, referred to as **grains**, are played back at varying speeds and pitches to produce new timbres. In essence, a recorded sound is manipulated to create new sounds.

## 🖑 GO TO SOFTWARE LESSON: *GRANULAR SYNTHESIS*

Using the FMT companion software, choose the lesson *Granular Synthesis*. If necessary, slowly adjust the main volume slider at the top left of the software.

- Click the button marked "Complete Sample" as shown near the orange circle *1* to play back a complete sample.

Granular synthesis can often employ many variables. The commonly used ones involve some way of selecting small sections of a sample and playing them back in novel ways like shifting the pitch while retaining the tempo or shifting the tempo while retaining the pitch.

- Click the preset "One Section Transposed Down" near orange circle 2.

We can see that a selection has been made from the sample. From this selection, numerous grains play back on top of each other and in varied orders.

- Change the selection region by clicking on the sample window near orange circle 4, then change the transposition by clicking the onscreen keyboard or the slider near orange circle 5.

Notice that the time between grains ultimately determines the density of the sound, where a value of 1000 ms (one second) produces only one grain each second, while a value of 20 ms produces a "cloud" of sound. In granular synthesis, it is common to change values, like transposition, in real time using controls as is simulated by clicking the "sweep" icon near orange circle 7.

Controlling these synthesizer parameters and others with hardware leads us to a discussion of MIDI, a powerful computer language that uses numbers to represent musical parameters and concepts.

## SUMMARY

Synthesis is the process of creating new timbres or emulating existing ones. The various approaches to computer synthesis have focused on ways to produce interesting timbres in ways that are efficient in terms of processing power. There are more synthesis plug-ins and hardware units in existence than you will likely encounter in a lifetime, but an understanding of the basic concepts of how all synthesizers work will allow you to use these various systems for your own creative purposes. For example, an understanding of the envelope as it relates to the timbre's overall sound as well as its filters and subtle nuances will allow you to control the "shape" of a synthesizer in any software or hardware application. An understanding of overtones, filters, modulators, and other techniques related to each of the synthesis approaches described in this chapter will allow you to realize the sounds you hear in your imagination or on recordings.

## KEY CONCEPTS

- Additive synthesis is the process of adding waves to make new timbres.
- Envelopes and ADSR curves refer to the shape of a sound's volume and/or timbre over time.
- Physical modeling is an approach to synthesis that emulates the physical properties of sound sources.
- AM synthesis is a technique in which the amplitude of one oscillator is modulated by multiplying it by another.
- FM synthesis is a technique in which the frequency of one oscillator is modulated by multiplying it by another.

- Subtractive synthesis is a technique in which certain frequencies in a frequency-rich sound source—like white noise—is filtered to create new timbres.
- Equalization is the process of tone-shaping using level controls on specific frequency bands.
- Sample-based synthesis uses actual recordings of audio to simulate realistic timbres.
- Granular synthesis uses fragmented "grains" of recorded audio to produce varying and evolving "clouds" of sound.

## KEY TERMS

additive synthesis
ADSR/ADSR envelope
all pass filter
amplitude modulation
   (AM) synthesis
attack time
bandpass filter
beating/beat
   interference
bins
breakpoint function
carrier/carrier signal
carrier/modulator
   ratio
comb filter
DC offset
decay time

envelope
equalization (EQ)
Fast Fourier Transform
   (FFT)
filter
Fourier Transform
frames
frequency modulation
   (FM) synthesis
grains
granular synthesis
highpass filter
Karplus-Strong string
   synthesis
low-frequency
   oscillation (LFO)
modulation

modulator/modulator
   signal
phase
physical modeling
pink noise
Q (band shape)
release time
ring modulation
sample-based synthesis
sidebands
subtractive synthesis
sustain volume
tremolo
vibrato
waveform
wavetable synthesis
white noise

# CHAPTER 5

# MIDI

## OVERVIEW

In this chapter, we will discuss MIDI, a language that synthesizers and computers use to convey musical information. In the early days of developing synthesizers, it was common to use voltage to control oscillator systems. Today, we use digitally controlled systems to control oscillators and other synthesizer components. In the early 1980s, as synthesizers became more uniform in terms of their operation, a standard way of arranging to communicate among the various electronic components, called the **Musical Instrument Digital Interface,** or **MIDI,** was developed. MIDI information has been in use by musicians since the 1980s and is still a very important type of technology in studios and in live performance. By the end of this chapter, many of the benefits of using MIDI will become clearer.

## BEFORE MIDI

Throughout history, people have created new musical instruments, and these instruments generally reflect the technological resources available at the time. Early primitive instruments had few moving parts, if any. The Industrial Revolution made way for the modern piano to evolve using steel and iron. In the Information Age, it stands to reason that newly created instruments may largely involve computers and electronics. The development of new musical instruments in the 1900s certainly revolved heavily around the idea of using electronic components to create new timbres including keyboard synthesizers, electric guitars, and drum machines.

Early electronic instruments, such as the 1897 Telharmonium, used motors and other electrical equipment to generate waves at desired frequencies. In some instruments, like the Buchla 200 of the 1970s, the tone was shaped and defined by turning wheel-like knobs. Other instruments of the 1970s, such as the Moog (pronounced like *vogue*) and the Minimoog, resembled modern keyboard synthesizers and allowed oscillator pitches to correspond to keyboard keys built within the instrument.

Eventually, synthesizer manufacturers developed ways to have their instruments communicate information with each other. In the early 1980s, a nonproprietary mechanism that allowed synthesizers to communicate with each other was developed—Musical Instrument Digital Interface, or MIDI.

FIGURE 5.1: The Telharmonium developed by Thaddeus Cahill in 1897
(From Timohummel, 2006)

FIGURE 5.2: A Minimoog synthesizer with keyboard-like controls
(Courtesy PeterAlbrektsen/iStock)

## DID YOU KNOW?

### Switched on Bach

In the 1960s and 1970s, synthesizers and their unique timbral possibilities grew in popularity. Popular musicians incorporated synthesizers into their creative works, and boutique synthesizers like the Moog soon came into high demand, with notable use by the Beatles, the Doors, and other major acts. This interest was not exclusive to popular and experimental music but figured prominently in other genres as exemplified by the mainstream success of the 1968 album *Switched-On Bach*, which featured works by composer J. S. Bach performed on synthesizers by Wendy (Walter) Carlos.

Early synthesizers were "monophonic"; that is, they could only play a single melody line at once. In order to create *Switched on Bach*, Carlos had to record each part separately and then—through overdubbing—assemble a complete performance. The amount of planning and time that this took is nearly unbelievable, but the result was a seamless performance that stunned listeners of the day. Carlos's work was so popular that director Stanley Kubrick hired her to help score the film *A Clockwork Orange* (1971), for which she created a Moog rendition of Henry Purcell's *Music for the Funeral of Queen Mary*, along with some original compositions.

## THE MIDI PROTOCOL

MIDI is a language, or protocol, that computers use to convey musical messages. Modern synthesizers as well as nearly all computer music software applications deal with MIDI in some way. What are these MIDI messages? In short, MIDI is a system for representing musical elements like pitch, dynamics, and timbre with numbers.

MIDI uses the numbers 0–127 to represent various musical components. The lowest MIDI note, 0, is the pitch C at five octaves below middle C. The number 1 is the C♯/D♭ directly above that C, and so on. The MIDI note 12 is the C above the lowest C. Velocity is a measurement of pressure related to MIDI volume represented by the same numbers 0–127. A velocity value of 0 means that the note is off, whereas the value of 127 is the loudest volume that MIDI can produce. Therefore, the MIDI note 60 with a velocity of 127 could be described as middle C played with a very forceful intensity.

One feature that is so great about MIDI is that MIDI files are essentially text documents containing a list of numbers that say, "These were the notes you played; this is how hard or soft you played them; this is how long you held each note down; and this is the timbre you used." The resulting files are very small since the actual synthesis of those numbers into sound occurs within the DAW or synthesis engine. In contrast, when we record audio with microphones, the sound is sampled and stored at a very high rate to ensure that what is captured is

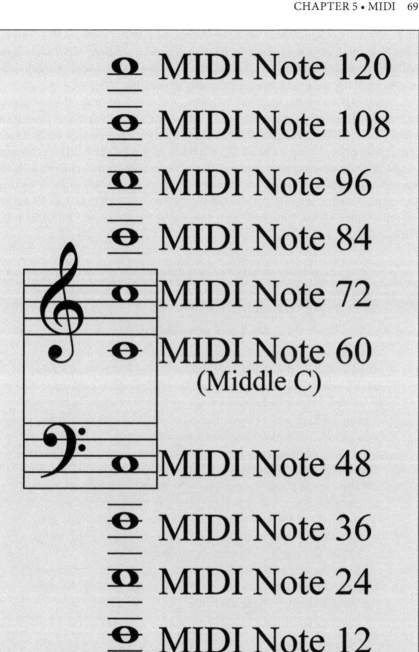

FIGURE 5.3: MIDI note C as it relates to the grand staff

an accurate representation of what the live sound actually sounded like. This results in audio files that are large in file size, much larger than MIDI files. Some MIDI keyboards used floppy disks and other storage media to allow users to read and write MIDI data, such as songs, directly to the disk.

Since MIDI messages are just numbers, a number of musical ideas can be executed with ease by simply applying a setting within the MIDI device. For instance, most MIDI keyboards allow transposition by a semitone, a musical half-step, by simply applying +1 to all MIDI pitches that are played. MIDI keyboards might also allow the simple harmonization of notes with the interval of a fifth, for example, by adding +7 to all MIDI pitches that are played. There are numerous techniques used to manipulate MIDI data, and modern MIDI devices introduce useful features all the time such as automatic accompaniment, smart diatonic harmonization, and more.

## DID YOU KNOW?

### MIDI and Accessibility

Most people find it easier to play a piano or keyboard in the key of C (using just the "white keys"). Composer Irving Berlin, on the other hand, learned to play piano using just the black keys; he used a special piano with a crank that allowed him to play in all the keys by literally moving the keyboard to the left or right! MIDI solves this problem quite neatly. With MIDI functionality, a person could conceivably play a variety of diatonic songs in different keys using only the white "C major" keys of the piano through the use of transposition changes.

Similarly, a pianist could "play" the guitar by simply changing the timbre settings through MIDI while still using a piano keyboard to "input" the notes. Different types of controllers have been developed to allow instrumentalists familiar with playing one instrument to be able to play an orchestra of others!

Consider the implications for music education and facilitating composition and performances with individuals who would otherwise have difficulty playing chords.

A typical **keyboard synthesizer** can be thought of as having at least two major components: (1) the keyboard portion, called a **controller**, which sends MIDI messages to (2) the **sound module**, which receives these MIDI messages from the keyboard and uses these data to synthesize the desired sounds. In a keyboard synthesizer, both components are contained in one instrument, but one may also purchase the components separately: a MIDI keyboard controller with no internal sound module and a sound module with no MIDI keyboard. For this purpose, MIDI devices generally have a **MIDI In jack**, or **port**, to receive MIDI messages from other devices, and a **MIDI Out** port to send MIDI messages to other devices. Sometimes a **MIDI Thru** port exists on MIDI devices, which typically duplicates the information received at the MIDI In port and passes the information "thru" without altering it. Thru ports can be useful if, for example, the selected patch in the sound module is set to alter the incoming MIDI messages in some way such as transposing pitches or harmonizing them. An unchanged copy of the original "unharmonized" signal could be sent through the "Thru" port to another synth module, where it might appear unchanged or harmonized differently. Today, it is common to use a personal computer and **virtual instrument software** as the sound module to synthesize incoming MIDI data from a MIDI controller as an alternative to using a stand alone MIDI sound module.

In the past, MIDI cables would be used to connect a MIDI keyboard controller to a computer using a MIDI-to-computer interface, but modern MIDI controllers connect to computers directly through a USB cable. However, MIDI controllers tend also to have a standard MIDI Out port in addition to a USB one.

FIGURE 5.4: A stand-alone MIDI sound module or "brain" (From Reccius, 2009)

MIDI keyboard synthesizers are typically designed to be flexible so that MIDI data from the keyboard portion can be sent via MIDI cable to other external sound modules, keyboard synthesizers, or even computers that include **software synthesizers** or virtual instruments. Musicians who are already satisfied with the sounds available through a particular sound module may decide to purchase an 88-key weighted MIDI keyboard controller without a sound module built in. They can then send the MIDI data to their favorite sound module. They may decide to use multiple MIDI controllers simultaneously, such as that same

88-key controller in conjunction with a MIDI foot pedal controller that resembles the bass pedals of an organ.

# 🖐 GO TO SOFTWARE LESSON: *MIDI*

Using the FMT companion software, choose the lesson *MIDI*. If you have a MIDI keyboard connected to your computer, use it to play some notes. If you do not have a MIDI keyboard, click the scale buttons at the top of the onscreen keyboard, or simply click on the keyboard itself. Notice that as you play MIDI notes, they are shown on the musical staff near the orange circle *1*.

- Click on the staff and observe that the selected note is highlighted on the large graphical keyboard.

Near the orange circle *3*, a diagram is shown to simulate the signal path of MIDI entering from the MIDI In port of a synthesizer from a keyboard controller. In this diagram, we are observing these values before they are synthesized into a sound. The pitch value will change, but the velocity value will remain at the default value set by this program: 100. A larger on-screen keyboard is used to represent these values on a musical keyboard. In this diagram, the MIDI Out represents your computer's internal synth module, which is what synthesizes the MIDI numbers as sounds that we hear through your computer's sound card. This is analogous to using an external MIDI sound module as the sound source. On a Mac, for example, your computer probably uses some variant of the AU DLS Synth or QuickTime programs to produce the sounds.

## Note On and Note Off Messages

To demonstrate the concept of MIDI note and velocity messages:

- Click on the "Note On" button near orange circle *5*, and observe the numbers changing near orange circle *4*, the "MIDI Output" section.

Clicking the first button simulates the middle C key on a keyboard, MIDI note 60, being played with a dynamic marking fortissimo, a MIDI velocity of 120. As long as the key is held down, the velocity value for this pitch remains at 120.

- Press the "Note Off" button to simulate the action of the middle C key being lifted.

Notice that the same MIDI pitch 60 is once again sent to the output, but this time it is paired with a velocity value of 0. Velocity 0 messages are known as "note off" messages and are used to silence notes.

- Click the buttons at orange circle *6* to simulate multiple pitches being played simultaneously.

Each time you hold a MIDI note down, it is sent to the sound module with a velocity value depending on how hard you pressed the key. When you lift off the note, it is sent to the output, once again, with a velocity value of 0 to stop the note from sounding. If the "note off" message is not received, the note will continue to sustain until a velocity 0 message for that pitch is received. Sometimes synthesizers, particularly software, will inadvertently produce a "stuck note" like this, where a note off message has been lost and a note is sustaining indefinitely. For this reason, some synthesizers have a "panic" button located somewhere that simultaneously sends a note off, velocity 0, message for all MIDI pitches.

- To simulate stuck notes, click and manually enter a velocity value of 100 in the box at orange circle 3, then click in the pitch box next to the velocity box, and drag the numbers up and down.

In this demonstration, MIDI pitches were created with a velocity of 100, but no note off messages were ever received, so the notes continued to sustain forever. To cease the sustaining notes:

- Click the Panic button at the left of the onscreen keyboard.

## DID YOU KNOW?

### Fixed MIDI Velocity Values

For the onscreen staff portion of the software, some of the values have been "hard coded," that is, they have been programmed into the software and cannot be changed. The MIDI pitch value may be changed when the user clicks on the staff. The pitch number is sent to the output section with a "hard-coded" velocity value of 64; no matter how hard you click on the staff, the velocity value is "fixed" at 64. The duration of each note created by clicking on the staff has been set to 500 milliseconds; after 500 milliseconds, the software automatically turns these notes off by sending the same pitch once again, but this time with a velocity value of 0. Velocity 0 messages are known as **note off messages** since they are used to silence notes. Some keyboards themselves do not offer "velocity sensitivity" and, instead, play all MIDI pitches back at a fixed velocity regardless of the amount of key pressure the performer puts on the keys.

## MIDI Programs

As digital keyboard synthesizers grew in the amount of features they could offer, specific sounds could be selected on a given instrument. For example, a synthesizer might have a group, known as a **bank**, of 12 sounds, each sound being referred to as a **patch** or **program**. Depending on which manufacturer made your keyboard, the first patch in the group might be a piano sound, while the second patch might be a trumpet sound. For a time prior to MIDI standardization, scenarios occurred where a composer might write a song on one MIDI keyboard, store the MIDI data on a disk, and bring the disk into a larger studio to work on

the piece with better sound modules. However, the composer would soon dis-
cover that patch 1 on his home keyboard was a piano sound but patch 1 on the
studio keyboard was a string ensemble sound. As a result, his piece would play
back with the right notes, but the wrong sounds. Eventually, a committee made
up of numerous synthesizer manufacturers agreed upon a standard mapping of
MIDI sounds and other MIDI values to form a standard called **general MIDI**.

MIDI patches are selected using a type of MIDI message known as a **program change**. Just like MIDI pitch and velocity messages, program changes are
used to communicate with the sound module. In the same *MIDI* lesson of the
FMT software:

- Near orange circle *7*, click on the slider to change the MIDI program, then
  play some MIDI notes to hear the different timbres.

## Controller Messages

The items near orange circles *8–10* reveal MIDI messages received from other
knobs and wheels on your MIDI keyboard. For example, **controller** values, or
**continuous control (CC)** messages, are another type of data used in MIDI. These
numbers can be used for a number of purposes like controlling specific effects in
external synthesizer modules. Controller values typically have some **controller
number** that identifies the individual control; then, some stream of numbers between 0 and 127 are received for that controller number. This can be easily demonstrated if your MIDI keyboard has some knobs on it.

- If your MIDI keyboard controller has knobs on it, turn a single knob and
  observe the data near orange circle *8*. Then, type that controller number
  into the topmost number box near orange circle *9*, and observe the data
  you are "listening to" on that controller number.

Some keyboards have a wheel that can be used to bend the pitch of certain
MIDI sounds.

- If your keyboard has wheels, move them and see what values are being
  transmitted.

Some wheels send bend data (see orange circle *10*), while others send controller messages.

- To see all raw MIDI values being transmitted by your MIDI device, click
  the button near orange circle *11* and press the buttons, knobs, and keys on
  your controller.

## MIDI Channels

Above orange circle *12* there is a pull-down menu that allows us to change the
MIDI channel. As MIDI synthesizers became more sophisticated, it became
desirable to play back multiple streams of MIDI notes simultaneously, each

transmitting different MIDI programs and other messages. In order to accomplish this, the MIDI protocol was designed to allow up to 16 independent channels of MIDI data to be transmitted simultaneously through one cable.

- Click the button near orange circle *12* to observe a pop-up illustration that demonstrates the way MIDI channels work.
- Click the Play button to begin playing a MIDI file with two MIDI tracks.

Each of the two MIDI tracks is set to a unique MIDI channel with a unique MIDI program.

- As the tracks play, change the MIDI programs.

Note that the two tracks will share the same timbre if they share the same MIDI channel. Note, also, that, according to the General MIDI standard, MIDI channel 10 is always reserved for percussion sounds.

## Piano Roll

As DAWs began to grow in popularity, the need for a visual representation of MIDI data became apparent. The **piano roll editor**, a system that uses bars at different heights, lengths, and sometimes even colors to represent MIDI data, emerged as a popular system of notation. The piano roll editor is still widely used in DAWs today, sometimes alongside traditional musical notation views.

### DID YOU KNOW?

### Edit Audio Like Piano Roll

MIDI editors allow you to transpose pitches with ease, correct wrong notes, adjust the length of notes, and more. It is often asked if these same tools exist for real audio files. "Can I import an audio file into a DAW and remove certain instruments, or edit pitches?" The answer is "kinda." As we will discuss in a general sense in the coming chapters, DAWs make it possible to adjust the tempo of an audio file without adjusting the pitch, and vice versa. Pitch correction software can do the same, but often for monophonic instruments only. When using these computer processes, some strange sounds called "artifacts" may be introduced. In terms of editing the individual pitches of a polyphonic audio file just as you would a MIDI file, it is not yet a standard option in most DAWs. However, some special programs, like Melodyne by Celemony, continue to push the envelope toward that goal without producing noticeable artifacts.

## 🖑 GO TO SOFTWARE LESSON: *PIANO ROLL*

Using the FMT companion software, choose the lesson *Piano Roll*. This software will use your computer's internal software synthesizer to synthesize the MIDI data played. Note the bars used to represent pitch duration horizontally and the pitch value vertically.

- Press the Play button near orange circle 1.

The piano roll editor can be thought of as reading through the MIDI data present on the track in the way that a music box or player piano would read through a set of grooves or perforated holes to play back pitches.

- Press the Stop button near orange circle 2.
- Click on one of the notes and slide it horizontally or vertically to change the pitch.
- Click on one more note and change the duration of the note.
- Press the Play button near orange circle 1.
- To save your modified MIDI composition as a standard MIDI file, click the Save button near orange circle 3.

Digital notation systems function similarly to the piano roll editor. They are simply graphical representations of MIDI data. MIDI data, of course, are a numerical representation of musical constructs.

## SAMPLING

In the late 1960s, as synthesis was continually growing in popularity, the idea of developing sample-based synthesizers emerged. The concept is simple: instead of synthetically combining waves together to emulate existing timbres, like a note on the piano, one might take a recording of a note on the piano and use the keys of a keyboard or some other button to play the recording of that note. The recorded sounds were known as samples, and a **sampler** was the device used to play back libraries of recorded samples.

### DID YOU KNOW?

#### The Mellotron in '60s Pop

The Mellotron was used on many pop songs in the late '60s, including the Beatles' "Strawberry Fields Forever," the Rolling Stones' "2000 Light Years from Home," and the Moody Blues' "Nights in White Satin" and "Tuesday Afternoon." Mike Pinder, a member of the Moody Blues, was also a salesman for the company that made the instrument. The Mellotron added to the psychedelic sounds of late '60s and early '70s progressive rock.

FIGURE 5.5: A Mellotron (From Andersen, 2007)

The Mellotron, for example, was an early sampler that resembled a keyboard. The performer would load tapes into the sampler with recorded sounds at different pitches. When a key was pressed, middle C for example, the Play button was pressed on a playback head for that sound. When the key was released, the playback head would quickly rewind the tape to make the sample ready to be played again.

One advantage of using samples of a sound over synthesizing the sound is the realistic quality of the sound that is produced. Companies that make sample libraries may record an instrument or an ensemble with high-quality microphones in a number of styles and dynamic ranges. For example, a string orchestra sound on a sampler was likely created by recording, or "sampling," an actual string orchestra playing every possible note sustained at a pianissimo dynamic level, then piano, then mezzo forte, the forte, and so on. Next, each note might be played sforzando and recorded at the same dynamic levels, then pizzicato, and so on. The inner workings of the sampler would have the task of interpreting key velocities and other MIDI messages in order to play the different samples, so that when the performer played softly, the "pianissimo" sample would be used. As you would imagine, sample libraries can contain very large numbers of samples.

Modern-day samplers use digital technology to play and store sound files on disks, hard drives, and other storage media. Computers and software-based sampler programs like Kontakt by Native Instruments or Sampletank by IK Multimedia contain vast sample libraries of many gigabytes. Programs like Mainstage, Live, and Logic also feature combinations of synthesized timbres and sample libraries allowing performance by MIDI controllers. Where early samplers required the performer to load a new tape each time a new sound was desired, modern-day samplers allow sample libraries to be loaded with Program Change messages just like the patches in General MIDI or used in combination with other sample libraries by sharing a common MIDI channel for a single controller.

Some sampler devices and software applications allow users to record their own samples directly. These approaches are very popular with many artists including DJs and broadcasters who may sample a small audio file of a speech, movie quote, or musical sound and then map that sample so that it can be played back at will by pressing a drum pad or a key on a MIDI keyboard.

## OTHER PROTOCOLS

The creation of MIDI is an important part of the history of human musicianship. It is used by performances in live situations in synthesizers, computers, and recording software as well as by composers and educators using notation software. In fact, the use of MIDI has become such a standard that it is used in other nonmusical contexts like lighting consoles and other applications that require some sort of digital synchronization.

Despite its popularity, MIDI still has a number of shortcomings. It is a relatively "low-tech" protocol by modern standards. The limitation of using 128 possible notes, for example, is a result of the fact that MIDI is an 8-bit protocol. Although the 128 MIDI numbers used for pitch, velocity, and other musical elements are enough to convincingly represent many aspects of a musical performance, there are some aspects of music performance that could benefit from being represented by more numbers (greater bit depth). MIDI data travel at 31.25 kilobytes per second, which is much slower than modern transfer speeds and limits the amount of information that can be conveyed without causing a delay, known as **latency**, or dropped information.

With the increased popularity of Ethernet connectivity, other musical protocols have been developed, including **Open Sound Control,** or **OSC**. Protocols like OSC allow greater amounts of information to be reliably transmitted with minimal latency. As technology advances, a greater number of musical variables can be controlled, manipulated, observed, and interpreted. These advancements will result in the creation of new software architectures and protocols, new performance venues, new musical instruments, and adaptations and enhancements to existing instruments.

## SUMMARY

The MIDI protocol is a widely used language that allows computers, software or hardware, to convey messages about musical things. This numerical "language" allows numbers 0–127 to be produced by a variety of "controllers," including MIDI keyboards, MIDI drum machines and modules, MIDI wind controllers, and more. On the receiving end, MIDI hardware modules and software synthesizers take those numbers and interpret them within the sound generation inner workings of the synthesizer and output them as audio. There are many different types of MIDI instrument controllers and synthesizers, both in hardware and software forms; mixing and matching a controller that you like and feel comfortable performing with and the sound module you enjoy listening to is easy.

## KEY CONCEPTS

- MIDI is a protocol that represents musical elements like pitch and velocity using the numbers 0–127.
- MIDI note on messages specify the MIDI pitch value being performed and a velocity value greater than 0.
- MIDI note off messages specify the MIDI pitch value being performed and a velocity value of 0.
- The MIDI protocol uses numbers to represent pitch, velocity, bend, and a set of 128 timbre presets.
- Piano roll editors display MIDI notes vertically according to pitch and horizontally according to duration.

## KEY TERMS

| | | |
|---|---|---|
| bank | MIDI In | piano roll editor (MIDI) |
| controller | MIDI Out | port |
| controller number (MIDI) | MIDI Thru | program change (MIDI) |
| controller/continuous control (CC) (MIDI) | Musical Instrument Digital Interface (MIDI) | sampler |
| | | software synthesizer |
| general MIDI | note off message (MIDI) | sound module |
| keyboard synthesizer | open sound control (OSC) | virtual instrument software |
| latency | patch/program | |

# CHAPTER 6

# MUSIC NOTATION SOFTWARE

## OVERVIEW

In this chapter we will discuss some of the basic concepts that apply to most music notation software applications. By the end of this chapter you will have done some basic notation editing using the free web application Noteflight as well as converting MIDI files obtained from the Internet into digital notation documents.

The two best known major commercial notation applications are Finale and Sibelius. Some users may prefer free notation software like MuseScore and Lily-Pond or the cloud-based software Noteflight. In reality, when discussing notation applications, we're ultimately talking about software that, at its core, functions like Microsoft Word with "note-shaped" fonts. In other words: most notation applications are superficially different and fundamentally the same. The differences tend to reside in the input mechanisms—for example, the ability to use MIDI keyboard support, microphone-to-pitch notation features, and computer keyboard commands—and the quality of the sound playback, including synthesis engines and large sample libraries. A list of popular commercial and free DAWs is available on the companion website for this book.

## BASIC NOTATION APPLICATION FUNCTIONS

Notation applications use note shapes to represent pitches that are played back in some way. While a main function of notation applications is to represent musical ideas in some presentable manner, the added ability to hear what you're composing in real time and through sophisticated playback mechanisms has become an increasingly important function. It is the reason why the Finale application, for example, in itself is only about 200 megabytes or so, but comes bundled with a roughly 2.5 gigabyte sample library. Notation applications commonly use MIDI as their main way of working with notes, either by using the computer's internal software synthesizers or through large sample libraries. It is the latter capacity that has helped Finale and Sibelius maintain their dominance over most other notation applications, which feature fewer sound libraries and less realistic playback mechanisms.

Sophisticated features and quality technical support, for all software applications, come at a cost and are often worth the price, in the long run, over free software. In this chapter, for convenience, we will discuss the free, cloud-based notation application Noteflight. The core concepts about notation applications learned through this discussion will transfer to other notation applications, like Finale and Sibelius, should you choose to use either one of those. If you'd prefer to use your notation application of choice, you may complete the next few steps as we discuss them and look for the equivalent menu items and tools in that application.

## NOTE ENTRY

Visit www.noteflight.com and create a free Noteflight account. Unlike software that must be installed on your computer, Noteflight is browser-based, with the majority of the application residing on a dedicated computer known as a server. Software of this nature is said to reside in "the cloud" as opposed to it being a resident on your local computer.

- Log in to *Noteflight.*
- Create a new blank score.
- Take a moment to explore each menu item within the application.

FIGURE 6.1: A blank Noteflight document

Like most notation software, Noteflight allows you to click on the blank score in front of you and position notes on the staff.

- Enter a note on the staff.
- Use the arrow keys on your computer keyboard to reposition the note on the staff.

Entering notes is the main function of every notation application. Applications like Finale and Sibelius offer very sophisticated note entry options, including MIDI instrument entry, the ability to detect incoming pitches through a microphone and convert those to MIDI notes, and other techniques for rapidly representing pitches on staves. For now, we'll continue entering notes manually by clicking on the screen.

- Click on the staff.
- Press the letter C on your keyboard to place the note C on the staff.
- Press the [ and ] keys to increase and decrease the rhythmic value, or simply click on the desired rhythm from the note palette.

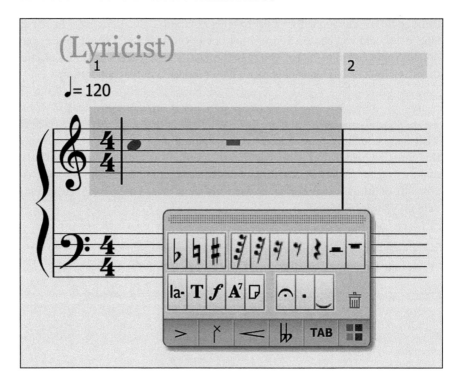

FIGURE 6.2: Clicking on a note reveals a note palette

FIGURE 6.3: The melody for "Mary Had a Little Lamb"

- Complete the melody for "Mary Had a Little Lamb" as shown in Figure 6.3.
- Click the *Play* button or choose *Play* from the main menu.
- Click above a placed note to add additional notes (chords) on that beat.
- Complete the piece as pictured in Figure 6.4.

FIGURE 6.4: "Mary Had a Little Lamb" notated on the grand staff

After you have completed the notation project, click File and Save from the main menu. If you haven't done so already, take a moment to explore the other options available from the Noteflight menu, including options to print your score, share your composition with others, add additional instruments, and change the key signature. Noteflight provides a variety of helpful tutorials for creating professional-looking scores using a variety of sophisticated features and tools.

## DID YOU KNOW?

### Tablature

Tablature is commonly used by guitarists and others who play stringed instruments instead of conventional music notation. Unlike notation that shows the notes to play, tablature shows how to actually play the instrument to produce the desired notes. It represents the fretboard of the instrument; in the case of the guitar, the six ledger lines represent the six strings of the instrument. Specialized notation on the tablature shows the player where to fret the instrument and which fingers to use. Sliding between notes, "hammering" on a string, and other fingering techniques are also indicated. These kinds of playing techniques cannot be shown in standard music notation.

Specialized programs have been developed with the ability to "read" tablature so that beginning guitarists can hear the music being played and mimic it as they learn a new piece.

Most notation applications also allow the ability to create tablature notation, or "tabs," in some way.

## IMPORTING MIDI FILES

One of the greatest features that notation applications have is the ability to import and export MIDI files. This means that you can notate a composition in some software application, and then export the MIDI data as a file to be imported into a DAW like GarageBand, Pro Tools, or Live. Because MIDI files are so small—generally about 100 kilobytes for an entire symphonic movement of Beethoven—at one time it was popular to load them onto cellphones to be used as ringtones or embed them into webpages that automatically played them when a user visited the page. Increases in bandwidth both in mobile devices and Internet browsing experiences have largely replaced these uses.

The Internet is full of MIDI files created through notation software and DAWs. One needs only to search "video game MIDI" or "Bach MIDI" to yield a wealth of results. Where did these files come from? People made them. A composition student may, in completing a homework project, notate the complete works of a popular artist or a forgotten composer and then post the MIDI files online. These files may be downloaded, copyright permitting, and imported into a notation application or DAW to make arrangements or other derivative works.

Let's import a MIDI file into Noteflight.

• Save your existing notation project.

From the companion website for this textbook, you may download a sample MIDI file, or simply spend a few minutes searching for and downloading a MIDI file from the Internet. Ensure that the file you download has .mid or .midi as the file extension. Audio files like .wav or .mp3 won't readily load into a notation application. (However, there are applications like *Melodyne* that attempt to facilitate MIDI-like operations on polyphonic audio files.)

From within Noteflight:

• Choose File>Import from the menu.
• Navigate to the MIDI file you downloaded or use the MIDI file provided in the chapter examples folder for this chapter.

Typically, when importing MIDI, you will be prompted to describe how you want to transfer the MIDI data in the file onto staves. The MIDI file may contain one or more tracks that all share a single MIDI channel; this is known as a **Type 0 MIDI file**. Alternatively, each track in the file may have a different MIDI channel assigned to it; this would be represented in the multitrack **Type 1 MIDI file**. Depending on how the MIDI file was prepared by its author, you may have better results importing the file into new staves by choosing Tracks Become Parts instead of MIDI Channels Become Parts.

• Use the default import options and Import the MIDI file.

Your imported MIDI data should appear in the software when the process is complete. At this stage, you may make arrangements for larger or smaller groups, change playback instruments, prepare versions for print, and so on. If your score did not translate properly to new staves, your import options may need to be finessed.

Some notation software supports a format known as **MusicXML**. This format surpasses the functionality of MIDI and allows users to save score information from notation applications like dynamic markings, articulations, and so on. Formats like MusicXML make it easier to bring notation documents in one program, like Finale, to another program, like Sibelius, and vice versa. With any of these methods, you can still expect to do some "touching up" to the files after they have been imported.

## IMPORTING MIDI FILES IN DAWS

Let's now take that same MIDI file you downloaded, or one that you created in a notation application, and open it in a DAW that can work with MIDI.

- Open GarageBand or Mixcraft.
- Find the MIDI file you used earlier, or another one, and drag it onto the main DAW timeline.

Notice that the MIDI data is parsed by the DAW and appears within the timeline. In some cases, the MIDI track may even contain information about the tempo at which the piece should be played back; some DAWs may attempt to match the tempo of the main session to that of the MIDI file or vice versa.

Once the MIDI data has populated the tracks within the DAW, you may change the instrument timbre for each track and perform other DAW-related functions. These techniques are discussed further in Chapter 7.

## FUTURE WORK

As you continue working with notation software, you may naturally gravitate toward a particular application that presents the layout and tools that matches your work flow. We have discussed the basic operations of note entry. Further investigation into the subtle nuances and advanced features available in a particular application is up to you.

## SUMMARY

In the same way that we no longer write stories on pieces of papyrus or etched into stone, musicians use digital notation software to preserve their compositions, leaving records of the various versions of their works as files until their final release. If only Haydn had had the convenience of copying, pasting, and transposing his recapitulations using digital notation methods, think of all the time he would have saved not having to do this by hand. Being able to hear what you compose by clicking a "play" button as opposed to having to rely on real-life musicians to come by and perform your piece is also an important step in the evolution of composition. The added ability to share scores easily with other musicians and create "rendered" audio files of compositions is a major advancement to the world of music making.

## KEY CONCEPTS

- Digital notation software applications facilitate notation in the traditional sense, but also add the power of desktop publishing and auditioning compositions through MIDI playback.
- MIDI Type 1 files have multiple instrument tracks on different channels.
- MIDI Type 0 files merge all instrument tracks into a single channel.
- MusicXML is a method for transferring digital notation documents between notation and other applications.

## KEY TERMS

MusicXML                 Type 0 MIDI file              Type 1 MIDI file

# CHAPTER 7

# SEQUENCING MIDI

## OVERVIEW

In this chapter we will examine advanced MIDI sequencing concepts using Ableton Live, a powerful digital audio workstation. This chapter will also serve as a thorough overview of the tools and functions available within this program and how they can be used to facilitate composition and performance. Ableton Live was chosen for this chapter because it is not specific to the Windows or Macintosh platform, allows cross-platform compatibility, and allows users to run a trial of the software without limitations given a free registration. Even if you are already familiar with Live or prefer some other DAW, you may find it useful to follow along in this chapter as we discuss concepts related to interactive music making using this tool. Although much of this chapter focuses on working with Ableton Live, most concepts learned through this exploration will transfer to other DAWs of your choosing like Logic and Pro Tools.

Take a moment to register (free trial), download, and install the latest version of Ableton Live for your Mac or PC from www.ableton.com. One main difference between the versions of Ableton Live available for download (Live Intro, Live, and Live Suite) is the library of samples, effects, and processing devices that come bundled within each version. In the case that an illustration in this chapter uses some content, such as a particular synthesizer sound or instrument, that is not available in your version of Live, feel free to substitute that content with other content as you see fit. Remember that one objective of this chapter is to illustrate concepts of sequencing MIDI as opposed to solely explaining how to operate a particular piece of software.

The companion website for this book contains the example files used in this chapter in case you get stuck. If you have not done so already, please take a moment to download these chapter example files.

## BASIC SETUP

Once you have installed Live, click the Live icon to open the program. The Live interface may seem intimidating at first glance, but in many ways it is similar to the FMT and Audacity software we've worked with so far. One of the most

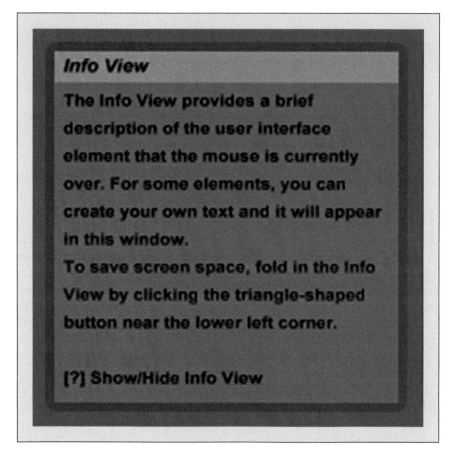

*Info View*

The Info View provides a brief description of the user interface element that the mouse is currently over. For some elements, you can create your own text and it will appear in this window.
To save screen space, fold in the Info View by clicking the triangle-shaped button near the lower left corner.

[?] Show/Hide Info View

FIGURE 7.1: Info View reveals a helpful description of whatever your mouse is hovering over

important features within Live is the Info View that appears in the bottom left portion of the program interface. This window, which provides a brief description of whatever your mouse is hovering over inside of Live, can be hidden or revealed by pressing the "?" key. It can also be enabled by selecting the View from the menu at the top of the program and selecting Info View. This feature alone gives Live a distinct advantage over other DAWs that require you to read numerous tutorials or explore intuitively in order to operate the software.

1. Toggle the Info View by pressing the "?" key or selecting it from the View menu.

At the top left side of the program is a menu of Browser items stacked vertically that, when clicked, allow you to see various content within the Live library including effects, synth instruments, loops, and more. These items are called Devices in Live. Notice that as you hover over these icons with your mouse, information appears in the Info View window.

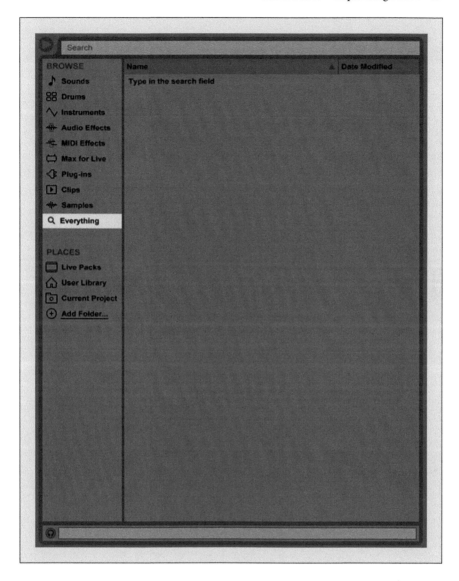

FIGURE 7.2: Browser reveals Live content when clicked

## The Live Browser

The menus labeled Sounds, Drums, and Instruments allow you to see the software-based musical instruments available for use within Live's library. The menus labeled Audio Effects and MIDI Effects allow you to see the various effects that can be used in Live such as reverbs, delays, arpeggiators, and chord generators.

    2.  Click on the various labels in the Browser.

The number of devices available for use within this library depends on your version of Live. However, the Live library can be expanded by downloading content

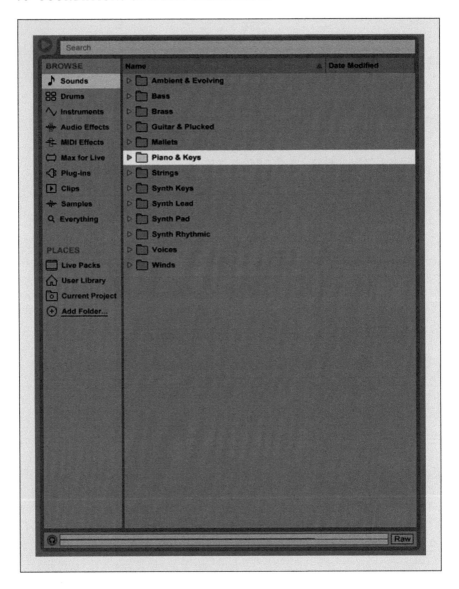

FIGURE 7.3: Live Device Browser shows the instruments, effects, and more bundled with Live

directly from Ableton. The library may also be modified from the Preferences window by going to Live>Preferences (Mac) or Options>Preferences (Windows) from the top menu, or by using the key command ⌘ + (Mac) or ctrl + (Windows). From the Preferences window, the Library tab will allow you to see the location of your library on your computer as well as the devices you currently have installed. Additionally, you may ctrl + click (Mac) or right-click (Windows) a menu item from the browser to import content from a previous version of Live.

## Max for Live

The menu item labeled Max for Live represents an arsenal of tools for use within Live that draw from the power of Max/MSP/Jitter, a powerful programming language that can expand the palette of compositional and performance options available within Live. Max/MSP/Jitter will be discussed further in Chapter 14.

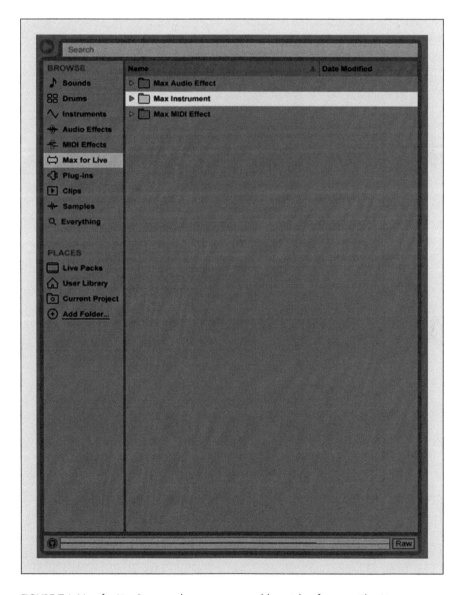

FIGURE 7.4: Max for Live Browser shows programmable patches for use within Live

## Plug-Ins Device Browser

The menu item labeled Plug-Ins allows you to view third-party plug-ins residing on your computer such as VST or Audio Unit plug-ins you may have installed. If these plug-ins do not show up in this browser window by default on your computer, view the File Folder tab within Live's Preference window. These plug-ins can be implemented into your projects just as easily as Live's devices.

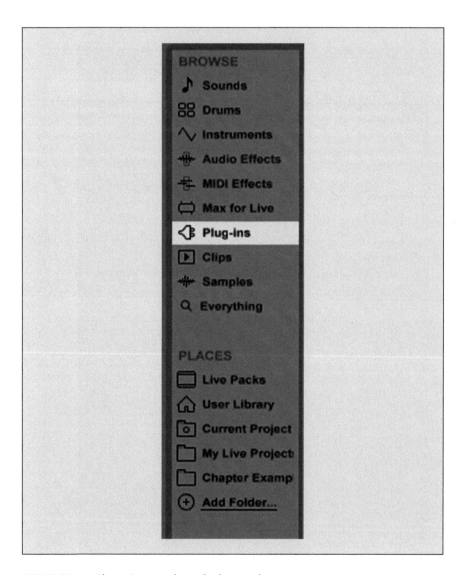

FIGURE 7.5: Live Plug-in Browser shows third party plug-ins

## Other Menus

The Clips menu allows you to see audio and MIDI files on your computer. These files, known in Live as **clips**, may include loops and other recordings.

The Samples menu is used to see small sound recordings on your computer called samples. These samples are often only one note or beat in duration and can be used in a variety of ways like creating a unique palette of sounds within Live's "drum rack."

You may search for devices and other content within the Live library and elsewhere by typing into the Search field at the top of the Browser.

## Places

Live allows you to view files and other content on your computer within the Places Browsers. These locations can be configured in a variety of ways to show commonly used file directories on your computer such as a folder that contains all of your Live projects. The Live Packs location is reserved to point to the contents of the Live library on your computer. Note the words "Core Library" appear at the top of the browser. This can be another way to view the content that is already accessible through the previously mentioned menu items.

The User Library Browser location can be set to folders of your choosing. If you don't already have a folder on your computer to store your Live projects, please create that folder now.

3. ctrl + click (Mac) or right-click (Windows) the User Library menu item and select "Add Folder . . ."
4. Create a folder on your computer named My Live Projects.
5. Select this folder as the Places location.

The folder My Live Projects will now be accessible from the sidebar menu area. As you create projects in Live, called Sets, you may save them to this folder for easy access.

## Adding Book Content

This book has chapter examples and other content available through the Oxford University Press companion website. Once you have downloaded and unzipped the Chapter Examples file to your computer, please add this folder to the Places Browser.

6. Unzip the Chapter Examples folder from the OUP website given above and copy this folder somewhere on your computer, but not in the "My Live Projects" directory.
7. ctrl + click (Mac) or right-click (Windows) the User Library menu item and select "Add Folder . . ."
8. Navigate to the Chapter Examples folder and select this folder as the Places location.

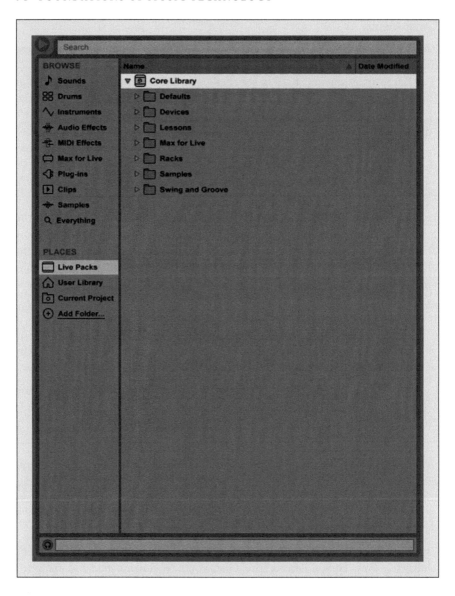

FIGURE 7.6: Live Packs menu item shows Live library files on your computer

The folder Chapter Examples will now be accessible from the sidebar menu area. As you continue reading through this chapter, we will refer to various files located in this folder.

## WORKING IN LIVE

Live has two main views in which you may work: Arrangement View and Session View. These views may be toggled using the tab key or by clicking one of the two

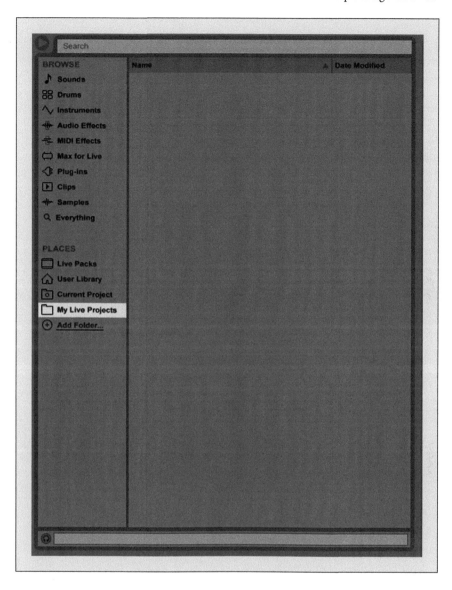

FIGURE 7.7: File Browser shows the newly created "My Live Projects" directory on your computer

icons in the top right portion of the program window. The views may also be changed from the View menu at the top of the program.

## ARRANGEMENT VIEW

We will begin looking at Live with the Arrangement View because it more closely resembles the typical DAW layout.

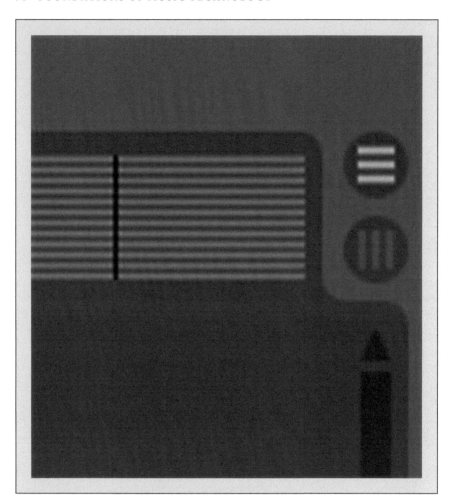

FIGURE 7.8: Icons to toggle between Session View and Arrangement View

    9.  Switch to the Arrangement View.

The arrangement view shares many of the same appearance properties of typical DAWs. The playback control transport is located in the dead center of this view. By default, there are even some Audio and MIDI tracks provided within Live, although there is, obviously, no musical content in this set yet.

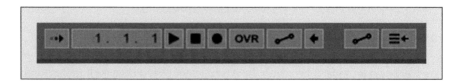

FIGURE 7.9: Playback control transport

10. Press the Play button to begin playback.

As the playback marker moves laterally in the main track display, note that the initial playback position can be changed by clicking at other points within the timeline and either clicking the Play button or pressing the space bar.

11. Press the space bar to start and stop playback.
12. Hold the shift key and press the space bar to start and pause playback.

## MIDI AND AUDIO TRACKS

Live allows us to work with two basic types of media: MIDI tracks and audio tracks. It's also possible to work with video, but for now our discussion will focus

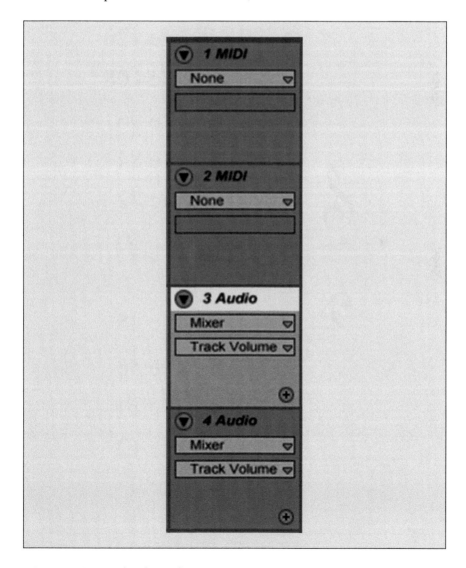

FIGURE 7.10: MIDI and Audio Tracks in Live

primarily on manipulating MIDI and audio. Notice that in the main track display, MIDI and Audio tracks have been added to this set by default. To add more MIDI or Audio tracks, choose Create from the top menu and add accordingly.

## MIDI

When we record audio with microphones, the sound is sampled and stored at a very high rate to ensure that what was captured is an accurate representation of what the live sound actually sounded like. This results in very large audio files. One feature that is so great about MIDI is that MIDI files are essentially text

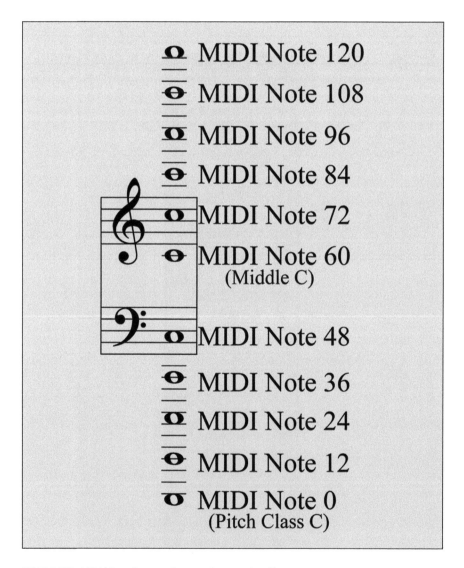

FIGURE 7.11: MIDI Note C as it relates to the grand staff

documents containing a list of numbers that say, "these were the notes you played, this is how hard or soft you played them, and this is how long you held each note down." The resulting files are very small since the actual synthesis of those numbers into sound occurs within the DAW.

Let's synthesize a MIDI file using the sounds given to us in Live.

13.   Select the Chapter Examples menu icon from the Places Browser on the left.

14.   Select the folder Chapter 1 and expand it to reveal the file piano riff 1.mid.

15.   Drag the file into the main track display area where the playback marker resides.

Live will ask you if you want to import tempo and time signature information that is stored within the MIDI file, but for now, we'll select no.

16.   Select No when Live asks you to import tempo and time signature information.

If you've already tried to play this file by pressing the Play button, you've probably realized that there is no sound. The reason is because, again, MIDI data

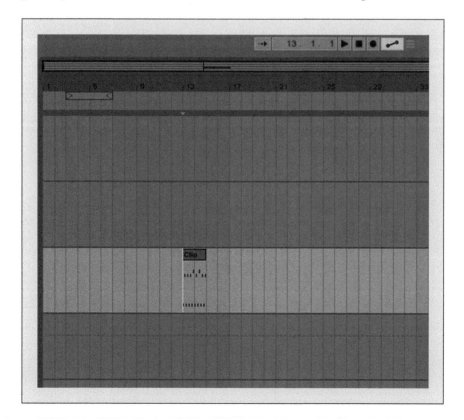

FIGURE 7.12: MIDI file represented in Live's track display

is just a bunch of numbers that Live will interpret and synthesize with any sound of your choosing. Let's choose a sound so that these MIDI pitches can be heard.

17. Select the Sounds menu icon from the Browser on the left.
18. Expand the folder Piano & Keys.
19. Select the sound Glass Piano.adg. (Note: You may use any sound you like or have available.)
20. Click and drag this sound onto the track containing the MIDI file.

Notice that when you selected this MIDI track, the instrument device Keys–Glass Piano now appears at the bottom of the screen in Live's Detail View and that the MIDI track has been renamed to reflect this instrument. If you don't see this area, you can expand or contract the Detail View using the arrow at the bottom right of the program screen or by choosing View from the top menu and selecting Detail>Show. Now that we have a sound to make sense of those MIDI numbers and map the data to an instrument timbre, let's play that file.

21. Click directly in front of the MIDI file.
22. Press Play to begin playing the file.
23. Press the Stop button after you have played the file.

## DID YOU KNOW?

### Using Substitute Sounds for Missing Media

Suppose your friend makes a really great composition in Live and wants to send you the set so that you can see what he did. However, when you open the set, you are prompted with a message in the bottom Status Bar that says "Media files are missing." This means that some of the media, perhaps some recorded tracks or loops, or even instrument devices, could not be found on your computer. There is no need to panic, as Live will prompt you to search for the missing media. In the case that a file such as a vocal track cannot be found on your computer, you may need your friend to resend it. In the event that you do not have a particular Live instrument installed on your computer, you may ask your friend where he obtained the instrument, or you may use a substitute instrument by locating the track that contains the missing device, selecting a similar instrument device from your own local Live Library, and dragging it onto the instrument window within Live's Detail View.

If you open the companion files that accompany this book, you will most likely not encounter this issue. If you did, however, open the Chapter Example file for this chapter and are unable to load the Live instrument used, you may use these steps to substitute for this missing media.

Now that we have some music working within Live, some of the processes you can perform with this file, referred to in Live as a clip, should be no surprise. For example, you can copy and paste this clip by clicking on the clip title and selecting these options from the Edit menu at the top of the screen or with the key commands ⌘ + *c* (Mac) or ctrl + *c* (Windows) for copy and ⌘ + *v* (Mac) or ctrl + *v* (Windows) for paste.

24. Click on the MIDI clip to highlight it.
25. Copy the clip using one of the methods described above.
26. Click at another point in time along the track display and paste a copy of this clip.

The contents of this clip as well as the way it functions within Live can be modified from within Live's Clip View. You can enter the Clip View by double-clicking on the top title part of a clip. This will switch the bottom view from the Detail View where we saw the MIDI track instrument to the Clip View.

27. Double-click the clip to enter Clip View.

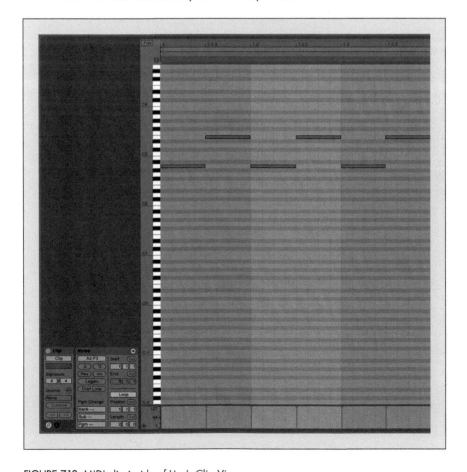

FIGURE 7.13: MIDI clip inside of Live's Clip View

## MIDI Pitch Editor

Because this clip is a MIDI file, the Clip View allows us to see the pitches represented in Live's MIDI Note Editor that some other DAWs refer to as a Piano Roll Editor. The MIDI Note Editor allows us to change the MIDI data within this clip and even add or delete MIDI notes. At the top left of this editor is a small circular icon with a tiny pair of headphones in it. Clicking on this circular Preview headphone icon will allow you to hear the MIDI data in the MIDI Note Editor when selected.

28.  Click the circular headphone icon. (Note: The icon will turn blue when enabled.)

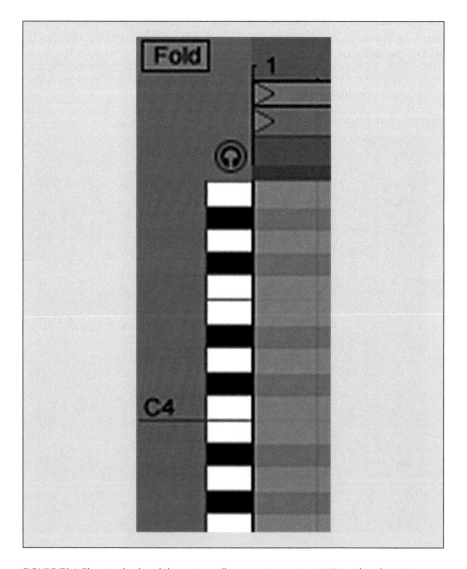

FIGURE 7.14: The circular headphone icon allows you to preview MIDI and audio in Live

The horizontal bars inside of the MIDI Note Editor represent MIDI pitches across the vertical keyboard at the left. Clicking on these bars allows you to delete, reposition, and perform other manipulations on this clip.

29. Click on the MIDI bars inside of the MIDI Note Editor.
30. Reposition a few notes if desired by clicking on the note and dragging horizontally or vertically.

To lengthen or shorten a note:

31. Click on the edge of a MIDI bar so that your cursor turns into a bracket, then click and drag while holding the mouse down.

Notice that while resizing or relocating notes, the notes seem to snap into place when they approach or cross a bar line. This is because, by default, Snap to Grid is enabled in the Options menu. If you prefer to turn this option off and move your MIDI files more liberally along the bar lines, you may deselect Snap to Grid from the Options menu or use the key command ⌘ + 4 (Mac) or ctrl + 4 (Windows).

32. Disable Snap to Grid using one of the methods described above and move one or more of the MIDI notes freely across bar lines.

To create new notes in the MIDI Note Editor, we will enter Draw Mode:

33. Press the b key on your computer keyboard and hover your mouse, now appearing as a pencil, over the MIDI Note Editor, clicking where you'd like to place a new note.
34. Press the b key again to allow your cursor to function normally. (Note that if you hold the b key, your cursor will function in Draw Mode only as long as you are holding the key down.)

## MIDI Velocity Editor

Beneath the MIDI Note Editor is the MIDI Velocity Editor, which, as you may have guessed, will allow you to edit the velocity for each pitch above it. The velocity value for each pitch is represented as a vertical bar which can be increased or decreased by clicking on the top point of the bar and dragging up or down.

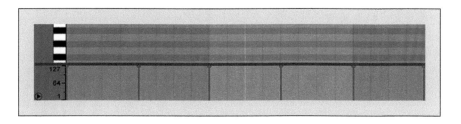

FIGURE 7.15: The MIDI Velocity Editor representing velocity values with vertical bars

35. Click on the top point of one or more velocity bars and drag them up or down. (Note the numerical change for the MIDI velocity value reflected at the left side of the MIDI Velocity Editor.)

Note that selecting all of the notes shown in the MIDI Note Editor by choosing Edit>Select All or using the key command ⌘ + *a* (Mac) or ctrl + *a* (Windows) will allow you to adjust the velocity for all notes in this clip simultaneously. This is also a great way to transpose all of the notes in a clip up or down by some number of semitones.

FIGURE 7.16: MIDI clip is set to loop

The small button labeled Fold located above the headphone Preview button will hide rows that do not contain MIDI clips. This can be used to make looking at data in the MIDI Note Editor a little easier. Be sure, however, to turn the Fold button off if you intend to move MIDI pitch bars from one note to another.

## Loops

While the MIDI Note Editor screen is still open for this clip, notice the Clips and Notes boxes at the bottom left. These boxes allow different parameters to be set for the selected clip. Note that the word Loop is highlighted.

The selected clip will **loop**, that is, repeat itself, when the clip's length is dragged horizontally within the track display.

36.  Select the clip within the track display.
37.  Hold your cursor over the top right edge of the clip until it appears as a bracket.
38.  Click and drag the clip to the right to extend the loop over several bars.

The looped pattern refers to the data within the original clip. This is important because any changes you make to the original clip within the MIDI Note Editor will appear in all of the looped iterations of that clip. This is good if you decide to change a note or two in that clip later on. If you'd prefer that changes to the clips not appear in the looped iterations, simply copy and paste an instance of the clip on the same track.

39.  Select the clip within the track display.
40.  Copy and paste a copy of the clip to the right of the original clip.

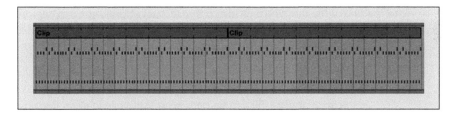

FIGURE 7.17: MIDI loop copied and placed alongside itself

There are now two instances of this clip. Changes made in one clip will not have any impact on the other. This is a good technique to use if you make a drum loop pattern that you would like to use to make derivative patterns from later without destroying the original. For our purposes, let's move this copied pattern to a new MIDI track and assign it a new timbre.

41.  Select the copied MIDI clip within the track display.
42.  Drag the clip to another track within the track display.
43.  Double-click the track name for this new track to close the Clip View and open the Track View. (Note: You may also accomplish this from the View>Detail menu item at the top of the program.)

44. Select the Sounds menu icon from the Browser on the left.
45. Expand the folder Piano & Keys.
46. Select the sound Keys-Tinefull Ambient .adg.
47. Click and drag this sound onto the new track containing the copied MIDI clip.

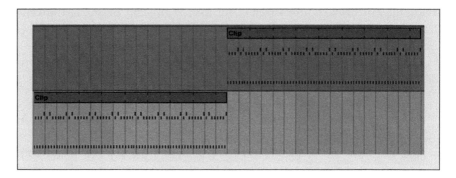

FIGURE 7.18: MIDI loop on different MIDI tracks

We now have pitch material on two different tracks with two different timbres. Let's edit the MIDI clip on this track to create some basic counterpoint.

48. Double-click the newly copied MIDI clip to open the Clip View revealing the MIDI Note Editor.

Among some of the more interesting compositional options one can explore within the Notes box are the buttons labeled :2 and *2; that is, Play at Double Tempo and Play at Half Tempo, respectively.

49. Click the button labeled :2 to change the MIDI values of the notes in the clip view so that they play at double speed.
50. In the track display, click at the beginning of this clip to move the playback marker to the front of it.
51. Press the Play button to hear the same melodic pattern played at double speed.
52. Press the Stop button when the track is done playing.

Notice that the second clip does, in fact, play twice as fast.

Additional processes available through buttons within this box allow the MIDI data to be manipulated in other novel ways. Let's now move this track so that at least part of the clip begins playing in sync with the first clip.

53. Select the copied MIDI clip within the track display.
54. Drag the clip to the left so that at least part of the new clip is overlapping the original clip.
55. In the track display, click at the beginning of the original clip to move the playback marker to the front of it.

56. Press the Play button to hear the same melodic pattern played at double speed.
57. Press the Stop button when the track is done playing.

This is starting to sound interesting, but the volume of the newly created track could probably be reduced. To adjust the volume of a track:

58. Go to View from the topmost menu and ensure that Mixer is checked.
59. Go to the track name for this clip and locate the orange panel containing the number 0.
60. Click on this panel and drag your mouse down to decrease the volume to −3.
61. Press the Play button to hear the changes.
62. Press the Stop button when you are done.

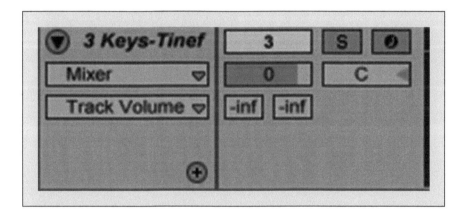

FIGURE 7.19: Track mixer section contains volume, pan, activator, and other elements related to the track

The mixer section of a track contains volume and pan level controls, a track activator to mute tracks, a Solo button to mute all other tracks, and other useful controls that we will discuss in the future.

## Adding Tracks

This set needs some bass and drum tracks. To create a new track, choose Create from the topmost menu and select Insert MIDI Track.

63. Create a new MIDI track.
64. Select the Sounds menu icon from the Browser on the left.
65. Expand the folder Bass.
66. Select the sound Wobble Bass.adg.
67. Click and drag this sound onto the new track.

## Inserting a New MIDI Clip

There's currently no MIDI data on the Bass-Wobble track, so let's create a new clip and draw in some pitches using the MIDI Note Editor.

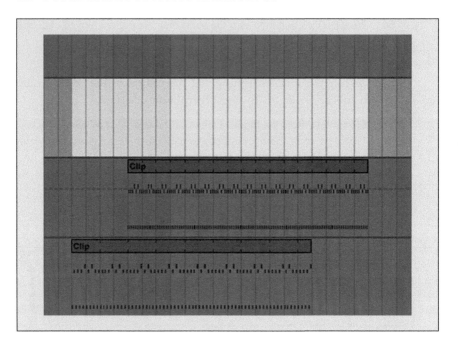

FIGURE 7.20: Selecting a region in the track display

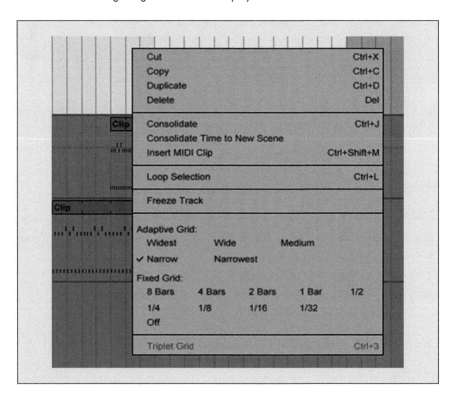

FIGURE 7.21: Inserting a new MIDI clip from the contextual menu

68. Select the track display for the bass track and select a region by click-ing and dragging your cursor to the right.
69. With the selection highlighted, ctrl + click (Mac) or right-click (Win-dows) the selection to show a contextual menu.
70. Select Insert MIDI Clip from the contextual menu.

We now have a blank clip by which we can add bass notes. Note that the clip length is the same length as the region you highlighted. Of course, we can change this region length from the Clip View as we saw earlier.

Let's add some notes:

71. Double-click the clip to enter Clip View.
72. Within Clip View, click the circular headphone icon to allow MIDI note previewing while drawing MIDI notes.

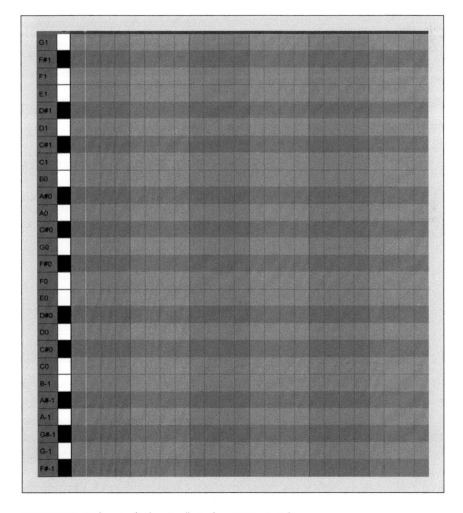

FIGURE 7.22: Pitches stacked vertically in the MIDI Note Editor

73. From the vertical piano roll on the right hand side of the MIDI Note Editor, locate the pitch marked A0.
74. Double-click in the first two squares directly to the right of the A0 marking at the beginning of the MIDI clip. (Note: These two squares should fill up half of bar 1 as delineated at the top of the MIDI Note Editor leaving two squares empty.)
75. Skip the two adjacent squares in bar 1 and click in the first and third squares of bar 2.
76. Play this set from the beginning to hear the changes stopping playback when you are done.

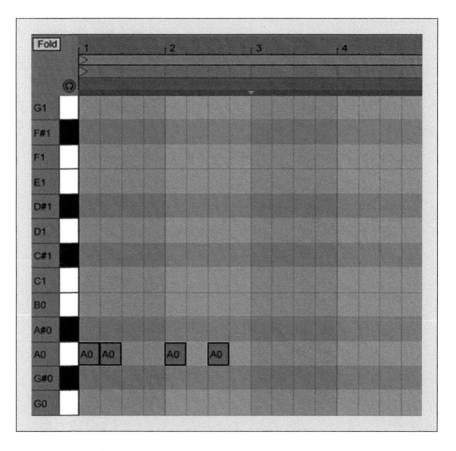

FIGURE 7.23: Bass figure drawn into the MIDI Note Editor

The bass pattern provides a nice, low-end complement to the other clips in this set. However, as you have probably noticed, even though the bass clip is set to Loop in the Clip View, the loop region itself is too large for the minimal amount of MIDI data we have entered. We can either write more notes to fit the length of the clip, or adjust the size of the clip to the amount of notes we've written. Let's choose the latter.

At the top left of the Clip View, note the two triangles stacked on top of each other just beneath the bars/beats numbers at the top. The top triangle is the Loop Start point. At the far right of the clip is the Loop End point. The length of the clip and, essentially, when and how it will loop, depends upon the position of the Loop Start and Loop End points in the Clip View.

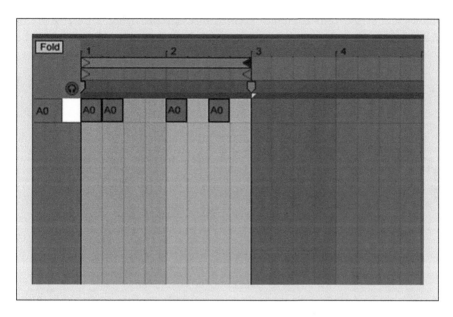

FIGURE 7.24: Adjusted loop region in the bass track's Clip View

77.   Click the Loop End point for this clip and drag it to the start of bar 3 at the far left.
78.   Press the Play button to hear the change.
79.   Press the Stop button after you have played the track.

Notice that the way that the loop appears within the track display has now been changed. Now that we have discussed how to do this, let's undo what we just did and save that process for another time when we need to use it.

The arrow beneath the Loop Start arrow is the Start Marker and controls from wherein the loop region the track will begin playing. We will leave this Start Marker in place so that this clip will play from the beginning.

## Recording with a MIDI Keyboard or the Computer MIDI Keyboard

Let's now add a drum part.

80.   Create a new MIDI track.
81.   Select the Drums menu icon from the Browser on the left.
82.   Select the sound Kit-Core 909 .adg.
83.   Click and drag this sound onto the new track.

If you have a MIDI keyboard connected to your computer, you'll be able to use it to play notes using this drum instrument as opposed to drawing them into clips like we've been doing. (If your MIDI controller is not working at the moment, we will discuss configuring it in Chapter 8. If you'd rather troubleshoot it now, you may open the Preferences>MIDI Sync menu to configure MIDI controller options.) If you don't have a MIDI keyboard, Live has provided a mechanism that allows you to use your computer keyboard to play MIDI notes. To enable this feature, go to Options from the top menu and check Computer MIDI Keyboard.

## DID YOU KNOW?

### Synthesized Sounds and Samples

Here's a quick review on how synthesizers are used to create different sounds. If you feel you've already mastered this information, feel free to move along to the next topic.

The sounds, or instrument timbres, that are played with MIDI information generally fall into one of two categories:

1. Instruments that are primarily created synthetically by manipulating wave forms or frequencies in some ways to create new sounds or to emulate sounds that already exist
2. Instruments that are primarily created using recorded sounds, called samples

Of course there are also hybrid approaches that combine both approaches.

In the synthesis approach to instrument creation, you might use a spectrogram to examine the frequencies present when a note is played on the piano and then attempt to add generated waveforms with oscillators to synthetically recreate that sound. When a MIDI key is pressed, the "synthesizer device" will understand the MIDI pitch that was pressed and generate a sound with those oscillators at a certain frequency based on the MIDI key/pitch that was pressed. Synthesis is now commonly associated with new, unique sounds as opposed to imitating existing sounds, especially given the increased popularity of the sampling approach.

In the sampling approach to instrument creation, instead of combining wave generators to imitate existing sounds, you might make audio recordings of someone playing each note on the piano. Then, when a MIDI key is pressed, a "sampler device" will understand the MIDI pitch that was pressed and trigger an audio recording of the piano playing that same pitch. The sounds are incredibly realistic because they are recordings, or samples, of actual instruments.

Early samplers, such as the Birotron or the Mellotron, used tapes to store the sample sound recordings. Now, software instruments feature "Sample Libraries" of several gigabytes that contain audio recordings of many different instruments. Each sampled software instrument contains numerous recordings of each pitch at varying volumes played in different ways.

To preview MIDI playback on a MIDI track, using a MIDI controller or a computer keyboard, ensure that the track is selected and that it is armed for recording by selecting the Arm Arrangement Recording switch in the Mixer section of the track. The switch will appear red when the track is armed.

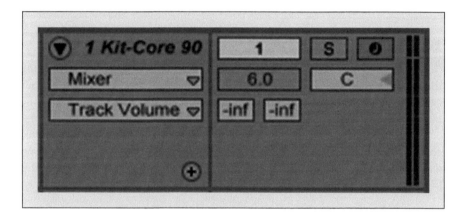

FIGURE 7.25: Arm a MIDI track for recording

84.   Ensure that the drum MIDI track is armed by clicking the Arm Arrangement Recording switch. (Note: Ensure that the mixer section is visible in View>Mixer.)

If you are using a Computer MIDI Keyboard, you may use only certain computer keys to play pitches. For example, the keys A–K map to the pitches of the C major scale. To transpose notes down or up an octave, use the keys z and x, respectively. Note that your current octave is shown in the Status Bar at the bottom left of the screen while you press the z and x keys.

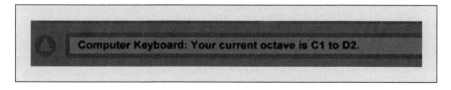

FIGURE 7.26: Octave of Computer MIDI Keyboard shown in the Status Bar

The Drum Rack device shown in the Track View shows a number of individual drums within a grid.

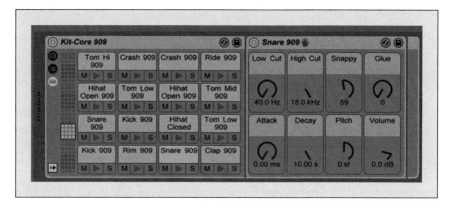

FIGURE 7.27: Individual drum samples within a Drum Rack device

From the Drum Rack device, you may sample different sounds by clicking the small Play button in each of the grid cells. Notice that when you move your cursor over one of these cells, the Status Bar reveals which MIDI note must be played in order to trigger the sample. For example, the Kick 909 sample is triggered with MIDI pitch C1. You may need to transpose down on your MIDI or computer keyboard to play this pitch. Once transposed to the correct octave, you will use the note C on a MIDI keyboard to play this kick drum; on a computer keyboard, it will be the *A* key.

85. Transpose your controller, if necessary, to the correct octave and play drum samples for this instrument.

Once you are able to get your controls working to play notes, recording them into the set is easy. With the drum track armed:

86. Using the keyboard to perform, determine a drum pattern to play that you feel fits with the musical material we already have in this set.
87. In the track display, click at the point in time where you would like to begin recording.
88. Press the F9 key to begin playback/recording or click the Global Record button in the transport dock at the top of the screen.
89. Press the Stop button to end recording.

FIGURE 7.28: Recording in progress via the Global Record button

It is advised that you enable the Metronome while recording so that you can keep in time by clicking the Metronome button at the top right of the screen (shown as two small circles). The icon will appear yellow when activated.

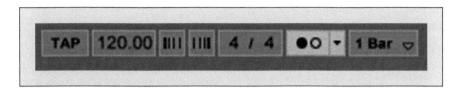

FIGURE 7.29: The Metronome button toggled to provide a click during recording/playback

If you messed up a bit in the recording process, don't worry. You already have enough skills to correct timing and pitch problems in the MIDI Note Editor with Clip View. Let's take a closer look at what you just recorded by opening the Clip View.

90.    Double-click the Clip title bar to open the Clip View.

I can see with painful clarity that what I recorded does not line up with the bars and beats grid provided.

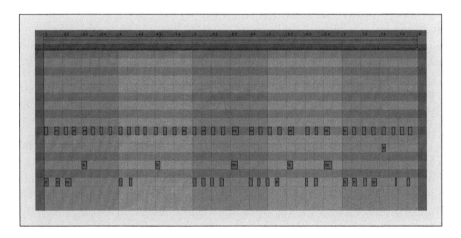

FIGURE 7.30: MIDI notes in the MIDI Note Editor out of beat as they were recorded

At this point, I can manually reposition all of the notes to my choosing or use a method called **quantization** to nudge the MIDI notes to the nearest bar. To quantize this clip:

91.    Highlight all of the notes within the clip.
92.    With the notes highlighted, ctrl + click (Mac) or right-click (Windows) the selection to show a contextual menu.
93.    Select "Quantize Settings . . ." from the contextual menu.

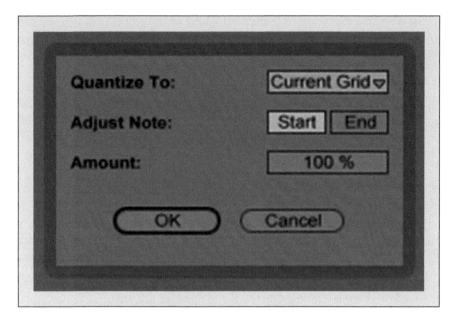

FIGURE 7.31: The Quantization Settings box controls the ways that quantization will function

The quantization process in Live can adjust the position of each MIDI note's start and end according to the beat spacing of the bars and beats grid. If you play a pattern of 8th or 16th notes and find that quantization creates a strange and unwanted accompaniment, you may select different rhythmic values from the "Quantize To:" pulldown menu in this box.

94. Click OK in the Quantization box to nudge the notes you played to the nearest bar and beat.

If this quantization process just ruined your recorded MIDI data, undo the process from the Edit menu and try the process again with different "Quantize To:" settings. (The Global Quantization button is located at the right of the Metronome.) Additionally, ctrl + clicking (Mac) or right-clicking (Windows) in the Track Display or Clip View will also allow you to adjust the beat grid.

The drum clip I recorded is not long enough to cover all of the music I have in this set, so I am going to click the Loop button within Clip View in order to use this clip as a repeating pattern. If desired:

95. Adjust the region of the recorded drum pattern within the MIDI Note Editor by adjusting the Loop Start and Loop End points.
96. Enable the Loop button for this clip.
97. Loop as desired within the track display.

As you continue to use this set, you may find it useful to loop a certain region of audio while adjusting volume, panning, or even notes in the MIDI Note Editor. To set the loop region to a specific clip:

98.   Ctrl + click (Mac) or right-click (Windows) the clip title bar for the drum MIDI track or another track.

99.   From the contextual menu, select Loop Selection.

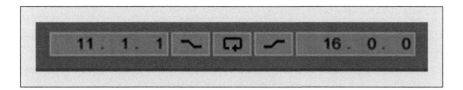

FIGURE 7.32: The Arrangement Loop settings specify the size of the loop region, punch in/out settings, and a Loop Switch

Notice that the loop region at the top of the screen now surrounds the length of clip you selected. This region can be adjusted from the Arrangement Loop settings at the top right of the program. Clicking the center icon called the Loop Switch will loop the selection as it plays back. This is a very useful feature for adjusting balance, panning, pitches, and more.

100.   Enable the Loop Switch and play the loop region noticing how it loops.

101.   Turn off the Loop Switch and notice how the track does not cycle back to the beginning as the playback marker reaches the end of the loop region.

## Changing Tempo

At the top left of the program, near the Metronome, is a button that says TAP with the numbers 120.00 next to it. Changing this numerical value will change the tempo of this piece. The tempo, at 120 by default, is measured in **beats per measure (BPM).** To change this number:

102.   Click the number 120 in the Tempo box and scroll your cursor up or down to increase or decrease the tempo.

103.   Play the file to hear the adjustment in tempo.

FIGURE 7.33: Tempo modification tools within Live

Additionally, you may click the TAP button repeatedly at the tempo of your choosing to insert that tempo value on your session.

## Saving and Cleaning Up the Set

For now, we will close our discussion of Live's Arrangement View. In Chapter 8 we will examine how Live's Session View functions. We will use the clips we've created in this chapter in our discussion of Session View, so let's quickly rename our clips so that our set is cleaner:

104. Ctrl + click (Mac) or right-click (Windows) the clip title bar for any one of the MIDI tracks in the set.
105. Select Rename and rename the track with a more appropriate name such as Keyboard Hook or Drum Pattern.
106. Repeat this process for each clip in the set.

Note that you can use the key command ⌘ + r (Mac) or ctrl + r (Windows) to rename anything in Live that can be renamed such as clips, tracks, and so on. Let's now save this set:

107. Click File>Save Live Set.
108. Save this project to the folder we created at the beginning of this chapter called My Live Projects.

## Exporting Rendered Audio

Now that the project is saved, you may render the entire set as an audio file.

109. From the top menu, click File>Export Audio/Video . . .

A number of options can be specified within this menu, including the audio settings and format. If it's not already apparent, the specific applications for changing these settings will become so later on in the text. Clicking OK will render the entire set as an uncompressed audio file.

110. Click OK and specify a filename for your audio file.

Note that highlighting a region in the Arrangement View prior to selecting the Export option will render only the highlighted region. This is useful if you intend to render only specific loops or sections of your set, and not the entire set.

## SUMMARY

Sequencing is a universal skill that is addressed in some way by every major DAW. The process is easy to grasp, and, with time, the various editing techniques become easier to work with and able to be executed rapidly.

There are many different DAWs. None is necessarily superior or inferior. Often, the particular DAW you decide to use may have more to do with the software preferred by your collaborators or some other particular feature or compatibility that appeals to you personally. Issues like technical support availability, including loop and effect libraries, are important parts of the decision-making process. For this book we elected to use Ableton Live because it solves the cross-platform compatibility (Mac vs. Windows) issue.

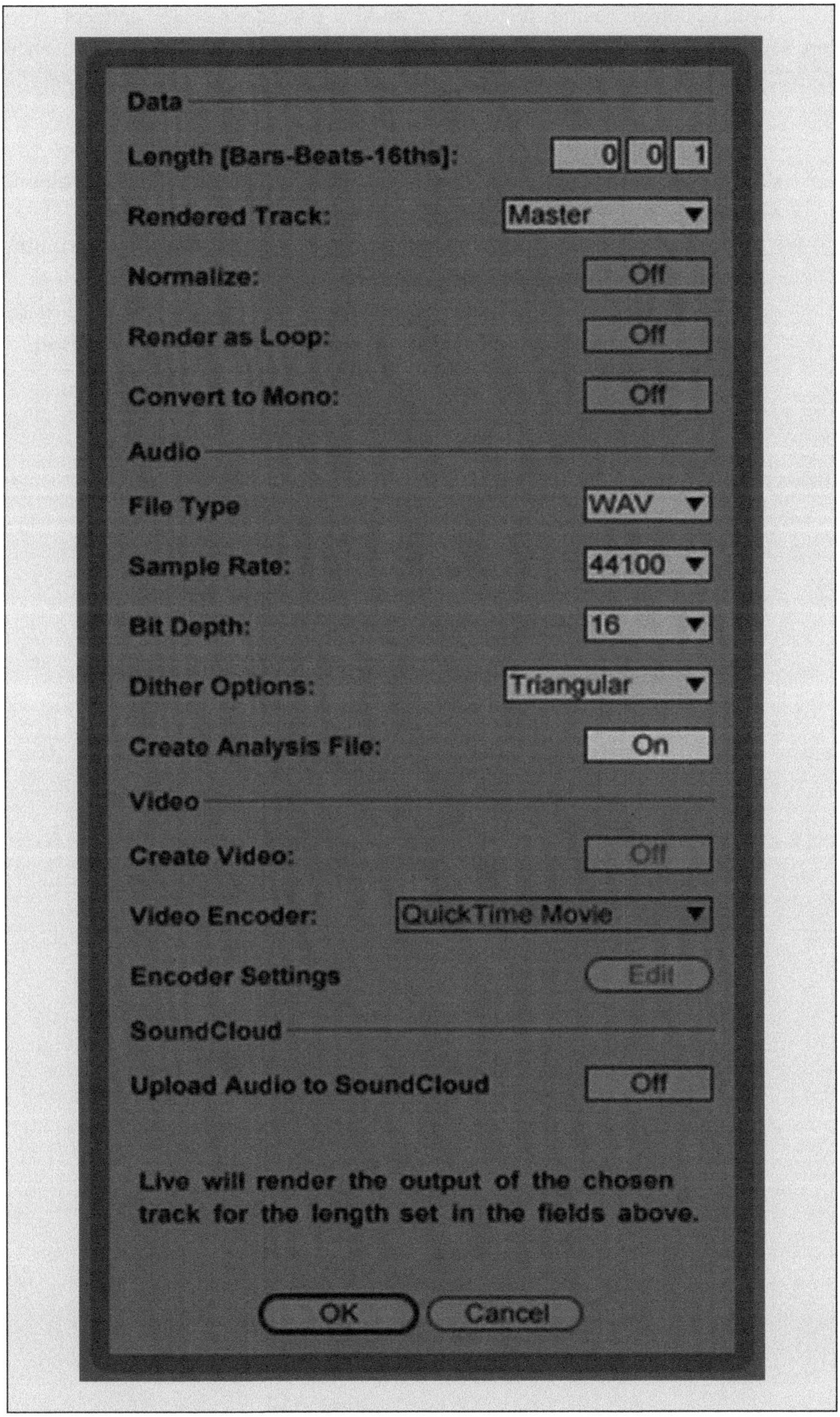


FIGURE 7.34: Export Audio/Video window

If you've enjoyed using Ableton Live and the pace at which the concepts were presented, you may enjoy the book *Interactive Composition* (Manzo & Kuhn, 2015).

## KEY CONCEPTS

- Sequencing is a function of all DAWs and allows mulitrack recording and editing of both MIDI and audio.
- Quantization is the process of "smoothing" MIDI data by repositioning notes to the nearest beat division.
- Recording MIDI and audio is generally a similar process in DAWs. It requires arming an individual track and clicking a Global Record button.

## KEY TERMS

| | | |
|---|---|---|
| beats per measure (BPM) | clip (Live software) | loop quantization |

# CHAPTER 8

# ACOUSTICS

## OVERVIEW

In the same way that a musical instrument's physical design and dimensions determines various aspects about its timbre, so the design and dimensions of a room shapes the timbre of the overall mix. For example, if you have an acoustic guitar, it will sound noticeably different if you stuff the inside of the instrument with cotton. You have probably noticed that a performance in a practice room sounds much different than one in a large concert hall. The reasons for this relate to the study of **acoustics** and, more generally, how sound travels.

In this chapter we will discuss the nature of sound travel and some techniques based on our understanding of acoustics that we can use in order to enhance music performance. By the end of this chapter you should feel comfortable understanding the ways that room designs will change how musical performances sound in that room. We will discuss what can be done to treat the room so that performances sound balanced as well as corrective and enhancement measures that can be taken with technology. Understanding acoustical phenomena has influenced the development of many audio effects, which we will discuss in Chapter 9.

## THE HEARING PROCESS

It begins with a sound. Some physical action, such as a hand clap or a struck tuning fork, causes air to begin moving. Air moves in a wave motion during which the molecules in the air are compressed together and then expanded, and then compressed, and then expanded, and so on. These processes are known as **compression** and **rarefaction**, respectively. Sounds travel differently through different mediums like air, water, and solids. Even temperature variations can change the ways in which sound propagates in a given room.

Sound waves enter the ear through the auditory canal and meet the eardrum, also called the *tympanic membrane*. The fluctuations in pressure from the wave cause the eardrum to move back and forth like a drumhead. In the middle ear, three tiny bones called *ossicles* connect the eardrum to another membrane called the *oval window*, and eventually the vibrations reach the *cochlea* within the inner ear. The cochlea contains three fluid-filled tubes through which the waves travel. The waves move like ocean waves through the fluid as opposed to the

## Conduction

Did you ever wonder why your voice sounds different on a recording than it does in your head? Sound travels differently through the air than through bone, a process called **conduction.** When you are hearing yourself speak, the sound is traveling to your ears through both air and bone conduction.

motion that they exhibited when traveling through the air. The fluid sweeps up and down the *basilar membrane,* causing it to move in accordance to the frequency of the fluid movement.

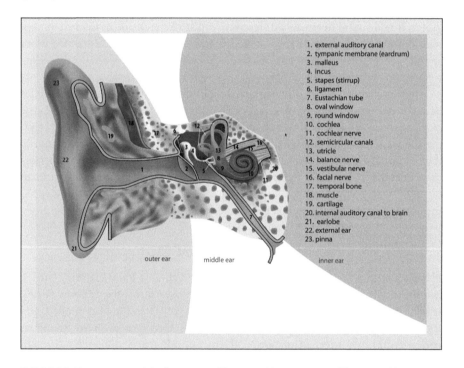

1. external auditory canal
2. tympanic membrane (eardrum)
3. malleus
4. incus
5. stapes (stirrup)
6. ligament
7. Eustachian tube
8. oval window
9. round window
10. cochlea
11. cochlear nerve
12. semicircular canals
13. utricle
14. balance nerve
15. vestibular nerve
16. facial nerve
17. temporal bone
18. muscle
19. cartilage
20. internal auditory canal to brain
21. earlobe
22. external ear
23. pinna

outer ear　　middle ear　　inner ear

FIGURE 8.1: The anatomy of the human ear (Courtesy Miro Kovacevic/Shutterstock)

From the point when the sound was created until the basilar membrane moved, the signal transmission had been entirely mechanical. However, lying alongside the basilar membrane are tiny hair cells, collectively known as the *organ of Corti,* that convert the mechanical energy to electrochemical energy. At this point, the sound as we knew it becomes a chemical signal that is sent to the brain for processing.

# ROOM ACOUSTICS

There are a number of variables within each acoustic performance environment that can "color" the timbre of the original sound source. For example, singing in the shower sounds different than singing inside the car. A recording of both performances would reveal differences in the overall energy of frequencies at different parts of the sound spectrum. In the same way that the size and shape of a cello's body yields a certain range of timbres and levels, so can the design of a room or concert hall.

Flat surfaces cause sound waves to reflect. An acoustical architect, acoustician, or acoustical engineer might design or treat a room with a combination of reflective materials and absorptive materials so that sounds made in the room will suit the intent of its use. For example, in the Middle Ages, cathedrals were designed so that sounds would echo, or reverberate. Composers for choir took advantage of these room acoustics by writing long sustained musical passages. Conversely, quick snare drum passages played in the same room would likely lose their articulation. Instrument designers build instruments with the same acoustic concepts in mind: Given the nature of this instrument as it involves strings, tubes, skins, etc., how can the instrument be designed so that the sound is loud, articulate, and produces a distinctive and balanced timbre?

## DID YOU KNOW?

### Singing in the Shower

We've all experienced the exhilaration of singing in the shower and enjoying the powerful sound of our own voice—only to be disappointed when we try singing in a different environment and realize that it doesn't sound quite as flattering.

There are three reasons that a shower stall presents such a great acoustic environment for would-be singing stars:

1. Greater Power: The hard tile walls absorb very little of the intensity of your voice. Because the space is small, the soundwaves bounce back and forth between these surfaces, gaining further power. The net result is that your voice sounds more powerful within the shower stall.
2. Added Reverb: Because many different sound waves are bouncing off the hard tile surfaces of the shower stall, not every sound reaches your ears at the same time. This delay creates an effect known as **reverberation** or **reverb**. This adds to the richness of your voice.

3.  More Bass: Your shower stall acts like a resonator box (like the body of an acoustic guitar, for example). Every space resonates at a particular frequency; when music is played that corresponds with the **resonant frequency** of the shower stall, it gets an extra boost. The typical resonant frequency of a shower stall is between 100 and 200 Hz; this corresponds to the lower notes or bass frequencies that we hear. So, when you sing in the shower, your voice sounds deeper, again giving the illusion of greater power.

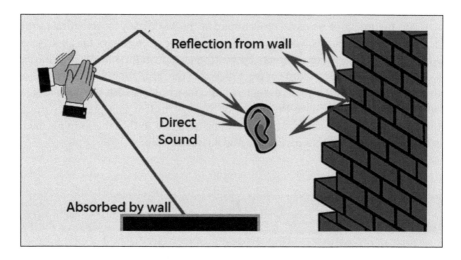

FIGURE 8.2: Delayed copies of a single sound source reach the listener's ear

An acoustically perfect room would mean that sound originating from some location in the room would spread, or **diffuse**, evenly throughout the room so that listeners would hear the sound in the same way regardless of where they stood in the room. This notion is largely idealistic. Structures inside the room such as posts, chairs, the balcony, and so on, cause the room to be nondiffuse, which results in sounds that are different depending on where the listener is standing.

## ☞ GO TO SOFTWARE LESSON: *SINE WAVE*

Using the FMT companion software, choose the lesson *Sine Wave*. If necessary, slowly adjust the main volume slider at the top left of the software.

Change the frequency number as shown near the orange circle *1* from 440 to 100. Notice that the length of each wave changes in size. As a result, lower-frequency waves are said to have longer **wavelengths** than higher-frequency waves.

Frequencies with a longer wavelength have a greater ability to bend around objects than higher frequencies do, a phenomenon known as **diffraction**. As a result, a listener sitting behind a column in the room might hear a performance that is bass-heavy or "muddy." In the same regard, drywall and drop ceilings beneath the balcony might absorb much of the bass frequencies, causing the listener to feel that the performance is "treble-heavy" or "too bright."

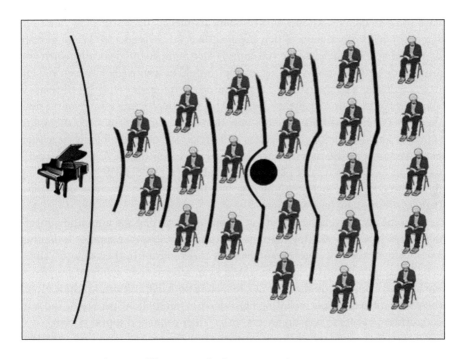

FIGURE 8.3: Sound waves diffract around a large post in the room

## DID YOU KNOW?

### Translating "Musician Speak"

Part of musicianship is learning to communicate musical concepts to nonmusicians. It is often necessary to explain informal musical nomenclature to nonmusicians and engineers alike. For example, comments like "the performance lacked oomph," "the mix sounds too boomy," or "the vocals are too tinny" give some vague, nebulous description that needs to be rearticulated in order to provide a clearer description of what is happening sonically. Phrases like "it just doesn't sound right" or "the band doesn't sound clear" are not nearly as helpful as phrases like "the vocals are not cutting through the mix" or "the keyboards are masking all of the mid-range frequencies."

# RESONANCE

If you play the bass guitar in a band, you may already be aware that there are certain notes that you can play that cause the drummer's snare drum to make sound without touching it—some frequency present in the bass note is causing the snare drum to make sound on its own, or **resonate**. Instruments and objects have some frequency, known as a resonant frequency, by which they vibrate in sympathy with other sources that produce that same frequency. We've already described how this helps make you sound like a more talented vocalist when you are singing in the shower. Another example would be a wine glass. When you tap it, you will hear a particular note representing the frequency at which the glass is vibrating. If that same frequency is played back through some sound source near the glass, the glass will resonate in sympathy with the sound source. If the sound source is amplified enough, the glass will break, as you undoubtedly have seen portrayed in comedic movies, cartoons, and television shows. A similar experiment can be conducted by playing middle C on a piano while gently holding down the C key one octave higher. As middle C is played, the note one octave higher will resonate in sympathy.

Rooms also have a propensity to resonate, increasing the amplitude of certain frequencies and making them more prominent. Room resonance is another variable for acoustical engineers and architects to address in their designs. However, for amplified music, audio engineers can also remedy resonant frequency imbalances using an equalizer, or EQ. In fact, in both live and studio applications, there are numerous tools including EQ, reference microphone packages, and self-correcting speakers to help engineers "tune" their room and sound system.

Some of the sonic qualities of a room can be measured with just a spectrogram and an **impulse response**. For example, one might enter two rooms, one large and one small, and then record the sound of a balloon popping in each room.

## DID YOU KNOW?

### I Am Sitting in a Room

One example of a composition that exploits the resonant frequency of a room is Alvin Lucier's 1969 piece *I Am Sitting in a Room*. In this work, a recording of Lucier's voice was played back into a room and recorded. Then that recording was played back and recorded. Each time a new iteration of the original recording was played, the resonant frequency of the room became more noticeably pronounced. The pitch fluctuations in his speech were ultimately lost, and only aspects of the rhythm of his speech remained.

Try searching YouTube using the phrase "I Am Sitting in a Room." You will find versions of Lucier's original as well as different homages to Lucier's original idea extended in various ways.

The impulse, the sound of the balloon breaking, will travel differently in each of the rooms, and a spectrogram would show the different frequencies present for both recordings. There are numerous tools available to refine this process.

## SOUND SYSTEMS

Using loudspeakers, microphones, mixers, and other audio equipment can certainly complicate an ensemble's mix. However, these technologies also provide a number of controls for enhancing the overall sound of the performance. In large halls, a quiet instrument or ensemble depends on the use of this technology to faithfully represent the desired sound. A sound system designed for orchestral music played in a very large hall should recreate the balance of the instruments heard on stage using the audio equipment. In this example, the sound system might not even be perceived as being present by the audience.

Some ensembles and rooms rely more heavily on technology to achieve an ideal mix. The sound systems in some concert halls include large multi-band EQs to help shape the sound with respect to the hall. Rooms that are somewhat "dead" and lack in natural reverberation may have a digital reverb effect in the signal chain of the sound system. The effect may then be applied to any channels coming through the soundboard to create the illusion that the sound source is reverberating naturally within the room.

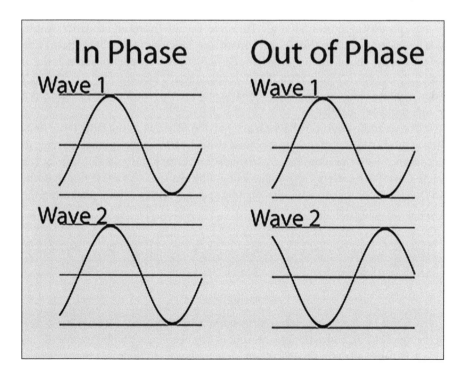

FIGURE 8.4: Two waves in phase and two waves out of phase (phase cancellation)

# PHASE CANCELLATION

Poor speaker placement can lead to the sound from each speaker hitting the listener's ears at different times. This produces a timbral effect called phase that is not desirable when it can't be controlled.

In Chapter 4 we added two simple sine waves together at different frequencies to produce vibrato, phase, and other phenomena. However, if two identical waves are used and one wave reaches its highest point at the exact time that the other wave reaches its lowest point, the two signals are said to be completely "out of phase." The result is that the two signals cancel each other out and no sound is heard. This is known as **phase cancellation**.

Phase cancellation is the process by which so-called "noise-canceling headphones" work and, in general relates to the study of all head-related transfer functions (HRTFs). Phase cancellation can be used for the removal of hum from sound signals and even to remove prominent center-panned instruments, like vocals and drums, from stereo audio recordings.

## ☝ GO TO SOFTWARE LESSON: *PHASE CANCELLATION*

Using the FMT companion software, choose the lesson *Phase Cancellation*. If necessary, slowly adjust the main volume slider at the top left of the software.

In this example, two waves are sounded completely out of phase. As the two signals travel from your speakers and combine in the air, they should cancel completely, producing no sound at all. However, because of room acoustics, unless you are demonstrating this concept in an anechoic chamber where there is no reverberation, the phenomenon will be demonstrated by reductions in volume in certain parts of the room. With the sound playing at a moderate volume through your speakers, walk around the room and observe this reduction in volume as a result of phase cancellation.

Today, audio engineers have an arsenal of tools, such as the DBX DriveRack line of products, to compensate for phase issues by timing the speaker delivery in accordance with the room design so that sounds reach the same location at the same time. Such systems also make using multiple speakers more manageable. In Chapter 2 we discussed multi-channel speaker configurations including the popular 5.1 and 7.1 setups.

### A Live Mix

Some loudspeakers themselves tend to boost more of the higher frequencies at louder volumes. An audio engineer might compensate by EQ-ing the main mix. However, people's bodies in the room tend to absorb high frequencies. An engineer might do a sound check with an ensemble playing in an empty room at moderate volumes before the concert and then get a very different mix when the ensemble plays in a crowded room at a louder volume. Often an engineer must use his or her ears in conjunction with the available technology to help shape the sound. Digital mixers allow you to store presets for mix configurations and EQ processing settings on channels, which can help engineers save time and energy.

In a 5.1 speaker setup, the listener faces three speakers, front-left, front-center, and front-right, with two speakers behind the listener, rear-left and rear-right. One subwoofer is placed somewhere else in the room. Since the low frequencies of the subwoofer have longer wavelengths, the listener does not need to sit in front of the subwoofer; it primarily needs only to be present in the room.

## PSYCHOACOUSTICS

Humans have two ears by which our brains receive sound. Just as high-quality microphones will deliver accurate representation of the sound source being mic'd, so our ears deliver information to our brains. The information includes the spatial placement of sound sources within the room or environment. If a car horn beeps 10 feet behind you, it is a noticeably different sound than a car horn beeping 10 feet in front of you. The field of **psychoacoustics** deals with perception of sound.

When mixing, a studio engineer will use the tools available to create or emulate a listening experience for the listener. We've already discussed the use of reverberation effects to simulate the sense that an individual is listening to music in a larger concert hall even if the recording took place in a small room. Panning specific instruments to either the right or left speaker will give the listener a sense of spatiality for individual instruments. For example, when mixing a rock song, an engineer may pan the drum kit mix so that the hi-hats are primarily present in the left speaker, pan the ride cymbal primarily to the right, while keeping the kick and snare drums in the center. This, in theory, would cause the listener to perceive, arguably subconsciously, that they are sitting where the drummer is seated. By contrast, an engineer may pan the drums so that the listener feels that they are sitting in the front row of the venue. Keeping the drum kit as a single sound source panned evenly across both speakers—essentially creating a dual mono mix—can make the drums sound dimensionless when compared to a stereo mix where parts of the kit are panned to different speakers.

### 👆 GO TO SOFTWARE LESSON: *MIXER*

Using the FMT companion software, choose the lesson *Mixer*. If necessary, slowly adjust the main volume slider at the top left of the software.

• Select "Main Stereo Outputs" from the menu shown near orange circle *1*.
• Next, select the "Play" button near orange circle *2*.

- As the music plays, pan channel 2 all the way to the left, referred to as "hard left," by selecting the *Pan* knob and dragging it to the left.
- Then, pan channel 3 all the way to the right, or "hard right."

Depending on the placement of your speakers, the vocal channel should sound like it is coming from the center of the sound source by comparison to the other panned channels. In actuality, the vocal channel is evenly distributed across both the left and right speakers.

Multi-channel configurations allow greater control over the spatial dimensions of mixes than a stereo mix. However, in stereo listening environments, with only front-left and front-right speakers, music that is evenly distributed across both speakers may be perceived as originating from a center speaker even though one is not present. This phenomenon is known as the **phantom center**. Because our brains are already producing this illusion, some engineers prefer to omit the center speaker from their 5.1 configurations. This may result in a 4.1 configuration where the front-center speaker is omitted and essentially replaced by the mentally constructed perception of the listener.

## LOUDNESS

Loudness is a subjective term; one person's "loud" may be another person's "moderate." The term "volume" is often used to describe the loudness of sounds. There are, however, a number of measureable characteristics that inform one's perception of "loud."

We understand that the amplitude of a sine wave refers to the strength of the wave and can be thought of in terms of its height as demonstrated in the *Sine Wave* software example. In this capacity, we can speak about amplitude strength in terms of a reference point; a wave with an amplitude of 0 has no wave height. Having a quantified reference point in discussions of loudness adds a measure of objectivity to our statements about how loud a sound is.

**Sound pressure**, for example, is a term used to measure sound levels based on such a reference point. In the case of sound pressure, the reference is a unit called the decibel, or dB. One might measure the **sound pressure level (SPL)** of a

### Our Adaptive Ears

Did you ever start up your car and get startled by the level of the music coming through your speakers? "Was I really listening to music this loudly?" you may ask yourself. Our brains adapt to loudness. This does not mean that hearing damage does not occur, only that we get used to loud sounds over time. Additionally, the "noise floor" from environmental sounds outside of the car as we drive may cause us to slowly increase the level of the car stereo to mask it. Before long, the level of sound inside the car is considerably louder than what one would deem a comfortable listening level.

microphone input and determine that a person's normal speaking voice measures at 60 dB. A link to the decibel level of daily sounds has been provided on the companion website, and an abundance of apps and hardware to measure sound pressure levels exist.

Perceived loudness is a tricky topic. Despite being able to objectively measure sound pressure levels, our perception of a sound's loudness may appear skewed given our own physiology. As you know, the range of human hearing is roughly 20 Hz to 20 kHz, yet our ears are most sensitive to frequencies within the range of 2 kHz and 5 kHz—roughly the 7th and 8th octaves of a piano. As a result, frequencies in this range may seem to be louder than they actually are; a sine wave at 3 kHz will seem louder than a sine wave at 1 kHz, even though it is not.

For example, in a live mix, a guitar player's overall level may seem in good balance with the other musicians when he's playing dropped-tuning power chords in the first few positions of the fingerboard, but his lead solos played in the highest register of his instrument may sound piercingly loud. Is it necessary to lower his overall level or just "shelve" the level in the most sensitive part of the frequency spectrum with an EQ? The same can be said for a drummer who has a good relative balance between the kick and snare drums and the rest of the ensemble but is perceived, collectively, as being "too loud" once the high-pitched cymbals are played. Is it true that "the drums are too loud" as a whole, or is it that only certain frequencies of the cymbals are too loud?

As was demonstrated in the *Hearing Test* software example in Chapter 1, natural hearing loss that occurs as we age will make higher-frequency bands seem to disappear. This may cause a sound engineer to compensate by increasing the higher frequencies in the mix. Despite their preference for what a live mix should sound like, an older man behind the mixer may tend to EQ the overall mix quite differently than a young woman simply by virtue of their amounts of hearing loss.

To better understand our sensitivity to certain frequencies, a number of **equal-loudness contour models** have been developed over the years. These models can be used to make EQ filters that shape the overall sound by altering the level of frequencies between 2 and 5 kHz to counteract the differences in sensitivity that human ears naturally have. Equal-loudness contours are particularly important to researchers who study sound perception but also have implications for mixing audio in live and studio situations.

## 🖐 GO TO SOFTWARE LESSON: *LOUDNESS*

Using the FMT companion software, choose the lesson *Loudness*. If necessary, slowly adjust the main volume slider at the top left of the software.

- Click the *Shepard Tones* button near orange circle *1*.

Roger Shepard is credited with creating a model similar to Escher's ever-ascending staircase in which the listener perceives a pitch to be infinitely rising (Shepard, 1964). With **Shepard Tones**, the only harmonics are multiples of the fundamental frequency that are powers of 2. All of the sine waves used in this example are equal in amplitude, although it appears that the frequencies at the higher end of the spectrum are louder even though they are not.

- Click the *Shepard Tones with Filter* button near orange circle *2* to apply a basic EQ-type loudness contour to this sound.

This filter simply tapers off the level of frequencies at the higher end of the spectrum, making the waves all appear to be equal in volume. This further enhances the illusion that the pitch rises infinitely.

One difficulty in discussing issues of "equal loudness" is that equal-loudness contours are developed through perception research. There is no absolute equal-loudness contour, only sets of contours that conform to different demographics such as age. A referenced unit of measuring sound pressure levels with regard to perceived loudness is the **phon**. As phons increase or decrease, the perceived loudness of frequencies also changes, thus equal-loudness contours change in response to the number of phons.

For about 23 years, the Fletcher-Munson equal-loudness curve was the standard contour for representing frequencies at a perceived equal-loudness. In 1956, the Robinson-Dadson contour (Robinson & Dadson, 1956) became the standard and remained so until 2003. The International Organization for Standardization created the ISO226:2003 contour (International Organization for Standardization) based on the Robinson-Dadson, which is, today, a recognized standard.

- Click the *ISO226 Curve* button as shown near the orange circle *3*.

Notice that the control for the ISO226 model is given using the phons unity of loudness measure. As you increase or decrease the phons using the slider near orange circle *4*, the equal-loudness contour shifts to boost or reduce certain frequencies differently. You may notice that the frequencies across the spectrum do, in fact, sound equal in loudness compared to the first two models.

The field of acoustics has many different avenues of study. With an understanding of just some of the properties of sound, we can use technology to enhance and compensate what happens to sound naturally in a room to reach our sonic goals. As we continue our discussion of sound, we will learn about audio effects and how they can be used to emulate naturally occurring acoustical phenomena like phase and reverberation, as well as ways to make many new timbral changes.

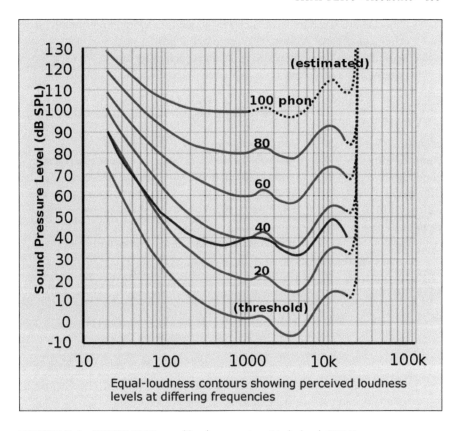

Equal-loudness contours showing perceived loudness levels at differing frequencies

FIGURE 8.5: An ISO226:2003 equal-loudness contour (Lindosland, 2005)

## SUMMARY

The nature of acoustics relates to how we hear sounds as well as how we perceive sounds. With technology, we can take steps to correct or even enhance the sound in a given room. This requires, of course, an understanding of how sound travels, which can be observed with a variety of technological tools and instruments. Once it is known how sounds travel in a room, an engineer can counteract and remedy potential problems using effect devices like reverb, timbral balance devices like EQ, and time-based correction devices as well as a variety of sound absorption and diffusion materials. A good mix, in many ways, comes down to having good listening ears to quantify what is being heard by the audience and what can be done to address the current state of the sound, technologically, acoustically, and musically.

## KEY CONCEPTS

- The process of hearing deals with wave propagation and conduction.
- The shape of the room has an influence on the way sounds are heard in that room.

- Objects have resonant frequencies by which they vibrate in sympathy with other sources that produce that same frequency.
- Sounds perfectly out of phase will cancel each other out.
- Loudness is a subjective term related to perception and psychoacoustics.

## KEY TERMS

acoustics

compression

conduction

diffraction

diffuse/diffusion

equal-loudness contour
    model

impulse response

phantom center

phase cancellation

phon

psychoacoustics

rarefaction

resonant frequency

resonate

reverberation/reverb

Shepard Tones

sound pressure

sound pressure level
    (SPL)

wavelength

# CHAPTER 9

# EFFECTS

## OVERVIEW

As discussed in Chapter 8, there are a number of naturally occurring sound phenomena that can be emulated using audio effects processors. For example, a singer in an acoustically "dead" room can create the illusion that his or her voice is in a much larger venue by using a digital reverb effect. In this chapter we will discuss many effects, what they do, and how they are generally used.

While the experimental use of an unknown effect can produce exciting and novel results, effects are best used as a means to facilitating a specific sonic goal. As you produce music, you may encounter some problems with the tracks that you are mixing: "the vocals aren't cutting through the instrument mix"; "the level of the bass is all over the place"; or "the piano is too bright." For each of these challenges, a number of remedies can be implemented before the performance takes place, such as ensuring proper microphone placement or using higher-quality equipment. However, audio effects also allow us to address these problems and manipulate signals to create new sounds.

We will discuss effects that influence dynamics such as gains, distortions, and compressors, tone-shaping effects like EQs and wah-wahs, and effects that rely on time like delay and reverb. By the end of this chapter you should have an understanding of how effects can be implemented into a live performance or recording situation as well as how to control and use each effect to produce an intended result.

## GAIN AND DISTORTION

Let's begin this discussion by reintroducing the topic of adjusting the level of the input signal through various gain stages that we first addressed in the discussion of mixers in Chapter 2. Boosting the overall decibel level of an input signal can be accomplished through a number of gain-related effects, but it is important to note that many of the other effects we will discuss have, within themselves, controls to adjust the input gain and the output gain. The nature of certain effect processes may have the propensity to increase the gain, so gain controls at both the input stage and the output stage are used. In other words, effects processors generally have the capability to ensure that the signal coming into them is strong but not so "hot" that it distorts and not so "hot" on the way out of the effect that the next effect or device in the signal chain will suffer from any sort of distortion. These controls are generally labeled "Input Gain" and "Output Gain" or simply "Input Level" and "Output Level." When the gain of a signal becomes too hot, the signal clips and distorts, often indicated with a red LED somewhere on the effect interface or level meter.

## ✋ GO TO SOFTWARE LESSON: *SINE WAVE*

Using the FMT companion software, choose the lesson *Sine Wave*. If necessary, slowly adjust the main volume slider at the top left of the software.

• Increase the level as shown near the orange circle *2*.

Notice that as you increase the amplitude of the wave, its top point reaches the vertical ceiling of the window. When the wave hits the ceiling, it does not break through but, instead, clips off. This clipping produces a distorted tone not unlike a square wave.

• Click the small *waveform select* icon at the bottom right of the wave display window and select a different waveform icon.

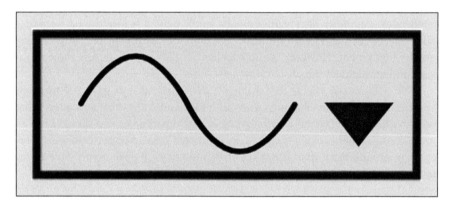

FIGURE 9.1: Waveform select icon within FMT software

Notice that the shape of the square wave depicts the wave as being "clipped" at the top even at lower amplitudes as opposed to the smooth arc of a sine wave. This gives the square wave its unique timbre. Intentional distortion like this is also present in FM synthesis techniques (see Chapter 4).

Professional audio equipment is typically designed with mechanisms that prevent damage to the components from signals that are or become distorted. However, as noted with FM synthesis, intentional distortion is a desired effect in many musical styles.

In the 1950s, rock guitarists began intentionally distorting their guitar tone through a variety of methods that included damaging the speakers and tube components of their amplifiers (Hicks, 2000) and, in general, playing at high gains (Rubin, 2007).

---

### DID YOU KNOW?

#### Rumble!

Link Wray's "Rumble" (1958) is one example of early mainstream guitar distortion types. It also is an early example of recorded feedback. Wray went so far as to poke holes in his guitar amplifier's speaker in order to get the sound that he wanted. The name "Rumble" referred both to the record's overall sound and the fact that it was thought to aurally simulate the sound of a street fight.

Contrast Wray's record with the more "melodic" distortion during the guitar solo of "Killer Queen" (1974) by the group Queen and the "heavy" modern guitar timbres of "Toxicity" (2002) by the group System of a Down. These are three different variants on the same distortion effect achieved by high-gain processes.

---

Over time, sophisticated methods of "smoothing" out the clipping of the sound wave were introduced to make the distortion sound more palatable while still maintaining the edginess of the distortion effect. With each varying method came new terms to describe the subtle differences, including "fuzz" and "overdrive." In general, distortion methods can be thought of in terms of distorting the signal in one stage while controlling the output level in another stage.

## 🖐 GO TO SOFTWARE LESSON: *EFFECTS*

Using the FMT companion software, choose the lesson *Effects*. If necessary, slowly adjust the main volume slider at the top left of the software.

- Press the play button near the orange circle *1*.
- Click the Distortion preset from the menu near orange circle *2*.
- Click the Bypass toggle to disable and enable the effect as the audio plays.
- Slowly increase and decrease the values of the controls for the Distortion effect.
- Click the Preset values for the effect as the audio plays.

### TONE-SHAPING CONTROLS IN EFFECTS

Coupled with this effect, as with many others, are "tone-shaping" or "tone-control" options. These are, in essence, EQs just as we discussed in Chapter 4. Because the effects themselves change the timbral qualities of the signal, it is sometimes desirable to EQ them to adjust accordingly. For example, a distortion effect may make the overall signal too "bright"; cutting the treble bands with a low-pass EQ filter will help balance the timbre. In the distortion effect, the *Tone* knob is a low-pass filter that, when turned to the right, allows the brighter frequencies to pass to the output.

## GATE

An effect called a *gate* is more of a utility than a timbral modifier. The function of a gate is simple: it prevents unintended noise, such as an air conditioning system or some hum from the lights, from coming through the microphone when the mic is not being used. From our discussion of masking in Chapter 1, we can understand that mild background noise on a mic channel will be less noticeable at times when a sound is coming through that channel than at times when the noisy channel is heard in isolation.

A gate works to prevent noise from being heard, blocking sounds below a specific decibel level. If the decibel level of your room noise is –30 dB, you would set the **threshold level** of your gate device to –30 dB. Any sounds that are louder than –30 dB would exceed the threshold level and, thus, be allowed to pass through the gate. The gate mutes the channel when the signal coming through the microphone falls below –30 dB. The assumption is that your noisy room isn't nearly as loud as the singer or instrumentalist behind the microphone will be.

## 👆 GO TO SOFTWARE LESSON: *EFFECTS*

Using the FMT companion software, choose the lesson *Effects*. If necessary, slowly adjust the main volume slider at the top left of the software.

- Click on the Noisy Speech button to change the audio playback file.
- Press the play button near the orange circle *1*.
- Click the Gate preset from the menu near orange circle *2*.
- Click in the box labeled Threshold and change the value to –39 dB.

Notice that parts of the noisy signal drop out as Threshold level changes. The level of the noise signal on the track does not exceed the level set by the threshold, but the speech portion of the track does. Gate effects are an important utility when working with imperfect audio recordings.

## COMPRESSION

The range of dynamics, loud and soft levels, in classical music recordings tends to be much larger than in popular music. Typical club music, for example, often has a very narrow dynamic range, whereas a performance of the prelude to Richard Wagner's opera *Tristan und Isolde* has parts that are very quiet and parts that are very loud. In these two scenarios, the dynamic range seems appropriate for the context: a club is a noisy environment where the music is intended to play at a constant level; a concert hall is a generally quiet environment where dynamic nuances may be more easily identified.

As an effect, a **compressor** limits the dynamic range of a sound source by adjusting the loud and quiet moments of the performance to a similar level. There are a number of reasons why you might want to compress the dynamic range of a signal. These reasons range from the desire to make a change in timbre as well as utilitarian reasons like the ease that comes with mixing channels with dynamic levels that don't widely fluctuate.

## 🖐 GO TO SOFTWARE LESSON: *EFFECTS*

Using the FMT companion software, choose the lesson *Effects*. If necessary, slowly adjust the main volume slider at the top left of the software.

- Press the *Nylon Guitar* button to use the guitar clip for playback.
- Press the play button near the orange circle *1*.
- Click the *Compression* preset from the menu near orange circle *2*.
- Click the *Bypass* toggle to disable and enable the effect as the audio plays.
- Click the *Preset* values for the effect as the audio plays.

A compressor has at least two main parameters: a **threshold** and a **ratio**. Just as with the gate effect, the threshold sets the dB level at which the compressor will begin compressing the dynamic range. A lower dB value will compress more of the signal, meaning that very quiet sounds, like breathing, will have their level noticeably increased.

Most effects have some controls that operate similarly to the parameters of an ADSR curve, as discussed in Chapter 4. To this end, the envelope of the effect, primarily at least attack and release, can be adjusted. In the compression effect, for example, a slow attack and release time will gradually mute and unmute the channel, respectively.

The other main parameter of the compressor is the ratio. The ratio determines how the compressor will compress sounds as they reach the threshold dB level. The ratio is expressed as, for example, 4:1 or 10:1, where the first number is the expected dB level of the sound source above the threshold level and the second number is 1 dB over the threshold level.

For example, in the software, the default threshold level is set to –24 dB, meaning that any sounds above –24 dB that enter the compressor will be compressed in some way. The ratio is set to 8:1, so any sounds that are –16 dB (8 decibels above the –24 dB threshold) will be compressed so that their new level is –23 dB (1 decibel above the –24 dB threshold). Adjusting the ratio value to 30:1 means that any sounds that are +6 dB (30 decibels above the –24 dB threshold) will be compressed so that their new level is –23 dB (1 decibel above the –24 dB threshold).

- Click the *Play* button once again.
- Change the *Ratio* value to 30:1 by clicking in the Ratio box and entering the value 30.
- Click the *Bypass* toggle to disable and enable the effect as the audio plays.

When considering timbre, higher ratios can produce a more "squished" sound. Increasing the ratio and decreasing the threshold levels will produce a very "squished" sound. Mild compression can produce a smooth "overdriven" sound and is often used to make vocals, drums, and other instruments sound a little bit more "aggressive" without having them wallow in distortion. Additionally, some compressors support **side-chain compression**, a technique used commonly in clubs to produce a pumping sound. Using this technique, the envelope of one signal, like a kick drum, shapes the envelope profile of the compression that is applied.

One common use of a compressor is taking an instrument with a very wide dynamic range and compressing the sound so that it is easier to mix. For basic mixing purposes, a ratio of 2:1 is a natural "over-easy" compression ratio that is ideal for singers, whereas a ratio of 10:1 may be ideal for drums. An attack level of 50 ms and a release of 200 ms is also a good "natural-sounding" starting point in most cases. Compressors work well in conjunction with gates, especially on tracks where the squishing of the dynamic range causes noticeable hiss.

Compressors often have attack and release controls, and may have additional parameters like "knee" to adjust the way that compression will be applied to the signal as it approaches the threshold. A "soft knee" will increase the compression ratio slowly as signals rise toward the threshold level, resulting in a more gradual type of compression.

## EFFECTS AND PERFORMANCE

It is also important to note that a performer may find that he or she performs differently when effects are in use. A singer, for example, may project his or her vocals more with the understanding that the compressor will "even it all out" and limit the dynamic range of a performance. It is also cautioned that musicians don't perform counterintuitively to what the effects are doing. For example, don't play quick scale passages with lots of reverb and expect the audience to hear each note articulated. Additionally, while distortion is used on guitars in rock music all the time, the result of playing 6-note open chords with lots of distortion is a vastly different sound than the commonly used three-note power chords with lots of distortion. The latter approach is often much easier to mix.

## OUTPUT GAINS IN EFFECTS

As you continue to compress sounds, you may notice that the overall level is decreased. To compensate, a "makeup" gain control is commonly implemented at the output stage. This allows you to compensate or make up for the level decrease that occurs by virtue of the effect process. A makeup gain at the output stage doesn't nullify the efforts of a compressor but, instead, increases the level of the compressed signal.

# LIMITING

Limiting is a type of effect process that goes hand-in-hand with compression, often at the final stage of audio production called the mastering stage. A **limiter** sets a ceiling for the maximum dB level that will be allowed. Any sounds above the set level will be decreased, or attenuated, so that clipping does not occur, through a process that operates similarly to that of a compressor. When tracks are being mastered at the final production stage, compression is used to ensure that tracks are at a high dB level. During this stage, EQ-ing is used to make sure that the tracks don't sound radically different at higher levels, and limiting is used to make sure that tracks can get very hot without clipping. In general, popular music recordings are much louder than classical music recordings due to compression and limiting processes and the perspective of what is an appropriate dynamic range given the genre.

# EQ

Equalization, or EQ, has been discussed several times in this book (see Chapters 4 and 8). Depending on the EQ device, the frequency range will be divided into a number of bands such as the three-band EQ in the software example. Additionally, there will be controls to adjust the center frequency by which the band is formed, as well as the Q, or width of the band.

# ☞ GO TO SOFTWARE LESSON: *EFFECTS*

Using the FMT companion software, choose the lesson *Effects*. If necessary, slowly adjust the main volume slider at the top left of the software.

- Press the play button near the orange circle *1*.
- Click the EQ preset from the menu near orange circle *2*.
- Click the *Presets* and adjust the controls of the effect as the audio plays.

Notice that for each of the three bands in this EQ, a control is given to adjust the center frequency of what one would consider "low," "mid," and "high," as well as a control to adjust the gain for each band. The Q control adjusts the bandwidth of the middle band. EQs can be used for enhancing the audio signal as well as correcting it, although there are a few different ways of thinking about EQ-ing. One approach is to EQ each track in the mix so that each one sounds good in isolation. An alternative is to EQ each track in the mix according to what will sound best in the overall mix.

The results differ in instances where, for example, a bass guitar sounds good in isolation but, combined with the low frequencies of the kick drum, produces a mix that is too "bass-heavy" and unbalanced. In such instances, an engineer might use an EQ on the master output channels as well. It should be noted, however, that using an EQ on a master channel ultimately changes the timbre of each individual instrument in the mix. Attempts to boost the low end on a bass channel will be nullified by a master EQ that is reducing those frequencies.

If you are able to download a collection of multitrack stems from an artist or a song that you know, you may be surprised to note the quality of each track in isolation. In popular music, for example, a vocal track in isolation tends to sound overly compressed and bright, whereas these attributes may be lost in the context of a mix.

## DID YOU KNOW?

### Limitations of EQ

EQ adjustments are made to enhance the way a track sounds by boosting certain frequencies in the audio signal. It should be noted that an EQ can only add or reduce gain to frequencies that are present in the mix. In other words, if you are adjusting the EQ on, for example, a mic'ed piano, and you're not receiving a strong high-frequency signal at the mixing board, you won't really be able to add those highs to the sound because they aren't really present in a significant way—you'd be adding noise or some overtones or artifacts of the signal. In that case, it would be better to adjust the microphone placement so that the signal is coming to the board with the higher frequencies represented. The same is true for "muffled" or "muddy" keyboard, bass, and guitar sounds; if a guitarist has his high-frequency content "shelved" so that the tone is more "mid-range" and "covered," an engineer can't readily make it "bright" and "high-range" by increasing the EQ high gain knob.

Drastic adjustments to the EQ of an instrument during a performance can produce a unique timbral effect. The build up and drop technique is a popular dance music compositional effect where a low-pass filter is used on one or more tracks to produce a "covered" tone. A DJ or instrumentalist might use a controller to gradually remove the low-pass filter as the music builds up to a musical climax. A wah-wah pedal is another type of EQ effect commonly used by guitarists to manually sweep between a covered tone and a normal, brighter tone through use of a foot pedal. An auto-wah operates similarly, but uses time, tempo, or some automatic variable other than a pedal to sweep between EQ states.

## DID YOU KNOW?

### EQ Effects

Changing tone color with equalization can provide a number of enhancements to your music. With fixed EQ setting, an EQ provides enhancement of specific frequency groups, but when used over time it can produce unique effects. In the last minute of Britney Spears's "Till the World Ends," a low-pass filter slowly allows the full range of the audio content to be heard; in conjunction with a compositional buildup, this produces a sense of spatial movement for the listener. In a quicker implementation, the lead guitar work in the song "White Room" by the group Cream demonstrates the use of a wah-wah pedal to produce a talking/pumping sound. These are just two contrasting examples of equalization being used to produce a timbral effect.

## DELAY

A **delay** effect produces a copy of a sound source at a specified amount of time after the original source has sounded and combines it with the original sound. It is akin to the concept of echo in which a sound source is repeated over time. The delay time is often used as the parameter for controlling the effect.

## 🖑 GO TO SOFTWARE LESSON: *EFFECTS*

Using the FMT companion software, choose the lesson *Effects*. If necessary, slowly adjust the main volume slider at the top left of the software.

- Press the play button near the orange circle *1*.
- Click the *Delay* preset from the menu near orange circle *2*.
- Click the *Bypass* toggle to disable and enable the effect as the audio plays.
- Click the *Presets* for this effect as the audio plays.

### DID YOU KNOW?

### Wet/Dry

Some effects have a parameter labeled **Wet/Dry**, where wet represents the gain of the signal once it has been processed by the effect and dry represents the gain of the input signal before it reaches the effect. The control is normally a single control by which you can control the mix of the signal, where 100% represents completely processed by the effect and 0% completely unprocessed by the effect.

Notice that the input signal is delayed and that a number of "copies" trail off with each repeat. The concept of delaying a signal is an important one and is used in many different effects.

# REVERB

If you have enough delayed copies of a signal, it produces an effect referred to as reverb. As explained in Chapter 8, a reverb effect is an example of an audio effect attempting to imitate a real-world acoustic phenomenon. A reverb effect can cause the listener to perceive a recorded sound source from originating in a cathedral or a large concert hall even if it was actually recorded in a small vocal booth.

# 👆 GO TO SOFTWARE LESSON: *EFFECTS*

Using the FMT companion software, choose the lesson *Effects*. If necessary, slowly adjust the main volume slider at the top left of the software.

- Press the play button near the orange circle *1*.
- Click the *Reverb* preset from the menu near orange circle *2*.
- Click the *Bypass* toggle to disable and enable the effect as the audio plays.
- Click the *Presets* as the audio plays.

Notice that adjusting the decay time changes the perceived size of the room. In general, reverb covers a multitude of sonic sins by providing supporting copies of the source signal. It can be used to add support for a singer whose vocal tone would be thin and weak otherwise. However, it can also "muddy" the tone of the input source if caution is not taken.

# CHORUS

A **chorus** effect is another example of a delay effect. However, the delayed copy or copies produced by a chorus effect are pitched slightly out of tune. The summation of these multiple copies with different tunings can produce the sound of an ensemble. The delay time of the pitched signal in a chorus effect is often subtle or unnoticeable when combined with the original, though the amount of detuning may be very noticeable.

## DID YOU KNOW?

### Why Pay for a Violin Section When You Can Overdub One Violinist?

From a purely business-oriented mindset, it would make sense to record a single violin part once and simply click the "duplicate" button 27 times inside of the DAW to create an ensemble sound with only one player. However, the quality that gives an ensemble its unique, full timbre is the slight tuning and delayed differences between those 28 players. As noted in Chapter 4, vibrato results when similar frequencies are summed. These small nuances in a large group make all the difference.

A chorus effect can be used to produce a shimmering "doubled" effect if the delayed copies are only slightly out of tune. A range of varied effects from "warbled" to "horror movie" is produced if the copies are set to different types of tunings.

## 🖑 GO TO SOFTWARE LESSON: *EFFECTS*

Using the FMT companion software, choose the lesson *Effects*. If necessary, slowly adjust the main volume slider at the top left of the software.

- Press the play button near the orange circle *1*.
- Click the *Chorus* preset from the menu near orange circle *2*.
- Click the *Bypass* toggle to disable and enable the effect as the audio plays.
- Click the *Presets* as the audio plays.

The chorus effect with a very slight detuning is often used to support weak vocals and give a unique timbre to acoustic guitars.

## FLANGER

Similar to the chorus, a **flanger** is a device that delays a signal by a varying rate producing a "comb filter–like" effect (see Chapter 4). The flange effect produces a "jet-engine–like" sound as the sound source shifts in and out of phase.

## 🖑 GO TO SOFTWARE LESSON: *EFFECTS*

Using the FMT companion software, choose the lesson *Effects*. If necessary, slowly adjust the main volume slider at the top left of the software.

- Press the play button near the orange circle *1*.
- Click the *Flanger* preset from the menu near orange circle *2*.
- Click the *Bypass* toggle to disable and enable the effect as the audio plays.
- Click the *Presets* as the audio plays.

## EFFECTS CHAIN

The string of effects applied to the audio source is known as the **effects chain**. Be it a channel strip on a mixing console or DAW or a pedalboard for guitarists and keyboardists, the order in which the effects are placed makes a big difference. It is important, then, to consider what each effect does when placing them in the chain.

In general, having a strong signal level to work with will make it easier to work with effects in the chain. Effects related to ensuring that the sound source is represented as it ideally exists—such as gains, autotuning pitch correctors, and compressors—typically belong at the beginning of the chain. Distortions might likely go next with the notion being that we'd prefer to add delay or reverb to a strong distorted signal as opposed to distorting a delayed or reverberated signal, thus nullifying the "trailing-off" aspect of those effects. Modulation effects like chorus, flange, and tremolo might go next after distortions, with delays and reverb closing out the chain. Individual EQs may exist within each effect in the chain. Of course, experimentation with different effect orders is fun and worth exploring.

## 👆 GO TO SOFTWARE LESSON: *EFFECTS*

Using the FMT companion software, choose the lesson *Effects*. If necessary, slowly adjust the main volume slider at the top left of the software.

- Press the play button near the orange circle *1*.
- From the dropdown menu above each "effect slot" near orange circles *2–5*, choose an effect and construct your own effects chain in whatever order you'd like.

## EFFECTS IN DAWS

DAWs provide users with the tools to use effects built into the software or to load third-party software effects, called **plug-ins**, into the DAW to be used alongside the native effects. The file formats for these plug-ins may include .VST or .AU, depending on the software manufacturer. There are also mechanisms in place to use other DAWs like effects through hosting protocols like ReWire. The point is simply this: many different plug-ins exist to facilitate your creative ideas and may be utilized within a DAW.

Once loaded inside the DAW, aspects of the effects, such as the Wet/Dry levels or EQ adjustments, may be adjusted or set to adjust in real time, a process known as **automation**. Automation allows you to draw or record parameter changes on a timeline that are adjusted by the DAW in real time.

### DID YOU KNOW?

#### Before Automation

Before automating effects, volume, and panning were possible, engineers would have to apply the changes to these parameters in real time while the final version of the recording was being mixed down to a stereo channel. In the 1970s it was not uncommon for each band member and engineer to be responsible for adjusting the knobs for a single effect as the final mixdown was being prepared.

## 👆 GO TO SOFTWARE LESSON: *AUTOMATION*

Using the FMT companion software, choose the lesson *Automation*. If necessary, slowly adjust the main volume slider at the top left of the software.

- Press the play button near the orange circle *1*.

Notice that the Wet parameter on the Delay effect is set to 0. The pink automation line displayed in the waveform viewer is automating this parameter.

- Click *Preset 2* near orange circle *2*.

Notice that as the playback head crosses over the automation line, the Wet/Dry value is changed.

- Draw in your own automation line by clicking in the window near orange circle 3.

Notice that as you draw and change the automation curve, parameters of the effect are changed over time. Some form of automation is available in most professional DAWs and allows parameter changes for effects, as well as panning and volume, to be changed over time.

As you continue to be creative with music technology, you'll want to explore these effects while also leaving time to explore the sonic potential that these processes possess. Consider the types of compositions and performances that can uniquely drive and take advantage of these types of effects.

## SUMMARY

Effects often imitate real-world acoustical phenomena. They generally fall into categories related to dynamics, like compression and gains, time-based effects like delays and reverbs, and combined methods, like a chorus effect that delays a signal and changes its pitch while combining it with the original signal. There are also several utilitarian effects like EQs and limiters. The manner in which the musical material is performed can sometimes be a factor in which an effect will help enhance it. To this extent, it is often a better approach to begin with a timbral idea in mind and seek the appropriate effects to facilitate that idea than to arbitrarily audition effects until you find the one that works for you. However, if working with effects is new to you, you should audition as many factory-made presets as you can for a given effect in order to familiarize yourself with the sonic potential available within your creative works.

## KEY CONCEPTS

- Effect processes can be used to imitate acoustical phenomena and manipulate source audio.
- Gain-type effects include distortion, compression, and volume effects.
- Time-based effects include reverb and delay.
- Mixed-methods effects include chorus and flange, which manipulate a delayed copy of a signal and combine it with the original signal.
- Tone-based effects include EQ and wah-wah.
- Automation allows effects to be manipulated over time within a DAW.

## KEY TERMS

| | | |
|---|---|---|
| automation | flanger | threshold |
| chorus | limiter | threshold level |
| compressor | plug-in | Wet/Dry |
| delay | ratio | |
| effects chain | side-chain compression | |

# CHAPTER 10

# SEQUENCING AND PERFORMING WITH AUDIO

## OVERVIEW

Technology is widely used in music performance. From the simplicity of using a reverb unit while singing to live looping—recording a pattern during a performance and overdubbing additional parts—technology can be used for directed musical outcomes. The computer, and specifically a DAW, as a performance instrument is unique in its versatility and delivers options that traditional instruments cannot rival.

In this chapter we will examine recording audio within a DAW using Live. We will also explore Live's Session View, a unique way of working with audio and MIDI with real-time accessibility for composition and performance. We will examine the basics of audio recording within Live and discuss the basics of applying audio effects to the signal source.

## SESSION VIEW

In Chapter 7 we worked primarily in Live's Arrangement View, which in many ways functions like traditional DAWs, allowing users to record, mix, and so on. Live's Session View provides a novel interface that allows you to interact with music material with a real-time composition approach. Let's examine this view by opening the project from Chapter 7: Sequencing MIDI. If you don't have this file handy, open the first file from the Session View Project in the Chapter Examples>Chapter 10 folder. This folder is accessible from the Chapter Examples location on the left-hand Places menu that we created in Chapter 7.

1. Open the file we made in Chapter 7 or load the file Session View 1 from the folder Chapter Examples>Chapter 10>Session View Project.

Before we look at Session View, let's export the clips we used in this project so that we can work with them within Session View.

2. Select the Places browser folder called Current Project at the left.
3. Click the clip title bar for any one of the MIDI tracks in the set and drag it to the right side of the Current Project browser window.

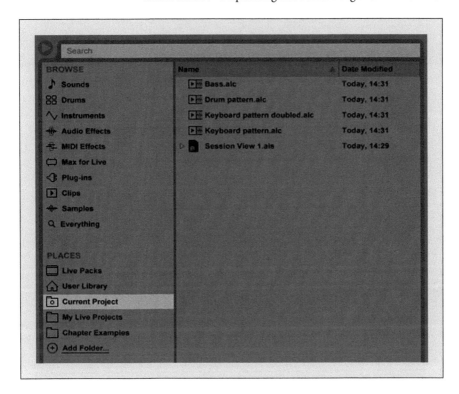

FIGURE 10.1: MIDI patterns as clips in the Current Project folder

4.  Repeat the process for each MIDI clip in the set until all of the clips are listed in the browser window.

Now that we've made these clips, let's make a new set and build a Session View project from the ground up.

5.  Choose File>New from the top menu to make a new set. (Note that you may be asked to save the changes you've made to the open document; choose No.)

Now that we have a blank set open, let's switch to Session View so that we can interact with these clips.

6.  Switch to Session View from the top View menu, the Selector icon at the top right, or by pressing the tab key.

At first glance you may not know what to do with Session View, so let's discuss the concept. Unlike Arrangement View, where the timeline moves forward on a linear plane playing the music material that you created, the Session View allows you to load multiple clips into the various slots for each track in your set and play them whenever you'd like. To demonstrate this concept, let's navigate to the location where you saved the clips that we made in the previous steps for this chapter.

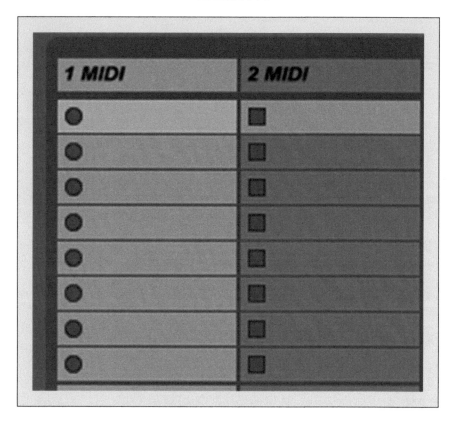

FIGURE 10.2: Clip slots stacked for tracks in Session View

7. From the Places Browser, navigate to the location on your computer where you saved the 4 clips made in previous steps. (Note: If you cannot access/find these clips, you may use the demo clips located in the Chapter Examples folder: Chapter Examples>Chapter 2>Demo Clips.)

The basic concept behind Session View is that you can stack multiple clips for a single track in which each clip contains different musical ideas. This means that if you have one track with a drum sound, you can load a bunch of clips into each clip slot for each section of your piece: an intro drum pattern, a verse drum pattern, a chorus drum pattern, and so on. Of course, Live gives you total control over how these clips are played (Do I use the mouse to start/stop clips? Do I press a keyboard key? Can I use a video game controller?), what happens to them during playback (Can I manipulate effects and filters? Can I change the volume?), and what actions take place after each clip is played (Do they loop? Do they jump randomly to another pattern? Do they play only once?). In essence, Session View takes the traditional functions of a typical DAW and turns it into a performable musical instrument.

To begin, let's double-click each clip you created earlier in order to create some new tracks within Session View with these clips loaded in.

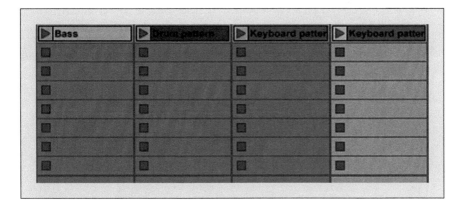

FIGURE 10.3: Clip slots loaded with clips on separate tracks

8.  Double-click each of the clips you created earlier from within the Browser at the right.

Notice that Live has created new tracks with each clip loaded into the first cell, known as a clip slot. The sounds we used earlier have been retained in these .alc format clips. (Note: If we had imported MIDI files directly onto these clip slots by dragging them from the browser onto new MIDI tracks, we would have to choose sounds to synthesize the MIDI data just as we did when we imported MIDI files onto tracks in Chapter 7.)

To play these clips:

9.  Press the Play button triangle at the left of each Clip Slot to play the clip in that slot.
10. Press any of the Stop button squares on a track that is currently playing to stop the clip from playing. (Note: You may also use the square labeled Stop Clips at the button right on the Master Track to stop all audio clips from playing.)

When you click the Play button for a clip, it begins playing looped. Each clip can play independent of the other clips on separate tracks. For example, you can press Play for each clip but then choose to stop, perhaps, just the drum clips or just the bass. In fact, we can make different configurations of clips on each row of cells and play all of the clips simultaneously.

## DID YOU KNOW?

### Performing Live with Sampled Audio

For songs like "Grand Designs" that contain synthesized sequences, the band Rush renders snippets of the recorded audio directly from the master studio recordings so that they can trigger the sequences during their live performances. The snippets of audio are loaded into Ableton Live, formerly a hardware sampler, placed off-stage, and triggered by MIDI keyboards, foot controllers, and other devices placed near the performers on stage.

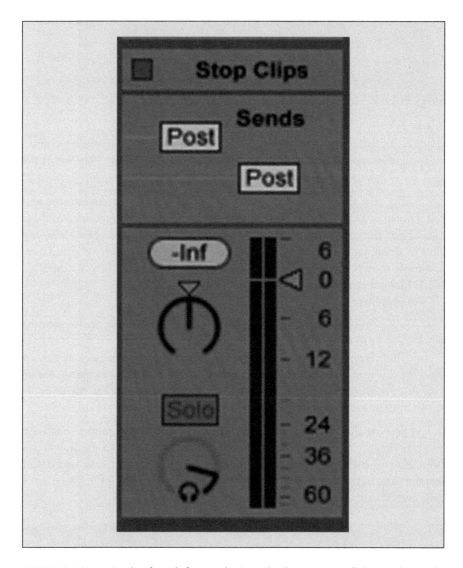

FIGURE 10.4: Master Track at far right features the Stop Clips button to stop all clips simultaneously

At the far right, you will see the Master Track complete with Play buttons of its own. Clicking one of these Play buttons will play, or launch, all of the clips in the horizontal row, called a scene.

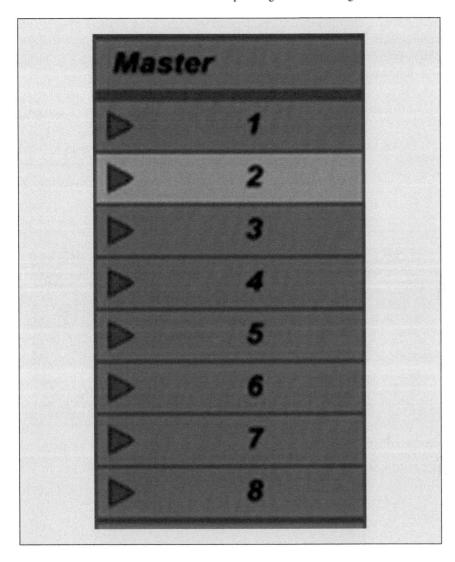

FIGURE 10.5: Master Track Play button allows entire row of clips to be played simultaneously

11. Click the Play button in slot 1 of the Master Track to launch all clips in the first scene.
12. Click the Stop Clips button to stop playing the scene.

In essence, **scenes** can be thought of in relation to the structure divisions, or form, of a piece of music. Perhaps you would like to set up scene 1 to be your intro by including just a few clips; maybe scene 2 has new musical material within its clips that you'd like to use as your verse; a third scene can contain other musical material as a chorus section. The concept of organizing musical content into scenes can be helpful in creating some semblance of structure within the composition, even if the composition is largely improvised.

Let's take a moment to copy clips from scene 1 to other scenes.

13. Copy some, but not all, clips from scene 1 to scenes 2 and 3. (Note: Be sure to think about each scene as having unique structural differences despite the limited number of clips we are working with.)
14. Ctrl + click (Mac) or right-click (Windows) the slot names for each scene on the Master Track and select Rename in order to label each scene according to its formal section (for example: scene 1 could be intro, scene 2 verse, scene 3 bridge, etc.).

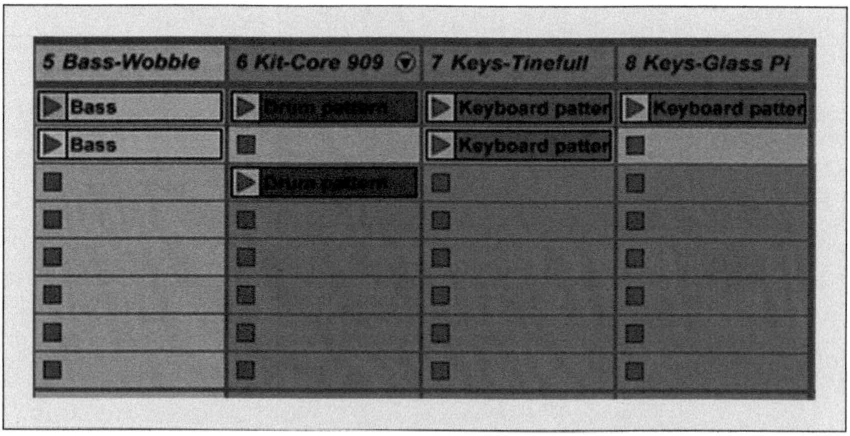

FIGURE 10.6: Multiple scenes representing the formal structure of this composition

15. Launch each of the scenes you've just created.
16. Stop the scenes when you are done.

Did you notice that when you pressed the Play button to launch a scene, it began playing on beat when the previous scene ended and not necessarily at the exact moment when you pressed the Play button? The way that Live knows what beat to come in on is determined, once again, by the quantization menu at the top left of the program to the right of the metronome. If set to one bar, the selected scene will begin playing one bar after the previous scene has ended. If set to none, the selected scene will begin playing instantly when the Play button is pressed.

17. Set the quantization menu value to none.
18. Play different scenes taking note that the alternation occurs immediately.
19. Reset the quantization menu value to 1 bar.

### Interacting with Technology

Many composers and performers compose technology-based works and then perform them live using a variety of methods, a concept we will discuss further in Chapter 11. Imogen Heap, for example, performs her a capella hit "Hide and Seek" by singing into a vocal harmonizer like the TC-Helicon VoiceLive. With this device, the notes of the device-generated accompanying harmony are determined by MIDI pitch messages she sends through a MIDI keyboard controller.

## RECORDING AND EDITING CLIPS

In the same way that we record and edit content on tracks in Live's Arrangement View, we are able to perform these operations and more within clips in Session View. Similar procedures for recordings apply in this context: Select a track to record to, arm session recording for the track, and click the Record button. In fact, as you may have noticed, if you arm a MIDI track for recording, you can use your MIDI keyboard or your computer keyboard to play notes using that instrument timbre.

In Session View, when a track is armed for recording, the appearance of the empty clip slots change from square clip stop buttons to circular record buttons. Clicking one of these record buttons for a given clip will record into that clip.

20. Select a MIDI track and arm it for recording by selecting the Arm Session Recording button on that track's mixer section.
21. Select an empty clip on that track and click the circular record button, then begin playing some notes on your MIDI controller or computer keyboard. (Note: You may find it helpful to turn on the metronome while doing this or even launching a scene.)
22. Press the Stop button at the top or the Stop Clips button at the bottom right when you are finished recording.

Editing the clip you just recorded is just as easy to do in Session View as it is in Arrangement View. Simply double-click the clip in order to open the Clip View.

23. Double-click the recorded MIDI clip to reveal the MIDI Note Editor within Clip View.

From within Clip View, you should already be familiar with the types of edits you can perform on this MIDI data. If necessary, disable the Fold button and enable the Preview headphone button to aid in this process (see Chapter 7).

24. Edit the recorded MIDI data as desired (this may include adjusting the clip length and loop section).

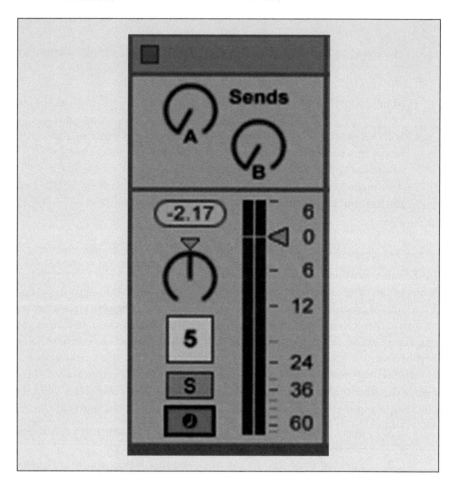

FIGURE 10.7: The session record button for a MIDI track is enabled to allow MIDI controller throughput

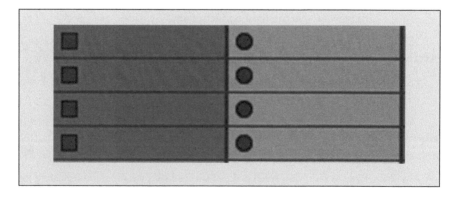

FIGURE 10.8: Empty clips show a track with stop buttons on empty clips on the left and a record-enabled track with armed empty clips on the right

For the sake of variety, instead of continuing to record MIDI, let's look at recording audio from a microphone into an audio track.

## RECORDING AUDIO

Recording audio from a microphone can be accomplished just as easily as recording MIDI. It also gives our tracks the added benefit of containing "real" sounds such as a track of your own voice or a guitar riff. In order to get started recording from a microphone, we need to make sure that your microphone is configured properly to work in Live, so let's check the Audio settings within the Preferences.

25. Go to Live>Preferences (Mac) or Options>Preferences (Windows) and select the Audio tab.
26. Select your computer's sound card from the Audio Device menu if it is not already selected.

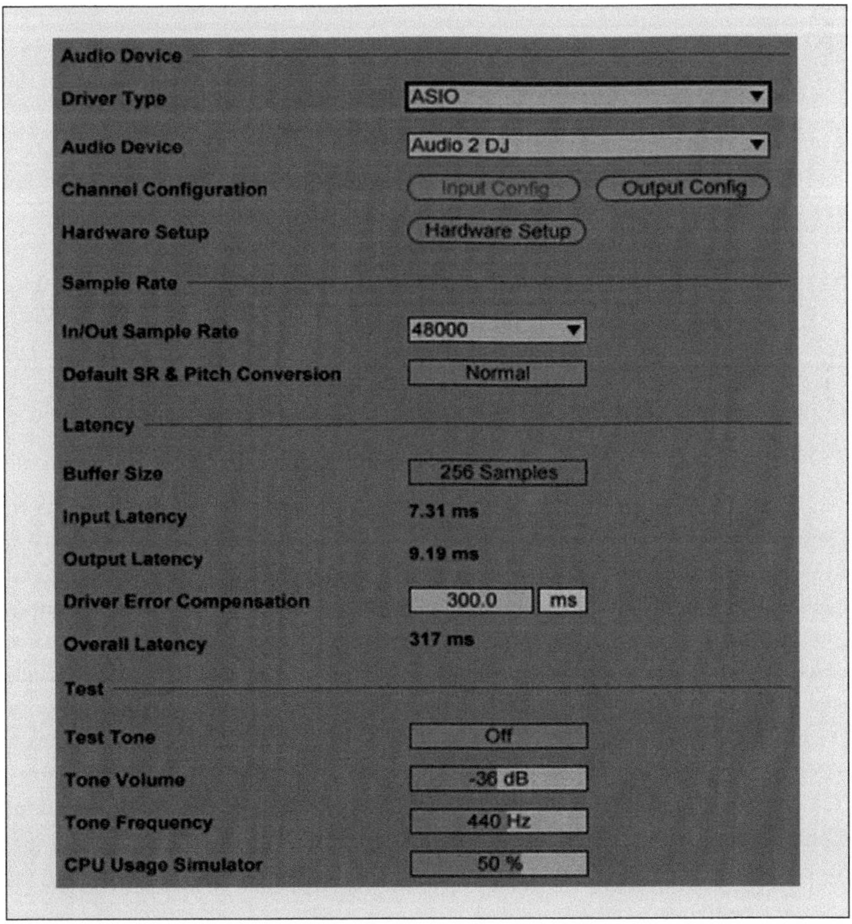

FIGURE 10.9: Audio preferences menu showing sound card options

It may be necessary to change your audio driver by selecting it from the Driver Type menu in order to reveal your sound card; this is sometimes necessary with ASIO sound cards on Windows or audio interfaces that have specialized drivers.

## AUDIO CHANNELS

Depending on the type of sound card you have in or connected to your computer, you will be able to record audio using a number of input streams known as channels. For example, if your computer has a built-in microphone, you can typically record two audio channels simultaneously as a pair or each channel independently. The pair of audio channels is referred to as a **stereo pair**, meaning the microphone can capture sound as a combination of two audio channels: one (mono) channel occupying sound captured from the left side of the microphone and one occupying sound captured from the right side of the microphone.

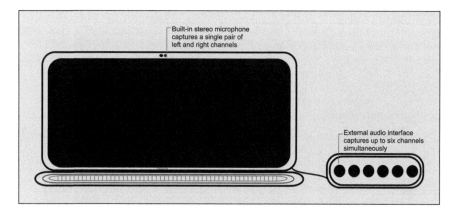

FIGURE 10.10: Computer with external soundcard can capture sound using its built-in internal microphone or one or more of the microphone channels on the external device

The more channels your audio device has, the more tracks you can record simultaneously. If you want to record yourself singing and playing guitar, you would probably want to connect a microphone to one channel to record voice and use one channel to record your guitar, either by placing a microphone in front of it or by plugging it directly into the audio device, if possible. Recording each piece of a brass ensemble would require many more microphones and an audio device that can support recording multiple channels of audio simultaneously. If your sound card only allows one channel to be recorded at a time, you can always record a track and then record another part afterward through **overdubbing**.

To view the available channels you can use for recording, select the Input Config button within the Audio Preferences.

27. Select the Input Config button within the Audio Preferences screen.

Depending on your audio device, the Input Config screen will allow you to record with a single stereo (two-channel) stream of audio or a single separated

| 1 (mono) & 2 (mono) | 1/2 (stereo) |
|---|---|

FIGURE 10.11: Input channel configuration within the Audio Preferences menu

channel from the stereo pair (left or right) on a track. Enabling both the stereo pairs and the individual channels for recording gives the most flexibility. (Enabling more channels allows greater flexibility but also uses a bit more of your computer's computational power.) For example, in a recording session you may want the flexibility to use microphones on channels one and two to record a stereo piano track from two different angles and then use just one of those microphones to overdub a vocal track on top of that piano track. For now, enable all of the inputs available as you can always change this later.

28. Enable both the stereo inputs for channels 1 & 2 as well as the individual channels 1 & 2.

29. Click OK and close the Audio Preferences menu.

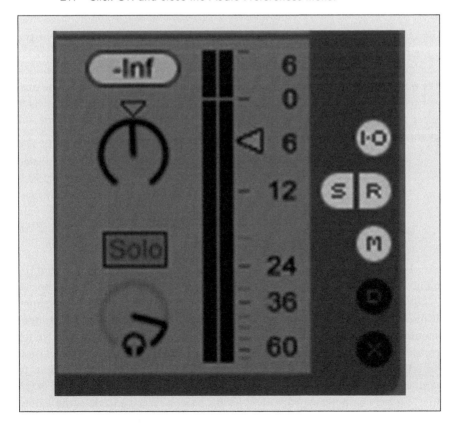

FIGURE 10.12: In/Out Section enabled for tracks by clicking the I-O button near the Master Track

Returning to Live's main window, we can configure the tracks to show the various input and output options available while recording by enabling the In/Out Section via the small, circular I-O button at the right of the Master Track's volume slider.

With the In/Out Section enabled, each track now shows an Audio From menu as well as an Audio To menu. The concept of signal flow from the microphone to the computer can be confusing, but Figure 10.13 shows how it basically works.

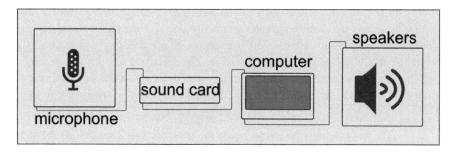

FIGURE 10.13: Basic signal-flow diagram explaining how audio is transferred to the computer

A microphone is connected to the computer on some channel of the soundcard/audio interface. The audio interface is connected to the computer via some cable such as a USB or FireWire cord; in the case of built-in microphones, the microphone is actually part of the computer. Within the computer, the program Live has options to receive and record the audio signal from the channels of these cards/audio devices and represent that audio on tracks. In Live, the specific channels of input are determined by the Audio From menu.

30.  If an audio track is present in your set, examine the menu labeled Audio From and select Ext. In. (Note: *Audio From* on Audio Tracks is different from *MIDI From* on MIDI tracks, but they conceptually function the same way to record data. If no audio track is present in your set, choose Create>Insert Audio Track from the top menu then follow the previous step.)

For our purposes, the audio track will receive external input from one of the audio channels that our audio device supports. The specific channel you choose, of course, should be the one that has a microphone connected to it; a microphone connected to channel one on your audio interface means that this track's input should be set to receive Audio From channel one. In Live, it's also possible for tracks to receive audio from other tracks, but we won't discuss that concept now.

Continuing through the signal path, the audio track is set, by default, to send audio to the Master Track. As you know, the Master Track is the "end of the line" for our computer's involvement in this process. You can control the output volume and a few other things on the Master Track, but, after that, the signal goes back out to the sound card/audio device to the speakers.

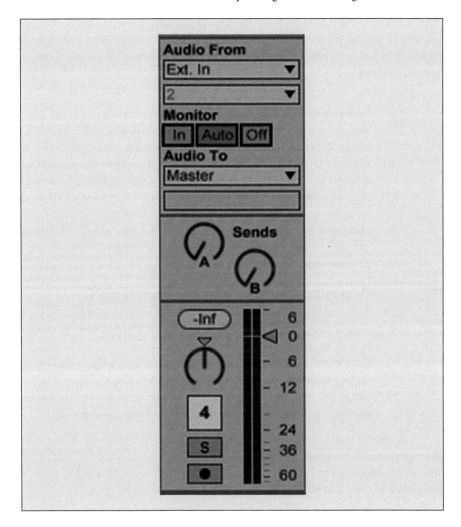

FIGURE 10.14: In/Out Section of an Audio Track

Before we arm the track for recording and press the Record button, the issue of monitoring should be addressed. In other words, would you like to hear what you're recording while you're recording it? The answer is commonly yes. Notice the Monitor section of the track shows the options In, Auto, and Off. Here's the difference between the three:

- The Off button turns off monitoring: while recording, you can't hear what's coming through the microphone.
- The In button allows the audio signal to constantly come through the microphone to the track even when the track *is not* armed for recording.
- The Auto button only allows the audio signal to come through to the track when it *is* armed for recording.

With both of the last two options, you should consider using headphones while recording, so that the sound of the other tracks in your set coming through the speakers is not accidentally captured by the microphone; this phenomenon is known as **bleed**.

Let's now record some audio from our microphone on an audio track.

31. Select an audio track in your set.
32. Arm the track for recording by hitting the Arm Session Recording button. (Note: Be careful that your microphone is not too close to your speakers or else loud feedback squeals will occur as the microphone attempts to capture itself; the use of headphones will help prevent this.)
33. Ensure that the Audio From is set to Ext. In. and that the Input Channel menu beneath it is set to receive on the channel your microphone is connected to. (Note: For built-in microphones, this is commonly channel one or two or the stereo pair of one and two.)
34. Ensure that the Monitoring is set to Auto.
35. Ensure that the Audio To is set to Master.
36. Select an empty clip slot on the audio track to record to.
37. Say or sing a few words into your microphone to ensure that the computer is receiving audio. You will see the meters within the track volume light up as you speak.
38. Click the circular Record Button on that clip and begin speaking or singing something.
39. When you are done recording into the clip, click the stop button on another clip slot or simply click the Play button on the same clip.

You should now have an audio recording in the selected clip slot. As you may have guessed, recording audio in the Arrangement View is done the same way; this is, of course, more like the traditional approach to using a DAW. Take a moment and copy this clip to one or more scenes in your set.

40. Copy this newly recorded clip to one or more of the clip slots in your existing scenes or create new scenes.
41. Record more clips if desired.

## ADDING EFFECTS

Unlike MIDI files, where we can drag various instruments onto our MIDI track to achieve different instrument timbres, we are limited, in some ways by working with recorded audio. For instance, if you record a MIDI pattern, you can easily play that pattern back with a piano sound or a trumpet sound with a few clicks; you can even quickly change the notes if you played a wrong one. If you record yourself singing, you may have a more difficult time making your voice sound like Pavarotti or Ronnie James Dio. However, even though we can't add MIDI instruments to audio tracks, there are a number of effects and other useful processes that we can add. We will discuss the concept of adding just a few effects to an audio track.

## DID YOU KNOW?

### Using a DAW and Effects as an Instrument

The artist Skrillex uses Ableton Live to host a variety of software synthesizer plug-ins like Native Instruments' Massive and FM8 in addition to Live's own Operator instrument to create his signature sound. In the studio and on stage, he uses these tools in conjunction with additional effects like the distortion plug-ins Ohmicide by Ohmforce and Trash by iZotope. Combined with power controller devices like "finger drum pads" and turntable-like interfaces, DAWs can be used in live contexts in powerful ways.

42.  Select the Audio Effects browser from the left side of the program.

The effects listed in this browser are depicted in folders; each folder contains presets that exemplify the versatility and overall "coolness" of each effect. For the audio clip we just made, let's begin by adding a delay.

43.  From the Audio Effects browser, select Ping Pong Delay. (Note: Again, you may substitute another effect for this one if desired or if the effect is unavailable.)
44.  Drag the effect from the browser onto the audio track containing the recorded clip.

Notice that the effect is shown in Live's Device View in the same manner that instruments are shown for MIDI tracks.

45.  Press Play on the clip to hear the delay effect.
46.  Press the Stop button when finished.

A delay is a copy of the original sound file played at an offset time as the original sound file. In some ways that we will discuss later, most effects are delays, but for now, know that the **Ping Pong Delay** is an effect that combines several delays of the audio on the track.

All of the effects that we'll discuss have a number of parameters that can be adjusted. Some will have the option to Sync some sort of timing function (such as the amount of time between delays of the signal) to Live's metronome time. A description of each parameter within a given effect is viewable from the Info View box at the bottom left of the program when you hover your mouse over a parameter knob.

47.  Hover your mouse over the Dry/Wet parameter knob.

The Dry/Wet of the effect is probably the most important effect parameter because it controls how much of the effect you would like to apply to the audio clip.

48.  Press Play on the clip to hear the delay effect.

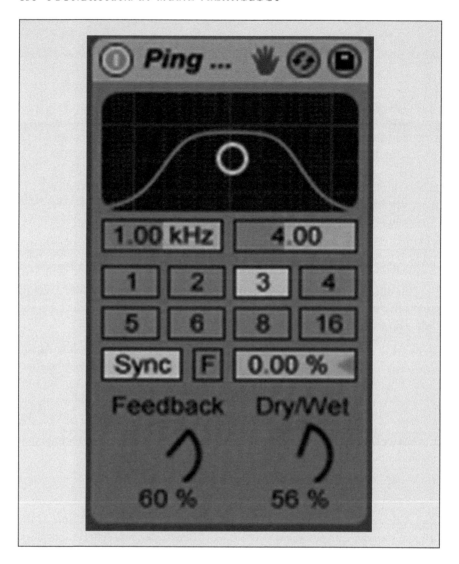

FIGURE 10.15: Ping Pong Delay shown for the audio track in Live's Device View

49. Decrease the Dry/Wet parameter knob to 0% while the clip plays.
50. Increase the Dry/Wet parameter knob to 100% while the clip plays.
51. Return the Dry/Wet parameter knob to 50% and stop the clip.

Notice that you hear more or less of the effect by changing the Dry/Wet pa-rameter knob. If you want to turn off the effect completely, simply click the Device Activator button at the top left of each effect. This will allow audio to pass through to the Audio To output destination bypassing the audio effect altogether. Let's deactivate the delay and add a new effect next to this delay.

52. Click the Device Activator button at the top left of the delay effect to deactivate it.

53. From the Audio Effects browser, select Chorus.
54. Drag the Chorus effect from the browser to the right of the delay effect that is present on the audio track containing the recorded clip. (Note: On the older version of Live, if you are not careful to place the effect *next to* the existing effect and not *on top of* the effect, you will replace the existing effect.)
55. Press Play on the clip to hear the chorus effect.
56. Decrease the Dry/Wet parameter knob to 0% while the clip plays.
57. Increase the Dry/Wet parameter knob to 100% while the clip plays.
58. Return the Dry/Wet parameter knob to 50% and stop the clip.

The Chorus effect, in essence, is like a very short delay between the original signal and the one after it. Additionally, the delayed version of the signal is slightly out of tune from the original, which produces that somewhat warbling sound. Increasing the modulation amount via the Amount parameter will increase the out-of-tuneness of this chorus.

In case you're wondering: yes, the order of the effects in the signal chain does make a difference. If we activate the delay effect, the signal path for this clip will be 1) delay and 2) chorus. The delayed signal will have the chorus effect applied to it. The other way around, the signal will be chorused, and that signal will then be delayed. It may seem like the same thing either way, but as you continue to learn more about effects, you will notice that the order in which you apply them within the path of the signal chain will make a noticeable difference.

59. Activate both effects.
60. Press Play on the clip to hear the clip with both effects applied to it.
61. Click on the Device Title Bar for the delay effect and drag it to the right of the chorus effect.

There is a subtle difference in the sound as a result of the ordering of these effects. As noted, the order of the effects will make a noticeable difference as we continue. For now, let's save our discussion of effects for later and discuss ways to interact with the clips in our set.

## KEY AND MIDI MAPPING

Not only is Live a novel DAW environment because of Session View, but it provides numerous approaches to interact with the computer in ways that far surpass other audio environments. One approach is the way that you can map most buttons, parameters, and knobs to MIDI buttons, sliders, and knobs. In fact, you can also map Live buttons to the keys on your computer keyboard. Imagine playing clips or scenes just by pressing the number keys on your computer keyboard! Let's get started with mapping.

In the top right corner of the screen are a number of buttons and indicators. Among them, the CPU Load Meter can help you keep track of how much you're taxing your computer's processors, and the MIDI track indicators.

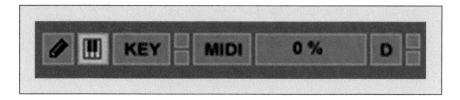

FIGURE 10.16: Indicators and buttons at the top right of the screen

The buttons marked Key and MIDI allow you to map Live control buttons, sliders, and knobs to computer keys and MIDI controls. Let's begin by mapping some scenes to be controlled by the number keys on our computer keyboard. From within Session View:

    62.   Select the button at the top right marked Key to enter Key Map Mode.

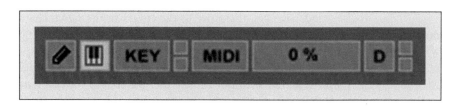

FIGURE 10.17: Key Map Mode enabled

Here's the not-so-tricky part: decide what controls you'd like to map, such as clip Play buttons or Scene Play buttons, device activators, and so on, and then decide which computer keys you'd like to map them to.

    63.   With Key Map Mode enabled, click the first Play button for scene 1.
    64.   Press the *1* key on your computer keyboard. (Note: At the left of the program window, you will see a list marked Key Mappings begin to populate as you assign keys to Live parameters.)
    65.   Select the button at the top right marked Key to exit Key Map Mode.

That's it, believe it or not. Once you've exited Key Map Mode, press the *1* key on your computer keyboard to launch scene 1.

    66.   Press the *1* key on your computer keyboard to launch scene 1.
    67.   Stop the scene when you are done.

Take a moment and map the other scenes to the remaining number keys. Be careful, however, because some of the computer keys are mapped to other things when Computer MIDI Keyboard is enabled.

    68.   Enter Key Map Mode.
    69.   Map other scenes, clips, and Stop buttons in your set to the number keys 2–9.

FIGURE 10.18: Scene 1 mapped to launch when the "1" key is pressed

70.  Exit Key Map Mode.
71.  Use the number keys *1–9* to perform your set.

How fun is that?! Let's, now, map our MIDI controller to other parameters such as Dry/Wet knobs and track volume sliders. In order to do this, we must first make sure that our MIDI device is configured properly to be used as more than just a note-playing instrument.

72.  Go to Live>Preferences (Mac) or Options>Preferences (Windows) and select the MIDI Sync tab.

| | Control Surface | Input | Output | |
|---|---|---|---|---|
| 1 | Axiom 25 Classic ▼ | USB Axiom 25 ▼ | USB Axiom 25 ▼ | (Dump) |
| 2 | None ▼ | None ▼ | None ▼ | (Dump) |
| 3 | None ▼ | None ▼ | None ▼ | (Dump) |
| 4 | None ▼ | None ▼ | None ▼ | (Dump) |
| 5 | None ▼ | None ▼ | None ▼ | (Dump) |
| 6 | None ▼ | None ▼ | None ▼ | (Dump) |

Takeover Mode  [None ▼]

| MIDI Ports | Track | Sync | Remote |
|---|---|---|---|
| ▷ Input: Axiom_25_Classic Input (USB Axiom | On | Off | On |
| ▷ Input: USB Axiom 25 (Port 2) | Off | Off | On |
| ▷ Output: Axiom_25_Classic Output (USB Axio | Off | Off | Off |
| ▷ Output: Microsoft GS Wavetable SW Synth | Off | Off | Off |

FIGURE 10.19: MIDI devices in the MIDI Sync tab of the Preferences menu

From this menu, you should be able to see your MIDI device. Note that in order to Track with this MIDI device—meaning "record notes into tracks"—you must enable the Track button on the Input device. In order to use this MIDI device to control parameters in Live, you must enable the Remote button Input device.

73. Ensure that both the Track and Remote buttons are enabled for your MIDI controller.
74. Close the Preferences menu.

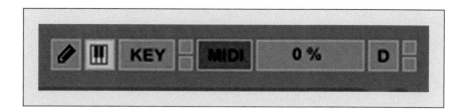

FIGURE 10.20: MIDI Map Mode enabled

The same procedures apply for mapping Live parameters to MIDI controls as they did for mapping computer keys. If your MIDI controller has knobs or faders on it, let's map those to control the volume of some of the tracks.

75. Select the button at the top right marked MIDI to enter MIDI Map Mode.

76. With MIDI Map Mode enabled, click the volume slider for one of the tracks in your set.
77. On your MIDI keyboard or controller, move the MIDI control that you'd like to map to this volume slider. (Note: At the left of the program window, you will see a list marked MIDI Mappings begin to populate as you assign MIDI controls to Live parameters.)
78. Select the button at the top right marked MIDI to exit MIDI Map Mode.
79. Play your set and use the MIDI control to change the track volume.
80. Repeat this process with other MIDI controls for other Live parameters. (Note: If a device, such as an effect or an instrument, is unseen, exit the Map Mode and select the track containing that device. Then, re-enter Map Mode.)

You have now created a performable DAW-type interactive instrument. Designing a system like this is one basic concept of performing interactive music.

## RECORD TO THE ARRANGEMENT VIEW

Performing interactively in Session View is one of the most appealing aspects of Live that sets it apart from most other DAWs. An additional feature in Session View is that your interactive performance can be recorded linearly into the Arrangement View. This allows you to edit your live performance later on in the Arrangement View.

To record your Session View performance, simply click the Arrangement Record button next to the Play and Stop buttons within the transport controls at the top of the screen.

FIGURE 10.21: Arrangement Record button enabled within Session View

81. In Session View, click the Stop All Clips button at the bottom right of the program above the Master Track. This will stop all clips from playing.
82. Click the Stop button at the top of the screen twice to reset the playback position to 1.1.1. This position corresponds to the linear position within the Arrangement View, specifically the first bar, beat, and beat division.
83. Click the Arrangement Record button.
84. Perform clips and slots as desired then click the Stop button.

Your performance is recorded verbatim into Arrangement View.

85. Switch to Arrangement View to see your recorded performance.

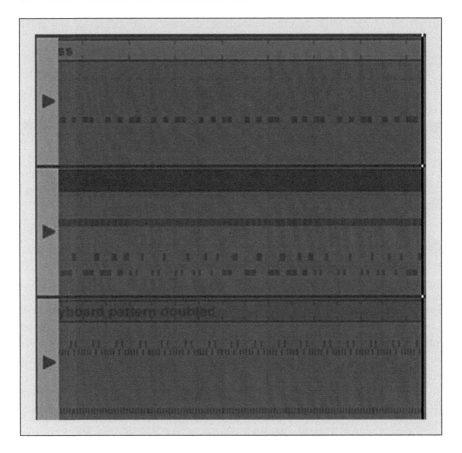

FIGURE 10.22: Session View performance being recorded in Arrangement View

With your Session View performance now recorded into Arrangement View, you can produce the tracks as you would any other by making edits, adding effects, and so on. Let's now save this set:

86.   Click File>Save Live Set.
87.   Save this project to My Live Projects.

A Live session called DubSession has been included in the Chapter Examples folder for this chapter. It contains a simple interactive composition by Will Kuhn performable through Live's Session View.

## SUMMARY

The notion of performing live with a DAW is becoming more and more common. In this chapter we used Ableton Live to facilitate live performance, but there are numerous DAWs and apps that may be more or less appropriate for you depending on your creative goals. The important thing to remember is that the DAW will only do what you tell it to do. A clear and well-conceived performance scheme is more readily facilitated by a piece of software than the idea that you'll "just start playing and see what happens," although there is also something to be said about the accessibility of technology that facilitates "play time." As you continue to work with DAWs and other technology in live performance contexts, consider the concepts we've discussed with regard to good signal-flow and recording practices and the creative use of effects as they relate to acoustical balance.

## KEY CONCEPTS

- DAWs are commonly used in live performance just as if they were any other instrument.
- Mapping is the process by which some musical action, playback mechanism, or data set, is assigned to keys, buttons, other controls, or another data set.
- Triggering effects and clips is a common performance action.
- Auditioning and changing effects on live audio input is easily facilitated within a DAW.

## KEY TERMS

| | | |
|---|---|---|
| bleed | Ping Pong Delay | stereo pair |
| overdubbing | scene (Live) | |

# CHAPTER 11

# TECHNOLOGY IN PERFORMANCE

## OVERVIEW

In this chapter we will highlight the influence that emerging technology has had on the types of performances that artists have conceived as well as technical innovations to the venues themselves. Some of the key innovators—including composers, performers, and technologists—will be profiled along with their work.

Consider the many new performance opportunities that have emerged as a result of advances in digital technology. Conceivably, the entire world can simultaneously view a performance using a computer or another mobile device. Technology can allow listeners to engage in a recording of your performances at their leisure; this is a much better alternative to having your fans come to your home and demand that you perform for them!

One obvious implementation of technology in compositions and performance can be seen in the work of DJs, interactive artists, and experimental ensembles with their roots in academia. Walk onto a college campus that holds music technology concerts, and prepare yourself for repurposed video game controllers as musical instruments, newly designed Theremins, musical gesture-tracking gloves, musical Tesla coils, and traditional instruments outfitted with technology, color-tracking systems. Yet, once the new instruments are made, how do we use those instruments to make a compelling performance, and what venues are suitable?

New software and hardware can help facilitate performances in ways that were simply impossible just a few decades ago. While the demand for the live performance model of the past may have diminished significantly in the early 2000s, as suggested by the number of professional orchestras facing bankruptcy (DiBlasio, 2013; Grannis, 2012; Kennicott, 2013), there are many new technology-based or technology-facilitated venues for live performance that have just come into existence.

## OLD VENUES WITH A NEW TWIST

To hear new Western art music in the Middle Ages, you would have to visit a church or monastery; during the Baroque time period, the theater also became a contender with the emergence of opera, ballet, musicals, and other mixed art forms. From the nineteenth century on, music conservatories and, as a later extension, academic institutions also grew in popularity as venues in which new music could be heard. Today, academic venues are important sites for encountering "new music." As an outgrowth of the combination of creating new music and the ties to academic research, particularly from the 1940s to present day, many new technology-based music innovations have been developed from the academy.

## DID YOU KNOW?

### Technology as a Facilitator for Performance

You don't have to throw out your traditional acoustic instrument and buy a DJ rig in order to implement technology into your live performance situation. In fact, you don't even have to change your style to take advantage of the ways that technology can help facilitate performance in traditional popular or art music contexts. In recording studios, in order to produce a certain sound, many music groups will overdub more parts onto a recording than they can possibly play in a live situation. So how do they perform those pieces live? Some groups accomplish this by performing some parts live on stage while remaining in sync, via a metronome, with a computer DAW that "performs" those additional tracks. Look for the computer, hardware sequencer, or even a mobile music player on stage, often near the drummer, for your favorite band. The sequenced tracks will likely go from the DAW to the main mix while the "click track" or metronome mix will go to the band's in-ear monitor mix.

## A LITTLE HISTORY: ELECTROACOUSTIC MUSIC

**Electroacoustic music** is a term used to describe the use of electronics in music creation. The term is sometimes used in different contexts to describe music that is either entirely created with the use of technology or music that combines a traditional acoustic instrumentalist with electronics in some way. *Musique concrète*, an approach to music creation begun in the 1940s by composer Pierre Schaeffer, involved manipulating prerecorded sounds to create new sounds. During this time, composers like Iannis Xenakis and John Cage were experimenting with chance, probability, and indeterminate music. The electronic and recording technologies available helped many electroacoustic composers facilitate their compositional objectives through "acousmatic" performances of recorded, or "tape," music, in which only loudspeakers were present on a stage as opposed to live performers. Composers began composing pieces with fixed, speaker-placement venues in mind such as Karlheinz Stockhausen's 1958 "Music in Space" concept of a spherical room outfitted with speakers capable of delivering a large multi-channel performance.

In America in the 1950s and 1960s, computer music pioneer Max Mathews at Bell Labs and others were writing sound generation and speech synthesis software and developing new performance instruments like the Radio-Baton. By the 1960s, composers like Morton Subotnick were working with instrument designers to create new works such as his 1967 *Silver Apples of the Moon*, again, for tape.

## DID YOU KNOW?

### Cutting Tape

Recording tape—first introduced right after World War II—helped revolutionize music making by offering the ability to edit a recording after it was made. An engineer could literally "cut" parts of the recording tape with a razor blade to remove a bad note or other mistake and then could "splice" in a separate recording to replace it. Recording tape also offered the ability to record to tracks, first on 2-track stereo machines, and then on 4-, 8-, 16-, 32-, and 64-track equipment.

Composers like John Cage became interested in the ability to create works by splicing together fragments of individual recordings. In his piece *Williams Mix* (1951–1953), Cage employed a team of friends to assemble the many fragments and then performed the piece on eight separate tape recorders played simultaneously. The ability to mix and match unrelated source materials was a great novelty and showed the potential for sound recording to go beyond merely replicating a "real" performance.

In contrast to the electroacoustic works that were intended to be listened to through speakers, composers like Mario Davidovsky composed works for electronic sounds and live performers of traditional acoustic instruments. His series of works called *Synchronisms* feature an acoustic instrumentalist performing with a tape of electroacoustic sounds, also created by Davidovsky.

These compositional innovations, particularly the technological resources, were fueled, in part, by academia. Research centers like the Paris-based IRCAM (founded by composer Pierre Boulez) developed both hardware and software to facilitate the creative objectives of composers and artists. The Computer Music Center (CMS) at Columbia University, the Princeton University Sound Lab, and the Stanford University Center for Computer Research in Music and Acoustics (CCRMA) are just a few of the research centers that drove and continue to drive electronic music composition and performance. The increased popularity in electronic music has, in recent years, led to the formation of new music ensembles such as the Princeton Laptop Orchestra (PLOrk) as well as groups such as the Society for Electro-Acoustic Music in the United States (SEAMUS), New Interfaces for Musical Expression (NIME), and new performance venues and events exclusively for electronic music concerts.

## DID YOU KNOW?

### Using Technology: Deception or Performance Aid?

Although it may seem like a trivial application, a singer or instrumentalist controlling a delay pedal while they perform makes the performance, by definition, an interactive electroacoustic event. In a live performance, some may consider a vocalist who uses a pitch-correction processor to be deceiving the audience, while others may view it as simply another effect that enhances the final sound, no different from adding EQ, reverb, and compression. After all, pitch, just like tone and dynamics, is but one variable a singer controls, yet it's much more common to hear performers use processors to correct tone and dynamics than to correct their pitch. Does ability matter with different performance objectives? Is a reverb plug-in deception? Is it deceptive to record a vocal take over and over until it's right?

## FILM, TELEVISION, VIDEO GAMES, MULTIMEDIA, AND THE STUDIO

As advances in technology continued to expand the palette of timbres and instruments available to performers, traditional instruments have also been transformed. In Chapter 2 we discussed the innovation of microphone and instrument pickup technology as they relate to acoustic instruments. This technology alone allows traditional instrumentalists to take advantage of the sonic possibilities of effects processors and digital sound manipulation. However, there are many new performance venues that have emerged as a result of technology in which an acoustic instrumentalist does not need to modify his or her instrument.

Individuals encounter music in a variety of ways. Researcher Mark Sloboda's *Exploring the Musical Mind* (2005) suggests that people intentionally use music for different intended outcomes. Many of these outcomes have been radically changed by the introduction of technology. For example, a person may listen to different music while exercising than she or he would at a dinner party or during a time of private worship or meditation. Each of these objectives presents with it a different context and a variety of implementations of music technology, from portable music players to tools for interacting with the music in some way.

For the performers themselves, the commercial demand for recorded music has drawn many ensembles from the sparsely populated concert venues to the studios. Big-budget films, television shows, commercials, popular music albums, and video game soundtracks have placed a demand on chamber groups and orchestras in ways that simply did not exist before technology. In terms of visibility, a single performance at a university may reach only a few hundred people, whereas a performance on a film soundtrack may reach millions.

It should be noted, however, that advances in synthesis engines and sample library technology sometimes rival the use of large ensembles in the studio. Composer Danny Elfman, for example, noted in a video interview by the Vienna Symphonic Library (2014), a popular sampling engine and library, that his compositional process for films includes the creation of synthesized and sampled MIDI mock-up scores. He claims that these mock-up scores are sometimes even used in combination with recordings of live studio performers when preparing the final production soundtrack.

## INTERACTIVE MUSIC

In the 1980s and 90s, buzzwords like "virtual" and "hyper" were all the rage when describing tech-based innovations in music; primarily in software. Today, the word "interactive" is often used to describe the connection between performers and tech-based instruments. The concept of performers interacting with technology does not need to exclude nonmusicians. Oh and Wang (2011) describe the rise of mobile devices to engage audience participation from the choreographed ringtones used in *Dialtone* (2001) to works by the Stanford Mobile Phone Orchestra, or MoPho.

Interactive galleries and works known as **installations** provide opportunities for nonperformers to engage in the music-making process by interacting with a constructed system. For example, Tod Machover of MIT and his Media Lab research group created an installation called *Toy Symphony* (Scanion, 2003) in which children and parents interact with a variety of music-making toys and technology-based instruments. Sound and visual artists at art galleries, clubs, and other performance venues frequently employ similar concepts to engage audience members in their compositions.

An interesting non-computer-based installation piece is John Cage's *As Slow as Possible*, or *ASLAP*. The notes of the composition are from a 1985 piano work of the same name. However, the composer's directive to play the piece "as slow as possible" is being facilitated by a 639-year-long performance of the piece on pipe organ (as shown in Figure 11.1) that began in 2001. You can visit the St. Burchardi church in Halberstadt, Germany, any time before the year 2640 to listen to the piece in progress.

DID YOU KNOW?

### Karaoke

For better or worse, depending on your experiences, karaoke machines are an example of interactive music performance systems that have created the demand for new performance venues. This technology ranges from software that claims to remove vocals from recordings to services like Music Minus One, which provide recorded accompaniment for each track in a composition in addition to notated sheet music that you can "play along" with. Musicians can now create their own backing tracks for performance, either through using pre-programmed rhythms and backing instruments to creating their own from scratch. Even the earliest electronic keyboards featured preset accompaniments that in essence offered canned accompaniments for aspiring musicians.

FIGURE 11.1: The pipe organ currently performing Cage's *ASLAP* (Wikipedia-ce, 2006)

## INTERACTIVE MUSIC SYSTEMS

**Interactive music systems** are hardware or software configurations used to produce music through interactions with electronics. Graphical programming languages such as Max/MSP/Jitter developed by Cycling '74 can be used to allow individuals to develop interactive systems in a visual programming environment that is different from traditional text-based programming languages (Manzo, Halper, & Halper, 2011). It is a popular programming language for use in creative works by composers, artists, and other multimedia designers given its vast set of programming objects that deal directly with audio and video. Through such an environment, individuals can create low-cost, easy-to-implement, and limitlessly customizable music applications for specific purposes to facilitate their performance objectives. The language has been used to allow composers, performers, educators, researchers, and therapists to design customized software that is specific to their needs instead of relying on the availability and features of commercial software (Manzo, 2006, 2007a; see also Chapter 14).

## FURTHER POSSIBILITIES

From mobile apps to music-oriented video games, a wealth of new music-making instruments and tools exist as a result of these new music technologies. With each application, the potential to use such tools to facilitate creativity for an audience also exists. Can you use QR codes to create an interactive "scannable" musical environment or gallery? In what ways can video game engines be used to create virtual reality and even augmented reality musical environments? Many performance venues of the past still exist as they always have, but the venues of tomorrow are still being created and defined.

As we will discuss in Chapter 12, interactive software and hardware systems have grown in popularity, particularly in their implementation by teachers for pedagogical purposes. This, of course, does not preclude the use of such systems from being used for performance. Consult the resource website for this book to see a list of just a few interactive music systems and tools ideal for facilitating unique tech-based performances and other musical applications.

## SUMMARY

New emerging technology has always influenced music performances. The advances of electroacoustic music in the 1950s and 1960s pushed art music in a previously unimaginable direction. Manipulating sound recordings and configuring multi-channel installations allowed composers to think beyond the terms of what an acoustical space and instrument ensembles would allow in terms of timbres. When we consider the evolution of Western art music from antiquity through the Romantic time period, we see natural refinement, new instrument creation, theoretical and pedagogical considerations, and key works that shaped the course of this history. In comparison, the history of electronic music as an outgrowth of the Western art music tradition is still in its infancy. We have a brief history of some key figures who contributed to its advancement. In the same way that we still hear works by J. S. Bach performed in concerts but not necessarily those by Josquin des Prez, a figure of arguably equal importance, we have only a glimpse of what performances in the future will look like now that we are introducing technological advancements, specifically with computers.

## KEY CONCEPTS

- Concert venues, composition, and performance have been profoundly influenced by advancements in music technology.
- Electroacoustic music uses prerecorded, manipulated audio alone or in combination with live performers to create works with novel characteristics.
- Installations are interactive gallery-type environments by which one might observe or participate in an ongoing performance.
- The rise of technology in performance has led to laptop-ensembles, mobile device performances, and new technologies that bring increased accessibility to music performance.

## KEY TERMS

electroacoustic music         installation                    interactive music system

# CHAPTER 12

# TECHNOLOGY IN EDUCATION

## OVERVIEW

This chapter explores how tech-based instruments can be used to strengthen musicianship skills of students in traditional band, choir, and orchestra classes as well as general music classes. These implications have potential for other educational contexts including special needs classes, research experiments, and other learning environments.

From making a collection of videoed instrumental lessons that you post to YouTube to writing a customized piece of software that helps your students perform, a variety of technology-based tools exist that can be used in a pedagogical context. Even the notion of recording a school ensemble performance can have multiple uses: for distribution and memorialization on websites and other media or for facilitating productive criticism that can be directed toward future performances. There is an overabundance of technology software in existence for you to explore. We will consider both the technology tools, such as instrument controllers, hardware, and software, as well as the performance contexts by which these tools are used. Later in this chapter we will primarily discuss the differences between technology that is used to facilitate musicianship and the type of musicianship that is inspired by what technology readily offers.

## TECHNOLOGY FOR A PURPOSE

The types of technology used for music education purposes can be thought of, generally, in the terms of how they may be used. In this utilitarian sense, we may consider at least three categories as they relate to tools that aid, instruct, or facilitate (1) composition, (2) performance, and (3) education. Within these categories, subcategories might include (A) self-directed activities, and (B) teacher-directed/facilitated activities. The companion website for this book as well as many other sources (Freedman, 2013) contain lists of some of the technologies that can be used to this extent. Some specific examples will be described in general terms below though new technologies emerge constantly.

### Composition

Technologies like Finale, NoteFlight, and Sibelius help facilitate composition through notation. DAWs like GarageBand and Mixcraft can also be used for composition but don't require a prerequisite knowledge of traditional music notation like notation software does. Groovy Music by Music First is a sequencer for kids, which uses animated characters and icons to represent musical ideas. These applications are accessible enough so that a student can learn about composition in a self-directed and explorative way such as placing loops onto a timeline in some devised form, and then modifying those loops. In this scenario, students would likely benefit from the guidance of a teacher regarding the compositional process itself moreover than an explanation of the mechanics of using the software. Composing with software and with technology-based musical instruments like mobile apps has become such a ubiquitous part of society that even nonmusicians use mobile app versions of drumkits and synths to "make beats" and other sounds in creative ways. Such technologies could certainly be used as a starting point for further discussions about musicianship.

## Performance

Technologies that facilitate performance may include all technology-based musical instruments, including mobile apps, like Morton Subotnick's "Pitch Painter" app, or new electronic interfaces and instruments, like the guitar-shaped button controllers by Misa Digital. Tech-based instruments would also include instruments that make performance easier, such as so-called "Adaptive/Adapted Instruments" used to facilitate performance by folks with special needs. For example, the Skoog (Schogler, 2010) is a box-shaped instrument that allows individuals to play music in an accessible way. Similar projects like AUMI (Pask, 2007), a gesture-based software application, and EAMIR (Manzo, 2007a), a DIY open-source set of apps, "map" motions tracked by the software to musical event playback. My Breath My Music Foundation (Wel, 2011), and Jamboxx also use adapted wind-based controllers in their accessible breath-controlled musical instruments. In addition to new musical instruments that assist performance, applications like SmartMusic by MakeMusic, the makers of Finale, is a system designed to help performers learn new repertoire in both a self-directed and teacher-facilitated way by tracking the pitch of the performer as he or she performs notated works into a microphone.

## Education

A wealth of self-directed, tutorial-like software applications exist. For example, Music Ace is a stand-alone application that allows a student to learn musical concepts in a self-directed manner. Similarly, EarMaster Pro is among the many ear-training software applications used in a similar self-directed manner. Nothing precludes an educator from working using these types of programs with their students, but the main use of these types of applications is by students working at their own pace. Music instruction software is a fairly recent development, yet a wealth of information exists in the literature documenting the use and characteristics of technology-assisted instruction (Rudolph et al., 2005; Sheldon, 1999; Watson, 2005).

Software like Riffstation by Sonicladder can be used to help listeners identify the guitar chords and solos of recordings. Similar audio processes, like slowing down a track without changing pitch, and looping repeated sections, are available in many DAWs and can provide opportunities for student-directed analysis of existing works. Of course, if the teacher does not specifically require students to spend time at home or in the music lab working with these programs, it may not be likely that students will gain any benefit from them. Just purchasing the software and making it available on school lab computers will probably not motivate students to use it.

The actual classroom use of such pieces of technology, as well as the technologies themselves, may vary greatly from teacher to teacher. A band or choir director may find the only "technology" that supports his or her methods is to record the ensemble as they perform and listen to the recordings in the class while making critical comments. Other ensemble directors may find it helpful to make full YouTube channels of videos that demonstrate how to play each instrument, so that class time can be spent on performing the literature instead of repeatedly showing beginners how to hold and clean their clarinet. In all cases, there is likely some technology that exists that can assist your pedagogical objectives be they composition, performance, or education in general.

## TECHNOLOGY-BASED MUSICAL INSTRUMENTS

Musical concepts are often introduced to beginning music students with the aid of instruments of simple design such as in the Orff approach. These Orff instruments are easy to play, in principle, but limited in terms of the number of musical functions one can perform compared to other acoustic instruments like the violin. In many ways, Orff instruments are like the adaptive Instruments that we discussed earlier. In fact, even the concept of frets on string instruments is a sort of "adaptive" method of helping the performer play in tune in an accessible way.

## INTERACTIVE MUSIC SYSTEMS

An interactive music system is a hardware or software configuration that allows an individual to accomplish a musical task, typically in real time, through some interaction and can very well be another type of "adaptive instrument." The accessible design of these systems allows them to be used in novel ways to allow individuals to compose and perform with greater ease than traditional instruments. Although commonly associated with composition and performance, interactive music systems can also be used to perform musical analysis, instruction, assessment, rehearsal, research, therapy, synthesis, and more.

In the general sense, interactive systems can be thought of in terms of "controls," like buttons, switches, and pedals, that somehow reflect changes in musical "variables," or things that change. In other words: a variable is something that changes; a control is something that changes a variable. In music, there are many variables, such as pitch, dynamics, and timbre, that change as a result of the instrument's **control device**, also known as a **control interface**.

The control interface for a violin is typically a bow. Without buttons, knobs, or sensors, the bow is capable of controlling numerous variables through a single, simple, interface. For example, if you angle the bow differently as it hits the strings, the timbre will change; apply more pressure and the dynamics will change.

We can compare the violin to a modular synthesizer like the Buchla 200e (as shown in Figure 12.1). The Buchla is also capable of controlling numerous musical variables. In fact, the Buchla is capable of creating more diverse timbres than the violin. However, controlling musical variables on the Buchla, with the control interface of knobs, buttons, and patch cables, involves more gestures than the violinist's bow.

For the intent of performance, some control interfaces are more accessible than others for real-time use. With a computer, you can arguably achieve any sound imaginable if you tweak the right numbers and press the right buttons. It is a well-designed control interface, however, that allows a performer to readily control musical variables in a less cumbersome way than clicking on menu items from pull-down lists and checking boxes.

## DID YOU KNOW?

### Mapping

In computer science, the term "**mapping**" is used to describe the correspondence of one set of data with another set. The potential mappings of musical variables to software controls has been the subject of recent experimental research (Arfib, Couturier, Kessous, & Verfaille, 2002; Goudeseune, 2002; Levitin, McAdams, & Adams, 2002). Hunt and Wanderly (2002) conducted studies in which participants performed music-making tasks using four control interfaces representing two mapping types: one-to-one and many-to-one. **One-to-one mapping** allows single musical variables to be controlled by a single control mechanism of an interactive system. **Many-to-one mapping** allows numerous musical variables to be controlled by a single control mechanism in an interactive system; this is similar to the example of a violin bow controlling numerous musical variables that we described earlier. In this research, the interfaces with many-to-one mappings were more engaging for subjects performing the musical activities, yet both types of interfaces allowed subjects to perform the required tasks.

Throughout history, people have created new musical instruments, and the instruments created generally reflect the technological resources available at the time. Early primitive instruments had few moving parts, if any. The Industrial

Revolution made way for the modern piano to evolve using steel and iron. In the Information Age, it stands to reason that newly created instruments may largely involve computers and electronics.

Tod Machover, whose *Toy Symphony* installation was discussed in Chapter 11 and is known for many great technological contributions to music including the Hyperinstruments group (Machover, 1992), raised an interesting idea about how technology could be used to build musical creativity:

> Traditional instruments are hard to play. It takes a long time to [acquire] physical skills, which aren't necessarily the essential qualities of making music. It takes years just to get good tone quality on a violin or to play in tune. If we could find a way to allow people to spend the same amount of concentration and effort on listening and thinking and evaluating the difference between things and thinking about how to communicate musical ideas to somebody else, how to make music with somebody else, it would be a great advantage. Not only would the general level of musical creativity go up, but you'd have a much more aware, educated, sensitive, listening, and participatory public. (Oteri, 1999)

FIGURE 12.1: A Buchla modular synthesizer (Tiemann, 2006)

With practice, an individual can control most variables of an instrument well and at very fast speeds. However, how hard it is to learn to play an instrument or control interface will affect how widely it is used—in particular, for those individuals who lack formal musical training and those who have physical or mental impairments.

## SEPARATING COGNITIVE FUNCTIONS
## OF MUSICIANSHIP FROM PHYSICAL ACTIONS

If you've ever tried to teach a beginner to play music, you've likely encountered at least two general challenges. This first can be bundled into cognitive functions and includes getting students to think about what they're doing and how what they're doing relates to the sounds they're trying to make. The second is related to physical actions and includes issues of dexterity, breathing, posture, and so on. With a hypothetical and purely cognitive instrument, a performer would just think about a note and the desired timbral properties, and it would sound; there would be nearly no physical layer, in the "instrument" sense, between the cognitive function and hearing the note.

The paradigm of instrument design up until just recently has been focused primarily on principles of acoustics (Hunt & Wanderly, 2002). Instrument designers had to find a compromise between building an instrument that is (1) physically performable in terms of size, weight, shape, and accessibility and (2) acoustically interesting in terms of body resonance, bore tubing, and so on. In other words, a violin designed to facilitate the full range of notes that a piano allows (1) would be unplayable in the same way due to its size, shape, and so on and (2) would not sound the same as other violins. Design concepts that inhibit string vibration or airflow in ways that compromise musical variables such as timbral qualities and dynamic range in undesirable ways are major concerns for makers of acoustic instruments.

On the other hand, with technology-based instruments, the physical actions necessary to perform a sound and the sound itself can be independent of each other. A synthesizer plug-in within a DAW receives information from a MIDI device and plays back a carefully designed sound, but the plug-in itself has no idea if the MIDI data originated from a MIDI keyboard controller, a MIDI drum controller, a MIDI wind controller, and so on. With electronic instruments, the mapping of musical variables to controls can be either similar to traditional instruments or completely unrelated and innovative. To this extent, instrument designers can pursue concepts that allow for novel idiomatic writing and performance without the acoustical concerns of sound reproduction. A person in a wheelchair, for example, can now simulate a drumset performance experience using a drumset app on a mobile phone to accommodate his or her physical needs.

Separating the understanding of musical concepts from being able to perform them on traditional instruments is important to educators because it allows **musicing** to occur (Elliott and Silverman, 2014). For example, students can be taught about harmony without making them wait until they have learned the performance skills on a traditional instrument in order to play chords. As technology continues to develop, the musical instrument as a physical "layer" between a cognitive process of "thinking musically" and the physical exercise of producing a musical event may become more transparent. If a musical concept, like "V- I cadences," for example, can be explained and demonstrated easier with a software app than it could with an acoustic instrument, why not use the software? Does learning one instrument preclude learning the other? Technology-based instruments can be designed with specific pedagogical activities in mind.

## Technology Dictating Pedagogy

To what extent do we allow music software to dictate how we teach musical concepts? Software developers typically design a program's layout to be accessible and intuitive, but in doing so they are bound to show certain biases toward the visibility of what are considered the more common features. In an instructional setting, if the feature that is going to help instructors explain concepts of rhythm or harmony is buried in the program's menus, they may be less inclined to teach those musical concepts right away to students because it takes too long to locate the material in the software. In other words, an app's or program's layout may require instructors to teach a number of software concepts just to get to the place where they could teach the concept they wanted to address in the first place. It's not the software company's fault; after all, they don't know what and how you teach. However, this presents a case where technology dictates the type of instruction that takes place instead of instruction dictating the type of technology that is used.

## Notation

The problem of technology dictating musicianship is not unique to software-based musical activities. Consider the way a beginning composer might avoid writing on ledger lines because it's unfamiliar terrain compared to notes and spaces that are on the staff. Perhaps a different or enhanced type of notation system could help making note-reading easier. Is there a reason we need to continue using a notation system that requires you to imagine what the ensemble will sound like when you look at the paper? Can the notation system be adapted and enhanced visually using technology? Think of your own uses: is the objective of your own notation efforts for preservation and "record-keeping" sake or to make performance direction clear to the performer? Are black and white pages the best mechanism to fulfill your objectives? What other technologies from around the 1500s do we unquestioningly hold near and dear (besides plumbing!)? Do we really need to continue solving performance issues related to page turns, or can technology be used to help our efforts? Can we end the indentured servitude page-turning careers of undergraduate music majors once and for all?

On the other hand, it's easy for software to confine us or dictate the way we teach. For example, if we want to teach a musical concept in a novel way using technology but can't find the technology to support the approach, it's possible that the novel approach will be dropped. What if that tech-based approach is more effective than the traditional approach? To put it another way: what do classroom activities look like when a teacher designs a lesson from the point at which pedagogical knowledge, content knowledge, and technology knowledge intersect (Shulman, 1986; Bauer, 2014)?

Teaching with technology can be seen as trendy and gimmicky. Suppose you decide to use a music-oriented video game in the classroom. A technology-based activity in a classroom setting can be fun, but at the same time it may be less effective as an instructional aid if the activity isn't framed in the right educational context; it could be seen as "play time" and the instructional objective might not be met. However, if the task is framed in the right context, the students might then learn something about music in a way that is more effective than the traditional approach. A good interactive music system in the classroom allows a user to do musical things with efficiency, ease of control, and clarity; it should not just exist for the sake of having technology in the classroom.

## EDUCATIONAL CONSIDERATIONS

In the typical American public school system, general music classes are no longer offered to students after about the 5th or 6th grade. Students are then offered an elective performing in the school's band, choir, or orchestra, or the option to withdraw from the school's music program altogether. Unfortunately, band, choir, and orchestra programs only reach a minority of middle and high school music students (Dammers, 2012; Williams, 2012), estimated at less than 20% of the school's student body, and data suggest that the percentage of students studying music is shrinking (Elpus and Abril, 2011). The remainder of students may, instead, pursue musical opportunities apart from their school such as starting garage bands, taking private after-school lessons, or watching YouTube videos and playing along with their own instrument.

To reach these other potential music students and offer classes that address different musicianship concepts than a typical ensemble class, some high school general music classes are incorporating technology to develop tech-based music classes (Kuhn, 2012). These tech-based general music classes are a promising addition to the music curriculum and uniquely suited to reach many of the nontraditional music students (NTMs) who are not actively engaged in the traditional programs of bands, choirs, and orchestras. A recent survey indicated that 14% of U.S. high schools offer technology-based music classes and most of these classes were created in the last ten years (Dammers, 2010). While 56% of principals at schools without technology-based music classes feel that it would be feasible to offer such a class, individual music teachers with vision and technological skills are still needed to make these classes a reality.

### DID YOU KNOW?

#### Teaching Digital Natives

As a beginning teacher, it can be scary to teach "technology-based" music classes or lessons; no educator wants to be in the situation where a student knows more about technology than they do. In my own experience, having tech-savvy students in your class can be an incredible benefit. These students can be utilized as immediate "tech support" when something goes wrong in the classroom; let them troubleshoot for you and their peers when problems are encountered. More importantly, because these students already understand the *technological* side of things, an educator can focus on explaining the *musical* side of things to them, which I guarantee these students don't understand nearly as well as you do. Musical concepts, as you'll recall, are the sorts of things you know a lot about.

## INFORMAL MUSIC LEARNING THROUGH TECHNOLOGY

Lucy Green has done considerable work on self-directed and truly "informal" music learning by observing the ways that popular musicians learn to perform (2002). As you would imagine, church musicians can't stop the service so that the newbie bass player can learn to play with the experienced musicians, nor can they slow the songs down so that the new singers can hold their own in the choir. Popular musicians learn in an immersive environment where much of the education occurs informally and experientially as opposed to in a classroom context.

Green (2008) described a successful teaching strategy hinged on students listening to music that was culturally familiar to them and learning to play the music informally "by ear" in the way that many popular musicians have learned to perform. The strategy involved a teacher handing the students instruments like a guitar or bass, sending them to a practice room with a recording of the song of their choice, and telling the student to figure the song out on their own. In this "informal music learning" strategy, teachers function as facilitators for student-directed learning. Green described the ways in which students succeeded to learn to play instruments by listening to music and figuring out the notes and chords without teacher intervention. Teachers assisted students with conceptualizing aspects of form, harmony, and other musical concepts as the students' experiences with music caused them to ask questions about these concepts.

Teachers in Green's study found the strategy to be a success. This finding comes despite the difficulties of playing an acoustic instrument as opposed to a more accessible tech-based instrument. One might then ask: To what extent could the strategies carried out by Green be facilitated more effectively with instruments that are easier to play?

Many teaching strategies have aimed to reach students through activities that were artistically and socially relevant to the students but fewer with the use of technology-based instruments or methods. The Manhattanville Music Curriculum Project, or MMCP (Thomas, 1970), was a teaching strategy aimed toward student-centered instruction. It targeted students with declining interest in school music programs, unlike Green's project, which was primarily an alternate way of instructing students who were already part of the school music program. It is unclear if interactive music systems, had they been implemented, could have been a viable mechanism to achieve the objectives of MMCP. This is an area of research that we are only now beginning to explore. However, it is clear that the creation of software systems specifically tailored to each student can be used to provide student-centered instruction in a self-directed learning environment. Teachers would serve as facilitators for the acquisition of musical skills to allow composition and performance of music that is artistically, personally, and socially relevant to the students.

One project that tested this approach was the Interactive Music Technology Curriculum Project (Manzo & Dammers, 2010), or IMTCP (www.imtcp.org), and related subsequent studies (Manzo, 2014). These projects successfully used accessible interactive music systems to facilitate composition and performance with nonmusicians and musicians without composition experience. The technology was developed by EAMIR, an open-source app and development kit project aimed at making accessible tech-based musical instruments for special learners and nonmusicians. In IMTCP, the participants were middle school and high school students participating in a week-long summer camp. They were presented with basic information about diatonic chord functions, chord progressions, harmonic ear-training, and standard harmonic patterns. Then they were given tech-based musical instruments and asked to make use of this knowledge by composing original music. In latter studies, the tech-based instruments were comparatively as effective as or more effective than traditional chordal instruments like piano in helping undergraduate students recognize and identify common chord progressions in popular music. In both studies, the primary musical "instrument/interface" used was a standard, unmodified ASCII computer keyboard that allowed the students to play diatonic chord functions by pressing the number keys 1–8 through custom EAMIR software apps.

## TECHNOLOGY IN PRACTICAL EDUCATIONAL USE

What are the other implications for the use of technology in education? Are we beyond the point where we simply marvel over new apps and technologies when they are released? Can we think low-tech pedagogically while thinking high-tech when it comes to facilitation? Are there new ways of teaching that emerge through technology? Is our job as educators simply to "create awareness" of new gadgets and apps with the hypothetical assumption that someone somewhere is using that technology in a useful way?

Consider the televised "Young People's Concerts" hosted by conductor Leonard Bernstein at Lincoln Center in the late 1950s. During a typical broadcast, Leonard Bernstein would conduct the New York Philharmonic performing classical music for a televised audience of families. Excerpts of important works were performed, and Bernstein would take short breaks from conducting to turn, face the audience, and talk to the kids and their families about what they were hearing: the instruments, the mood, and so on. With the orchestra seated right behind him, Bernstein was able to demonstrate various musical aspects of the performance as he explained them.

Now, we might consider this televised show to be rather "low-tech" in comparison to what else is out there, but, regardless, it was an implementation of technology that facilitated a mass demonstration and explanation to kids about orchestral music. Consider the technologies available today that were unavailable in the late 1950s. Did the success of the program rely entirely on the technology? Of course not! It was the content of the presentation that steered the ship, but technology was the sea. A team of producers, technologists, camera crews, engineers, and so on helped translate the experience for the viewers and broadcast the series to over 40 countries.

Now, consider a fundamentally solid concept like the "Young People's Concerts" and the ways that a similar concept could be enhanced by all of the present-day apps, and controllers, and effects, and so on. Do we really need more sophisticated technology to enhance our creative objectives? Are all of these apps just novelties, or can someone somewhere make a meaningful piece with them, or create a unique performance opportunity, or help explain some tricky theoretical concept? As educators, are we using technology for technology's sake, or can it be used to facilitate something greater?

## SUMMARY

We have more technology to assist our teaching objectives than ever available before. From real-time musical instruments and apps to software applications and recording technology that foster self-reflection and serve as tutorials, we have covered all the bases, and yet we continue to develop new tools every day. Technology is an excellent facilitator and, possibly, a motivator for learning musicianship skills. Technology allows for the possibility of new ways of learning that are defined by what the technology is capable of facilitating. Author and educator Barbara Freedman says, "teach music and the technology will follow" emphasizing the role of technology as a facilitator for one's musical objectives. Author and educator Will Kuhn says "teach technology and the music will follow" emphasizing the role of technology as a facilitator for exploration into music-making that would otherwise be difficult. Both are correct. Ultimately, the burden of learning is on the student, but numerous types of technology exist that can help both students and educators to support this process.

## KEY CONCEPTS

- Technology in education is evidenced in a variety of ways, including composition-supporting technologies, new technology-based instruments, and assistive learning software.
- Adaptive instruments are generally acoustic instruments designed to make performance more accessible.
- Interactive music systems are technology-based systems that typically facilitate composition or performance.
- Educators may use technology to separate cognitive functions of music learning from the physical gestures associated with performance.

- Tech-based music classrooms are becoming an increasingly popular method of engaging students who wouldn't otherwise participate in their school's music programs.
- The accessibility of tech-based instruments could facilitate informal music learning.

## KEY TERMS

adaptive instruments

control device/control interface

interactive music systems

many-to-one mapping

mapping

musicing

one-to-one mapping

# CHAPTER 13

# TECHNOLOGY IN COMPOSITION

## OVERVIEW

In this chapter we will discuss some aspects of electronic music composition, namely algorithmic composition and some aspects of electroacoustic music composition. Whether the ultimate extent of the technological impact on your compositional habits is the use of digital notation software or the creation of new timbres, consider the ways in which technology can be used to make your compositional workflow more efficient and boundless.

As discussed in Chapters 11 and 12, many tech-based musical instruments, controllers, and other performance systems have been created and continue to be created each day. Composers are needed to champion these innovations and create some compelling music with and for these new technologies.

## ALGORITHMIC COMPOSITION

The term **algorithmic composition** is used to describe music that is composed using some sort of process. It commonly refers to music composed with the use of computer algorithms or processes. However, algorithmic composition is as old as composition itself.

One of the earliest examples is found in Guido d'Arezzo's treatise on medieval music *Micrologus*, written around 1026. As an example of one of his approaches to algorithmic composition, as shown in Figure 13.1, Guido notated a scale on the staff and wrote a different vowel beneath each pitch. Then, using some Latin text, he matched the vowel sound of each syllable in the text to the pitch in his scale that used the similar sounding vowel. In effect, the word *alleluia* might be used to yield the pitches C for syllable *a*, D for syllable *e* (from "lle"), G for syllable *u* (from "lu"), and A for syllable *a* (from "ia").

Another type of algorithmic technique, often credited to Mozart, was used to compose a minuet by reordering precomposed measures of music through controlled chance. In one such technique, a number of 2-bar "opening" phrases were composed along with an equal number of 2-bar "closing" phrases that end in some form of cadence. Each opening and closing phrase was given a letter as an identifier and placed in one of two hats. As guests entered the party, each drew a slip of paper with a one-letter identifier written on it from one of two hats that referred to one of the opening or closing phrases. The order of the

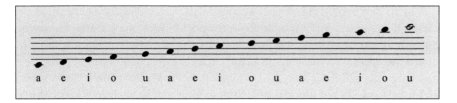

FIGURE 13.1: Guido d'Arezzo–style algorithmic composition

letters, then, indicated the order in which the phrases should be played. When all the guests had arrived, a musician would then perform the new piece composed algorithmically through recombination of the precomposed phrases. Mozart's so-called *Musikalisches Würfelspiel* (K. 516f), or "music dice game," used a similar controlled-randomness approach by rolling dice.

## Early American Algorithmic Composition: David Cope

David Cope (b. 1941) is a composer best known for his algorithmic compositions. He is the author of numerous books and articles on the subject of algorithmic composition and artificial intelligence and has lectured extensively on their role in the artistic process.

Although he is well known for his computer music, it should be noted that Cope has primarily composed music that is traditionally notated and that could be played by an acoustic instrument. This is a departure from other "computer music" contemporaries of Cope such as Mario Davidovsky, whose collection of *Synchronisms* employed electroacoustic techniques and processes by which a performer interacts in some way with an electronic sound source.

Much of Cope's early music falls into the posttonal category or **posttonal cycle**, as he refers to it (2010). His earliest work in this category, from 1959, is his first of ten symphonies. He has written ten piano sonatas and a wealth of chamber music to date. As the term suggests, the music of Cope's posttonal category is heavily chromatic and rhythmically complex. Although Cope describes all of his music as being algorithmic in some way, his works prior to the early 1980s were composed before his venture into using computers to facilitate his algorithmic composition techniques.

## Algorithmic Cycle

In 1981 Cope was commissioned to write an opera and, as he described in a lecture (2008), did many of the things a professional composer would do while preparing for such an undertaking: he analyzed scores of other composers like Verdi, Wagner, and others and began immersing himself in the literature. However, Cope began experiencing serious writer's block and found himself in a pattern of sketching, composing, and, yet, eventually trashing weeks and months worth of ideas. In his words, had his writing process continued this way, he would have abandoned composition altogether. The unlikely factor that changed his writing was in fact algorithmic computer composition.

In his first book (1991), Cope explained that in the 1980s he had heard about personal computers and thought about the possibilities of a computer assisting his compositional process. It was during this time that Cope temporarily abandoned the opera commission and began exploring the possibilities of computer-assisted composition. He identified two approaches to his algorithmic composition endeavors: **rule-based algorithmic composition** and **data-driven algorithmic composition**.

## Rule-Based Algorithmic Composition

Using a rule-based algorithmic approach, the composer of the algorithm would carefully code rules about music elements such as voice-leading, harmonic direction, and other elements in the same way a teacher might explain these rules to a beginning composition student. The use of context-dependent choices based on previous choices, or **Markov chains**, was becoming a growing area of research for those interested in artificial intelligence, and composing pieces based on rules appeared to be a good first step for Cope. He began learning the programming language *LISP* (derivative of "LISt Processing"), one of the oldest programming languages still used today, primarily by researchers in artificial intelligence. This approach can be heard in Cope's composition *Gradus* (1991).

### DID YOU KNOW?

#### Markov Chains

A Markov chain is a mathematical system that deals with making choices based on randomness or by memory of previous choices. Consider a composition program that randomly chooses a note from the possible 12 notes in one octave. This is a first-order Markov chain that considers the possible options within the current state of the system and randomly chooses one. A second-order Markov chain applied to that decision-making algorithm would remember the previous choice and consider it, in some defined way, in the decision-making process of which note to choose next. It could, for example, be set to not repeat the previous note. A third-order Markov chain would remember the previous two choices and consider those in the decision-making process, and so on. Thus, an infinite-order, or $n$th order, Markov chain would continue to remember choices and consider those previous choices in some way within the decision-making process. Composers like Xenakis, Cope, and many more have used these approaches to composition.

While Cope saw the benefit of composing algorithmically in a rule-based approach, he also saw major flaws in the subjective nature of such an approach.

He abandoned it in favor of a way more similar to Mozart's party game the *Musikalisches Würfelspiel*, in which music is derived solely from existing data as opposed to subjective rules.

## Data-Driven Algorithmic Composition

Cope began to think about the Mozart technique and how it could help him begin his opera. He decided to take the renowned opera works of famous composers and, instead of manually analyzing rules and idioms about their works, have the computer objectively analyze characteristics about the works devoid of any of the biases he or any other composer possessed. In this way he could create new music in the style of Wagner or Verdi that resembled characteristics about their music—derivative works in extremely close emulation.

In order for this type of data-driven approach to take place, Cope would need a large sample of music from which he could have the computer analyze and obtain data. Though operas are in abundance, there are many complexities to the forms and works within one opera, let alone the works of many operas or across composers, so Cope thought to begin writing LISP code to create new works based on the Bach chorales.

There are at least 335 Bach chorales (Boyd, 2000, p. 6), which seemed a large enough sample size from which Cope's software could infer data. The process of organizing each Bach chorale in the computer was not unlike that used in the *Musikalisches Würfelspiel*. Cope analyzed each beat of a given Bach chorale and entered the notes at each beat into a computer table. Eventually, Cope had a database of each chord at each beat of every known Bach chorale, how it was voiced, and, most importantly, where it came from and where it went next in terms of harmony.

His LISP code was then somewhat simplistic in nature. The computer program randomly chose a starting chord for the to-be-composed chorale from one of the 335 possible starting chords in the Bach chorales. From the chosen starting chord, the computer then looked at all of the chords like the one chosen from the Bach chorale database and where each chord went next. From the potential list of "second" chords, the computer chose one chord from the database as the next one to be played. Then, the program looked at the current chord and, considering the previous two chords that occurred in the database, chose another chord from the list of possible "third" chords. Eventually, the program chose chords until one of the destinations for the chosen chord cadenced and ended the piece.

Cope called the software *Emmy* (1980) for Experiments in Music Intelligence (EMI). Using it, he generated 5,000 chorales in the style of J. S. Bach that all sound convincingly like J. S. Bach. His idea of recombining musical ideas in this way launched his career as a pioneer in computer music and led to over a decade of articles and books on the subject in which he was considered the foremost authority.

The opera he was commissioned to write in 1981, *Falling Cradle*, was completed in two days in 1989. Many of his chorales composed "after Bach" were later given text and performed internationally. Other works included music in the style of Bach inventions, Beethoven piano sonatas, and Chopin nocturnes, all described in his book *Computers and Musical Style* (1991).

## Issues of Authorship

In his book *The Algorithmic Composer* (2000), Cope distinguishes between composers who use algorithmic processes in their music and those, like him, that compose algorithms. One question that seems to follow the work of composers like Cope is the issue of authorship and originality. Cope argues that since he is the author of his own algorithmic processes, compositions made with that algorithm, even if created by others, are the work of Cope since they are his techniques.

However, with compositions like *Emmy*, the issue arises: Did Cope compose those chorales or did Bach? As Cope explains, Bach did not write those compositions because they simply use chords that Bach also used in an order that Bach would have used them. However, Cope notes "in the style of Bach" in the transcriptions of these pieces, much in the same way that Bach would write "after Vivaldi" in pieces he composed written in the style of Antonio Vivaldi.

### DID YOU KNOW?

#### Authorship, Ownership, and Copyright

Mash-ups, remixes, and loop-based compositions like those made with GarageBand and Mixcraft are all subject to the questions of ownership (and copyright) as they relate to recombinance. But how far back does this question lead? Can anyone make a claim to authorship of a simple rock beat? If the answer is no, is it necessary to create an original recording of that beat in order to preserve an artist's legitimacy and integrity, or may the convenience of using a professionally recorded drum loop be considered? If sampling drums is acceptable, why not pitched instruments? Is the combination of notes to form new ideas what makes a musical work an "original" composition?

What about the creative mechanisms involved? A composer decides which notes he or she would like performed at which time, but does the composer need also to create the instruments for this performance? What about a luthier who makes an instrument that produces a one-of-a-kind timbre: Should he or she be paid royalties each time the timbre is used on a recording? If an artist uses a software synthesizer, should he or she have been responsible for tweaking the settings or the patch and making it his or her "own" in order to stake claim to "ownership" of the composition, or will simply the notes played be sufficient? Should composers have to program their own synth software? Build their own computers? Invent mathematics? Create the universe?

We may denigrate pop artists for "borrowing" musical ideas and patterns from other artists—such as the "sampling" of Queen's "Under Pressure" bassline in Vanilla Ice's "Ice Ice Baby"—but accept "borrowing" when it's done by the great composers in music history. For example, the famous opening few measures to Wagner's *Tristan und Isolde* are strikingly similar to Liszt's "Ich möchte hingehen" and Chopin's op 68.4 (Hofmann-Engl, L., 2008). A less extreme imitation occurs in many of J. S. Bach compositions in which the composer notes "after Vivaldi" to mean in Vivaldi's style. Perhaps it's our way of thinking about the past that makes it acceptable that classical composers imitated and even quoted each other's works regularly.

Recent examples of copyright lawsuits in popular music include Avril Lavigne's song "Girlfriend," which is said to be based on the Rubinoos's "I Wanna Be Your Boyfriend"; some critics note ironically that both infringe upon the Rolling Stones's "Get Off of My Cloud." Jorge Ben Jor filed a lawsuit against Rod Stewart for borrowing from "Taj Mahal" when Stewart composed "Da Ya Think I'm Sexy?" Yet ownership issues arise even in art music. For example, a lawsuit was filed against composer Mike Batt for his work "One Minute Silence (after Cage)." Batt credited the work to Batt/Cage to acknowledge his debt to Cage's landmark work 4'33", a conceptual piece in three movements of silence marked "tacet" (Latin for "silent"). Nonetheless, Peters Editions—Cage's publisher—sued him for copyright infringement and won.

In his book *Computer Models of Musical Creativity* (2005), Cope described what he considers to be an important part in valuing the authorship of algorithmic music: finality. After the *Emmy* code had been written, creating one new piece versus creating 5,000 new pieces was simply a matter of changing a number before he hit the return key.

As Cope notes, one of the reasons we value the works of composers is that they are somewhat limited in their quantity. If the *Emmy* software continued to write new music in the style of other composers forever, Cope felt that the works would never be valued to their full extent. For this reason, Cope describes how he deleted all of the computer libraries *Emmy* used to compose music in an attempt to metaphorically kill the composer *Emmy*.

Cope has since created software to assist his composition in a completely different style than the recombination methods used with *Emmy*. In 2005 Cope began developing a new piece of software called *Emily Howell*, an amalgam of the name *Emmy* and his own middle name. Unlike *Emmy*, the composition process used with *Emily Howell* is an interactive one in which the software provides suggestions for new material and development based on Cope's existing works and measures within the working composition. Composing with *Emily Howell* is thus more like composing with a collaborator. For this reason, Cope has credited *Emily Howell* as a contributing composer for his works *Shadows* (2005) for disk clavier and *Land of Stone* (2007) for chamber ensemble.

## ALGORITHMIC COMPOSITION METHODS

In *Interactive Music Systems*, Robert Rowe (1993) describes three methods of algorithmic composition:

1. **Generative** methods use sets of rules to produce complete musical output from the stored fundamental material.
2. **Sequenced** techniques use prerecorded music fragments in response to some real-time input. Some aspects of these fragments may be varied in performance, such as tempo playback, dynamic shape, slight rhythmic variations, etc.
3. **Transformative** methods take some existing musical material and apply transformation to it to produce variants.

According to the technique used, these variants may or may not be recognizable related to the original. For transformative algorithms, the source material is complete musical input.

All compositions are generally, in some regard, algorithmic even if they do not use a computer; a computer, however, can help to make the composition process much more efficient. Estonian composer Arvo Pärt's *Cantus in Memoriam Benjamin Britten* (1977) is a prolation canon, an imitative compositional device in which each instrument performs—in this case the descending notes of the A minor scale—at different harmonic rhythms. In this composition, once the composer decided on this process, the nature of composing the piece on staff paper was largely a matter of adhering to the process and putting the notes into the right place. Of course, there are numerous musical judgments that the composer also made in addition to carrying out the process. The point of this analogy is that when the composer decided on a process, he had at least two choices: do it by hand, which he did, or, if he had known a programming language, as in the case of David Cope, use a computer to carry out the task. The latter would have been much more efficient and would have structurally yielded the same piece.

## SOFTWARE AND TOOLS

There are numerous software applications on the market geared toward assisting the composition process. The extent of the assistance, however, varies greatly.

### Precomposed Loop and Pattern Software

DAWs like GarageBand, FL Studio, Mixcraft, Band-in-a-Box, and many more offer users a library of precomposed patterns, loops, and other bits of royalty-free audio that can be used in the creative process. To this extent, the use of these loops can be, for example, to alter them beyond immediate recognition through effects, splicing, and other process or to use them as the basis for further compositional development by layering additional parts on top of them.

## Sound Manipulation

As mentioned in Chapters 9 and 11, sound can be manipulated using a variety of techniques and technologies. Even the simple act of slowing down the playback of a recorded note or phrase can result in very interesting timbres. The combination of computerized sounds with traditional instrumental sounds is a popular technique employed by many electroacoustic composers, such as in the works of Mario Davidovsky, yet many composers prefer to use only computerized sounds.

Luke Dubois's work *Billboard* (2005), for example, uses a technique he termed "time-lapse phonography" by which, for example, the samples of audio within a recording are processed so that an average of the frequencies in the piece is established. In *Billboard*, recordings of songs reaching number 1 on the *Billboard* music charts from a given year are "averaged" in this manner by a computer process so that all frequency values for the song will play back for a number of seconds representing the number of weeks the song charted at number 1. For example, for Hanson's 1997 hit "MMMBop"—a song that remained at number 1 for 3 weeks—all frequencies present in the song are played back for three seconds. It should be noted that this process is much different than simply "fast-forwarding" a song; all frequencies in the original recording are averaged so that they play back in a condensed time. *Billboard* processes each year of hits as "movements" and spans a number of years. Dubois's work *Academy* (2006) used the same process but combined video of Academy Award–winning films. For example, the "Titanic" movement, available from Dubois's website, shows averaged values of video from the entire film. In this process, main characters that move around frequently in each frame are blurred when frames are averaged, and background characters that often stay in fixed positions and locations are less obscured.

## Composer of Algorithms and Algorithmic Composition

Some DAWs and notation programs offer compositional aids that vary, randomize, and apply grooves to your recorded music. These are, of course, algorithmic processes that result in algorithmic composition. But what if you want to compose your own algorithms and truly create your own processes?

In this case, we look to programming languages for help. A variety of programming languages have been used to assist in the creation of composition algorithms. As mentioned, David Cope used LISP; others prefer C and C++. In the mid-1980s, a media-oriented programming language began to emerge now known as Max/MSP/Jitter.

In Chapter 14 we will explore a few basic aspects of music making using this programming language. Don't worry if you have never programmed before. Max/MSP/Jitter, as you will find, is easy to understand and provides a unique technology-based opportunity to composition by creating your own compositional processes.

## SUMMARY

Composers have generally always thought about composition in terms of some "process" or "algorithm." The rule-based approaches to composition during the classical era—like "avoid writing parallel fifths and octaves" and other general practices—are testament to this. Even if the process is that there is no process, a defining mechanism by which music is intended to be performed still exists. Both Cope and Pärt used clear processes for creating their works along with some sense of intuition in terms of direction and the overall compositional direction. Cope's work, however, was facilitated by computer-based technology. Both composers had to reconcile the advantages and disadvantages that come with these approaches. For DAWs and other forms of music technology, creating new music is made easier through the technology itself but still requires much effort from the creator in order to refine the work and push it into a compositional direction.

## KEY CONCEPTS

- Composers generally follow some rules, processes, or "algorithms" in their creative works.
- Algorithmic composition is not new, but computer-based algorithmic composition is.
- Rule-based approaches to algorithmic composition rely on preexisting guidelines by which one may compose.
- Data-driven algorithmic composition is based on sampling and analyzing some set of existing works as models for derivative works.
- Technological advancements have resulted in a variety of tools and apps that can facilitate novel compositional ideas.
- Issues of authorship exist in recombinance works, as well as the distinction between the composer of algorithms and algorithmic composers.

## KEY TERMS

algorithmic composition

data-driven algorithmic composition

generative algorithmic composition

Markov chains

posttonal cycle (Cope)

rule-based algorithmic composition

sequenced algorithmic composition

transformative algorithmic composition

# CHAPTER 14

# INTRODUCTION TO MUSIC PROGRAMMING

## OVERVIEW

Today, there are software applications for just about everything, so you may wonder why it would be necessary to learn how to create your own. After installing a software application, it's normal to look at the program and ask: "What does it do?" "How can I perform with this?" and "How can I make a demonstration or instructional activity for my class using this software?" There's certainly nothing wrong with this approach, but what if you already have some musical ideas in mind and are looking for a way to express them using the efficiency and interactivity of technology? Existing software may not be able to address the particular musical objectives that you want to facilitate from the angle that you prefer. For this reason, understanding a little bit about how to program can help you design small applications for composition, performance, instruction, or research and also provide some insight into the ways that existing software is designed.

This chapter introduces the powerful visual programming language Max/ MSP/Jitter, or simply "Max." There are a number of programming languages that have implications for use in musical activities such as Pure Data (PD), CSound, SuperCollider, ChucK, and more. Max is among the most popular, flexible, and powerful and provides excellent support.

By the end of this chapter, you should have some understanding of how to program small music-making applications. Of course, this book only scratches the surface of the limitless musical opportunities available once custom programming is an option, but you should at least have a better understanding of the scope of unique project concepts you may have in mind. This chapter will also help to reinforce the notion of signal flow.

## PROGRAMMING LANGUAGES

A **programming language** is a means to specify processes performed by a computer. It is somewhat similar to the language we speak. Each word in the language serves some function and the ordering of each word follows a syntax from which we derive meaning. In a programming language, these words are commonly referred to as

**functions** or **objects**. Each object has some purpose germane to the programming language. For example, an object called *number* might allow a user to specify a number. Another object called + might be used to add that *number* to another *number*. The objects, each with a specific purpose, work together to create some intended outcome; this is how a program works. In this case, the program we defined added 2 numbers together.

In a typical programming language, there are numerous objects each with a specific function. One difficulty in the beginning stages of learning to program is that you do not know the fundamental objects that form the basic vocabulary of that programming language. In this chapter we will begin by developing small music programs that use only a few objects.

Another difficulty lies in thinking about the steps involved in creating a program. There are different ways to write programs that achieve the same result, but they all require that precise activity to be specified in order to produce that result.

## DID YOU KNOW?

### Taking It Step by Step

In an early experience as a kindergarten music teacher, the teacher stood at the door of the classroom and greeted the students as they entered the room. "Good morning, let's take out our books and start class." At that moment, they hadn't yet put their backpacks down, walked to their seats, or sat in their chairs. It was obvious that they were not ready to begin class. Some students scrambled to find *any* book anywhere in the room. Some took all of their books out of their backpacks. One student began crying. It was a disaster.

The problem was that the teacher didn't clearly describe the individual processes that needed to take place. Instead of using a number of small processes in conjunction with one another, the teacher attempted to use one command that would do it all. It is important to think of the overall flow of actions before you begin to program: break down the objective into smaller tasks and create a procedure for accomplishing the objective.

In this chapter, we will be using a programming language called Max/MSP/Jitter, commonly referred to as simply Max. Max is different from most programming languages in that it uses a graphical interface to display each object as a small rectangle on the screen. This rectangle is called an object and is the basic unit of function in Max.

Objects typically have **inlets** on the top of the rectangle for receiving data *from* other objects and **outlets** on the bottom for sending data *to* other objects. Data is sent from one object to another by drawing a small line, called a **patch cord**, from the outlet of one object to the inlet of another object. With the objects connected via patch cords, it is easy to see the dataflow between each object in your program.

There are an unlimited number of programs you can write using Max. For the purpose of this chapter, we will write a small program to demonstrate how writing your own software can be used to facilitate very unique musical ideas or to express musical ideas in a very unique way. As you begin to learn the Max/ MSP/Jitter language and grasp the concepts of programming, you will quickly see how easily you can develop software applications to accomplish your objectives.

The steps involved in creating these programs are listed in a "cookbook"-style numbered list. If you get stuck or if something doesn't work correctly, go back and ensure that you have completed each step exactly as described, and you'll find yourself back on track.

If you have not already done so, download and install the latest version of Max from www.cycling74.com. Max version 7 is used in the narrative that follows though other versions may also be used for this chapter with slight variations in direction.

## INTRODUCTION TO MAX

As we begin building some programs together, be brave. At times you may not understand the programming concepts at first, and it may feel like you're just blindly following instructions. Continue to follow each step in the programming process and these concepts will soon become clear.

In this chapter we will look at the basic tools of operation and navigation in the Max programming environment. A document in Max is referred to as a **patcher** or, simply, a **patch**. A patch is a blank canvas for programmers to put objects on. From within the Max application, click the menu item marked *File* at the top of the screen and select *New Patcher* or use the key command ⌘ + *v* (Mac) or *ctrl* + *n* (Windows). To create a new object, press the *n* key. When you do so, a small rectangle appears on the screen, allowing you to type in the name of an object in the Max language. You can also add an object by clicking the *Object* icon located at the top left of the patch window.

It's time to learn our first object called *button*. Note that the object names are case-sensitive.

1. Create a new object box by pressing the *n* key on your computer keyboard.
2. Type the word *button* in the new object box.
3. Hit the enter/return key.

If you've accidentally clicked away from the new object box without typing in the word *button*, you can double-click the object box to allow text to be entered once again. Once the word *button* has been entered, the *button* object appears on the screen as a small circle.

The top of the *button* object has one inlet for receiving data. If you hold your mouse over the inlet on top of the *button* object, a red circle appears around the inlet

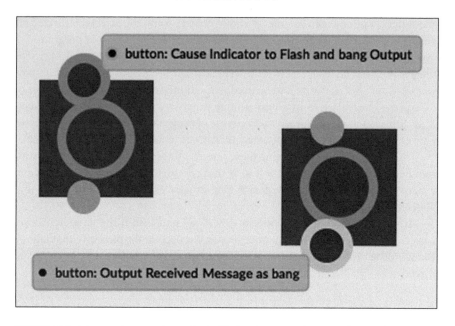

FIGURE 14.1: A button object with its inlet highlighted next to a button with its outlet highlighted

as well as a message window giving you some description about the data that the inlet can receive as shown in Figure 14.1. Now, hold your mouse over the outlet on the bottom of the object. A button sends out a message called a bang from its outlet.

If you are having trouble viewing the inlet, you can *Zoom In* and *Zoom Out* on a patch by clicking *View* from the top menu, or by using the key commands ⌘ + = (Mac) or ctrl + = (Windows) and ⌘ + − (Mac) or ctrl + − (Windows).

A **bang** is an event in Max that triggers an object to perform some task. The only task the *button* object performs is to send and receive bangs. The *button* is such a common object in Max that it has its own key command shortcut, the *b* key, for putting the object in your patch.

> 4. Add 5 more *buttons* to your patch by pressing the *b* key or by highlighting an existing *button* and copying and pasting it. Copying and pasting is accomplished in Max by going to the *Edit* menu or by using the key commands ⌘ + c (Mac) or ctrl + c (Windows) and ⌘ + v (Mac) or ctrl + v (Windows). You can also copy an object by holding the alt/option key and dragging an object.

To move *buttons* to different locations in your patch, simply click the center of the object and drag it to the desired location. You can also resize the *button* by holding your mouse over the bottom right of the object until your mouse shows two arrows at an angle and then dragging while holding the mouse button down.

We've been working in what Max calls the Patching Mode or Patching View. In Patching Mode you can create new objects, move them around, resize them, and connect them to each other. By going to the *View* menu at the top of the screen and unchecking the item marked *Edit*, the patch will become *Locked*, that is, the patcher will function as a program and cannot be edited in any way until the patch is unlocked again. You can lock and unlock a patch by clicking the small *Lock* icon in the bottom left of the patcher window or by using the key command ⌘ + *e* (Mac) or ctrl + *e* (Windows). You can also ⌘ + *click* (Mac) or *ctrl* + *click* (Windows) any blank space in the patch to toggle lock modes.

5.  With your patcher locked, click on the *button* objects you've made.

Notice that the buttons now blink when clicked. This is a graphical display of a bang message being sent or received from the *button* object. Unlock the patch and you can once again make edits in Patching Mode.

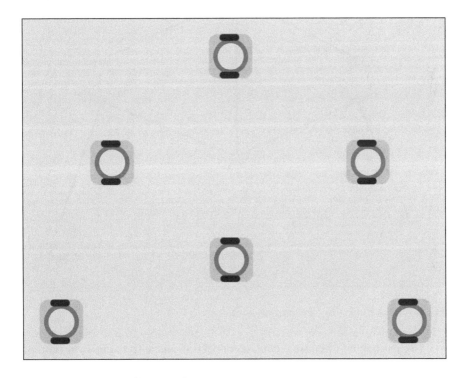

FIGURE 14.2: A group of buttons | button_tree.maxpat

Now let's send data from one *button* to another via *patch cords*. A patch cord to be created when you click on the outlet of an object. The cord will travel wherever your mouse does and will not disappear until you click on the inlet of another object or press the *esc* key.

Unlock your patch and:

6.  Click on the outlet of one of your top level *buttons* and move your mouse to the inlet of another *button* beneath it until a red circle appears above the second *button*.

Patch cords can connect from outlets to inlets and the other way around, though it is advised that you begin by only connected outlets to inlets. Once again, keep in mind that if you click on an object's outlet, the patch cord will follow your mouse until you connect it to another object's inlet or press the esc key.

7. When your mouse gets over the inlet of the second *button*, click your mouse and the two objects will be connected.

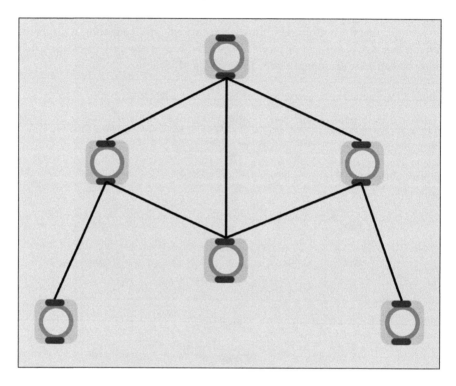

FIGURE 14.3: A button tree | button_tree.maxpat

In this chapter, when we reference connecting one object's outlet to another object's inlet, this is the process.

8. Lock your patch and click on the top *button* in your *button* tree.

The bang flows from the top *button* and triggers a bang to all of the connected *buttons*. If you click on a *button* beneath the top one, the top *button* does not turn yellow because it did not receive any data to its inlet. This illustrates the dataflow within Max. To save this patch, click File>Save from the top menu or use the key command ⌘ + s (Mac) or ctrl + s (Windows). When asked for a file name, name the file "button_tree." Notice that the Max filename extension ".maxpat" is given to your file. After you have saved the patch, close it.

Look at the following illustration and try to determine what will happen when you click on one of the *buttons*.

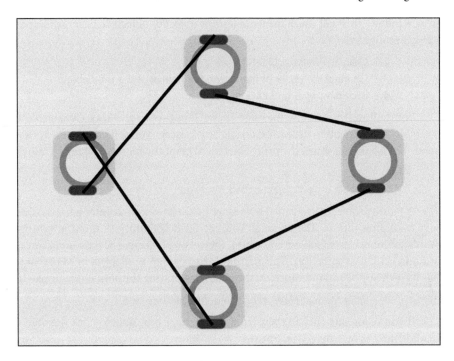

FIGURE 14.4: A button loop

When you click a *button*, a bang will flow from one *button* to another without any way to stop the data. The bang will continue to flow forever without any way of ever stopping. This causes an error called *stack overflow*. It's a concept similar to the way that feedback is heard when a microphone is too close to a PA speaker. Make sure that objects are not feeding data back into themselves. Errors like this one will cause an error message to appear at the top of the patch describing the problem and listing the culprit object. Clicking the error message will highlight the problem object in the patch. The error message may be cleared by clicking the small "x" on the right of the message. In some cases, you may be instructed to go to the *Edit* menu and click *Resume*.

## THE MAX WINDOW

Create a new patcher, and:

1.   Create a new object called *print*.

The *print* object is used to display some information in what is called the Max Console, or the Max window. Open the Max Console by choosing Window>Max Console from the top menu or by using the key command ⌘ + m (Mac) or ctrl + m (Windows). Important messages, like errors, for instance, will appear in the Max Console. If an error occurs somewhere in your patch, you can locate where the error occurred by double clicking on the error message (highlighted) in the

Max window. This will cause the troublesome object or objects to become temporarily highlighted.

2. Create a *button* object.
3. Connect the outlet of the *button* to the inlet of the *print* object.
4. Lock the patch and click the *button*.

You will notice that the message "bang" appears in the Max Console. The *print* object will print to the Max Console any message you send it. Since a *button* sends out a bang message, the *print* object will print the message "bang." Unlock your patch and:

5. Create a new object called *message*.

A *message* object, also called a *message* box, allows you to enter a message as text by typing into it. The message you type can contain just about anything: words, numbers, or words and numbers. Objects will receive the data in *messages* and interpret it in some way. The *message* is such a common object in Max that it has its own key command shortcut, the *m* key, for putting the object in your patch.

6. Enter the text *Hello World* into the *message* box.

If you've already clicked away from the *message* box, double-click the object to allow text to be entered once again.

7. Connect the outlet of the *message* box to the inlet of the *print* object.
8. Lock the patch and click the *message* box.

When the *message* box is clicked, the message *Hello World* will appear in the Max Console. You can bring the Max window to the front of the screen by double-clicking on the print object.

FIGURE 14.5: A print object receiving data from a message box | hello_world.maxpat

## Help Patchers

If you want help seeing how an object works, you can open up the Help file for each object in an unlocked patch by ctrl + clicking (Mac) or right-clicking (Windows) on the object and selecting *Open Help* from the contextual menu. (Mac users will have to use ctrl + click if right clicking has not been enabled in *System Preferences* or if their mouse or touchpad does not support right clicking capabilities.) You may also open Help by holding the alt/option key down and clicking on an object in an unlocked patcher.

Unlock the patch and:

9. Open the Help file for the *print* object.

In the Help file for an object, a description of the object is given along with fully working examples of how the object may function within a patch.

The interesting thing about Max Help files is that they too can be unlocked and edited just like patches.

10. Unlock the *print* Help file.
11. Highlight all of the objects in the Help patch and copy them using the commands ⌘ + c (Mac) or ctrl + c (Windows).

You can construct entire Max patches by copying working code from the Help files. To find out more information about an object including all of the available messages you can send to it, click on the *Open Reference* link within the top right corner of an object's Help file.

On the top menu of each Help file is a menu item labeled "?" This menu shows objects that are somehow related to the object whose Help file you are currently reading. If you select one of these objects from the menu, its Help file will open up. Looking through these related objects is a great way to learn the Max language fast. Also, if you are trying to find an object that operates similarly, but not exactly the same, to an object you know, you may find that object via this menu. You can also create a new object and type in the desired function you're looking for as if the new object box is a search engine!

12. Close the Help file for *print*.
13. Paste the contents copied from the *print* Help file into your patch using the commands ⌘ + v (Mac) or ctrl + v (Windows).

## Arguments

In your patch, notice that one of the *print* objects in the Help file contents you just copied contains the letter $x$ next to the object name. This is called an **argument**. Arguments are used to set or change variables for an object and are related to the types of data and messages the object deals with. In most cases, specifying an argument replaces some default value, if the object had one, with a new one. In this case, the $x$ argument will replace the default name "print" in the Max Console.

14. Change the *print* argument from *x* to a single word of your choosing.
15. Lock the patch and click the *message* box.
16. Open the Max window to reveal that the word you chose has replaced the word "print."

Look at Figure 14.6 and try to determine what will happen when you click on the *message* box.

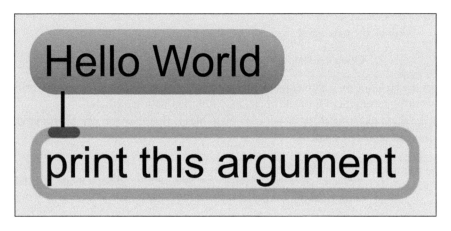

FIGURE 14.6: A print object with an argument | hello_world2.maxpat

The supplied argument is two words: *this* and *argument*. However, the *print* object only takes one argument, so the second argument, *argument*, is dropped. The message in the Max window reads: Object: thisMessage: Hello World.

### Separating Items in a Message

Now, unlock your patch and:

17. Double-click the *message* box containing the text *Hello World* and put a comma after the word *Hello*.

The comma is used to separate items in a *message* box. The *message* box now contains two separate items. Each item in the *message* will be printed to the Max window on a separate line.

18. Lock your patch and click the same *message* box.

Take a moment to save your patch as *hello_world.maxpat*. Close the patch.

### Numbers: Integers and Floating Points

Create a new patcher, and:

1. Create new object called *number*.

The *number* object, also called a *number* box, is such a common object in Max that it has its own key command shortcut, the *i* key, for putting the object in

FIGURE 14.7: Printing a list to the Max Window | hello_world3.maxpat

your patch. Think of the *i* as short for *integer* as opposed to the other type of number box we'll deal with in Max: the floating-point numbers; numbers with a decimal point. A *number* object simply holds a number.

2.  Lock your patch, and click on the *number* object.

Now, type the number *34* into that object. The number *34* will stay in that *number* box until you change it or close the patch. When the patch is closed, the number box will return to its default value of *0*.

3.  Click on the number in the *number* box and drag the number up or down to increase or decrease the value. You may also use the arrow keys to increase or decrease the value once you have clicked in the *number* box.

Unlock your patch and:

4.  Create three new *message* boxes containing the values *44*, *55*, and *42.85*, respectively.
5.  Connect the outlet of each *message* box to the inlet of the *number* box.
6.  Lock your patch and click each *message* box.

Notice that the value of the *number* box changes for each value you send to it by clicking a *message* box. Note that when you send the *number* box the floating point value 42.85, it drops the decimal point values completely. The *number* object only takes the integer part of a floating point number. It does not round the number up or down; it simply truncates it.

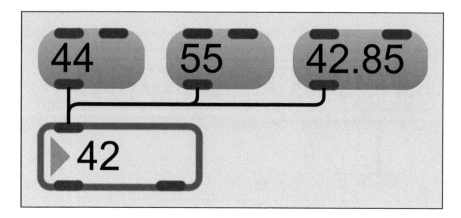

FIGURE 14.8: Connecting message boxes to number boxes | number_boxes.maxpat

Unlock your patch and:

   7.   Create a new object called *flonum*.

A *flonum* object is a floating-point number box. Floating-point number boxes can be used to show more precise numbers than integer numbers. Is the singer singing exactly at A 440 or are they singing at A 440.91? A *flonum* will represent this value more accurately than a *number* box since it can, unlike the *number* box, contain the numbers after the decimal point. The *flonum* object, sometimes called a *float*, is such a common object in Max that it has its own key command shortcut, the *f* key, for putting the object in your patch.

   8.   Create three new *message* boxes with the values *55.72, 44.35,* and *55,* respectively.
   9.   Connect the outlet of each *message* box to the first inlet of the *flonum* box.
   10.   Lock your patch and click on each *message* box.

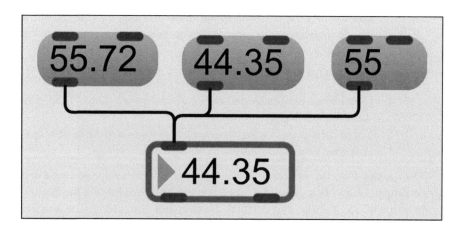

FIGURE 14.9: Connecting message boxes to flonum boxes | number_boxes.maxpat

The first two *message* boxes send the floating-point number to the *flonum* object. If you send a floating-point number with more than two decimal places, you will need to resize the *flonum* object to see these places by clicking on the button in the right corner of the object and dragging to the right. The third *message* box, 55, is still received by the *flonum* even though it is not a floating-point number.

## Aligning

You may have noticed that the patch cords in the chapter examples may look more segmented than yours. With *Segmented Patch Cords* selected from the *Options* menu, you are able to click at multiple points along the path between objects controlling the shape of the cable. You can also align patch cords by highlighting them (ctrl + clicking [Mac] or right-clicking [Windows]) it after they're connected to some objects and selecting *Align*, or by using the key command ⌘ + y (Mac) or ctrl + shift + a (Windows).

You can also *align* highlighted objects using the same key command. (This option is best used for objects positioned along the same plane. Highlighting everything in the patch and clicking *align* could make a mess.) You can highlight multiple objects, either by holding the shift key and clicking the desired objects or by drawing a marquee around them with the mouse. To highlight patch cords while you are drawing a marquee, hold the alt/option key. The *Arrange* menu also provides the option to snap objects in place according to a grid or even to snap objects in place relative to each other.

## Commenting

It is a good idea to make comments within a patch while you are writing it. As patches become larger, they can become difficult to read, and if you haven't opened the patch up in a while, it is easy to forget what you did and how certain parts of it function.

11.  Create a new object called *comment.*

The *comment* object, also called a *comment* box, allows you to type directly into your patch and document it. The *comment* object is such a common object in Max that it has its own key command shortcut, the *c* key, for putting the object in your patch.

12.  Create 2 new objects called *comment* containing the text *integers* and *floating point numbers,* respectively.
13.  Label the *number* objects as integers and the *flonum* objects as floating-point numbers by moving the *comments* near these objects.

In general practice, it is important to be descriptive when documenting your patch.

14.  Create a third *comment* object, which we will use for the title, and enter the text *ints and floats.*

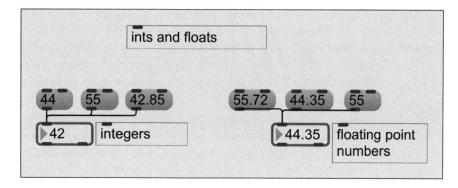

FIGURE 14.10: Commenting your patch | number_boxes.maxpat

## Inspector

It would be nice to see our title comment "ints and floats" in a somewhat larger font. To change properties about this or any object, go to the *Inspector* by ctrl + clicking (Mac) or right-clicking (Windows) an object and selecting *Inspector* from the contextual menu while the patch is unlocked. With an object highlighted, you can also use the key command ⌘ + *i* (Mac) or ctrl + i (Windows) or click the *Inspector* icon located on the right side of the patch window. Another method of getting to the *Inspector* is to hold your mouse in the middle of the left side of the object, click the arrow icon that appears, and click the *Inspector* icon.

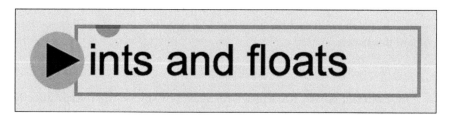

FIGURE 14.11: The Inspector icon at the center left of the object | number_boxes.maxpat

15. Open the *Inspector* for the *comment* box containing the title "ints and floats."

From the *Inspector* menu, you can select tabs for which to edit the object's properties. The tab *All* is selected by default and contains all of the property options of the other tabs.

16. In the *Inspector*, scroll down to the line marked *Font Size* and increase the font to *30* by double-clicking the default number and typing in the number *30*.

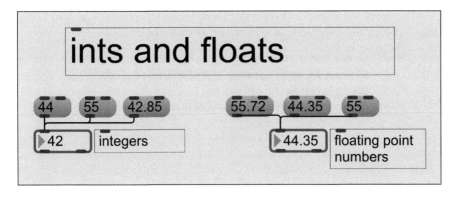

FIGURE 14.12: Changing an object's properties through the Inspector | number_boxes.maxpat

Take a moment to save your patch as *number_boxes*. Close the patch.

## GENERATING MUSIC

Now we will create a program that randomly generates pitches at a specified tempo. The program will have the ability to change a number of musical variables including timbre, velocity, and tempo. We will also write a program that allows your MIDI keyboard to function as a synthesizer. These two programs will be the basis of future projects related to composition and performance.

Because you've already learned a number of objects in the previous steps, let's agree that when asked to create an object that you already know, like *button*, it will be sufficient to say "create a *button*" instead of repeating the process of creating a new object box and typing in the word *button*. Combining steps in this way will help us to get through the instructions with greater speed while reinforcing understanding of how certain objects work. In this way, the instruction "create a message box containing the numbers 41 and 38" actually combines several smaller, and hopefully intuitive, instructions into a single step. I will slowly stop mentioning key commands and other shortcuts for objects and tasks that have already been introduced.

### The RAT Patch: Creating Random Atonal Trash

Create a new patch and:

1. Create a new object (press *n*) called *random*.

The *random* object takes a number as its only argument and randomly generates a number between *0* and one less than the argument when it receives a bang in its inlet.

2. Give this *random* object the argument *128*. (Note: If you already clicked away from the object, double-click it in order to, once again, enable typing within the object box.)

Be sure to put a space in between the word *random* and the argument *128* or Max will look for an object called *random 128* that does not exist.

3. Create a new *button* (press *b*).
4. Connect the outlet of *button* to the first inlet of *random 128*.
5. Create a *number* box (press *i*).
6. Connect the outlet of *random 128* to the inlet of the *number* box.

FIGURE 14.13: Outputting random numbers from 0 to 127 when a bang is received | the_RAT_patch.maxpat

### Zeroing In on Zero

Do you remember that kid that you went to grammar school with that asked you to count to 10, and when you started counting "1, 2, 3 . . .", he stopped you and laughed as he declared "No! You forgot the number 0!!!" I'm sure you remember that kid, or maybe you were that kid. Well, in Max we almost always start counting at the number 0, not the number 1. With the argument *128*, the *random* object will randomly output a total of 128 possible numbers starting at 0, which means that the range of numbers being randomly generated from *random* will be between 0 and 127.

7.  Lock your patch and click the *button* to see random numbers between 0 and 127.

## Synthesizing MIDI Numbers

With these objects, we are able to generate random numbers, which is not a very musical task. However, since MIDI uses numbers to represent pitches, there's no reason why we can't use those random numbers as pitches. We would then hear each random number as a random pitch. In order to accomplish this, we need to format those pitches into a MIDI message that includes some information about the velocity of the random pitch and how long the note will sound. An easy way to do this formatting is with the *makenote* object. The *makenote* object takes two numbers as arguments to specify a default velocity (first argument) and default duration (second argument), which will be associated with the random pitch value. The duration value is how long, in milliseconds, the note will last until *makenote* sends out a velocity *0* value to turn the note off. Unlock your patch and:

8.  Create a new object called *makenote* with the arguments *100* and *500*.
9.  Connect the first outlet of the *number* box to the first inlet of *makenote* 100 500.
10. Create two *number* boxes.
11. Connect each outlet of *makenote* 100 500 to the inlet of the two newly created *number* boxes, respectively.
12. Lock your patch and click the *button*.

You've likely noticed that although we see the numbers change, there is no sound. Remember, we've only now organized a bunch of messages; we haven't included an object to allow us to hear the note through our computer's soundcard. With the objects we've assembled this far, clicking on the *button* will generate a random number between *0* and *127*, the full range of MIDI pitches. The random number will be treated as the pitch in a MIDI message and partnered with a default velocity value, which we have supplied as *100*. The note will last for *500* milliseconds, after which the *makenote* object will output a velocity value of *0* for that pitch turning the note off.

Look at the *number* box connected to *makenote*'s last outlet as you click the *button*. It outputs the velocity value of *100* for half a second and then sends the "note off" message: velocity 0. The *makenote* object keeps track of what numbers

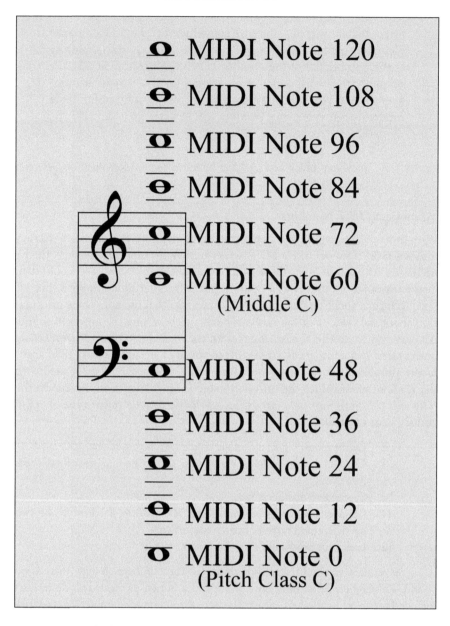

FIGURE 14.14: Pitch class C and corresponding MIDI note numbers | the_RAT_patch.maxpat

it receives and ensures that all notes are given a "note off"/velocity 0 message after the duration value—in this case, *500* milliseconds.

Now, let's actually hear what this sounds like by adding the object *noteout* so that *makenote* can communicate with our soundcard.

If you hold your mouse over the two outlets of the *makenote* object, you will see that it sends MIDI pitch numbers out of the left outlet and MIDI velocity numbers out of the right outlet. The *noteout* object takes pitch numbers in its leftmost inlet and velocity numbers in its middle inlet. Unlock your patch and:

13. Create a new object called *noteout*.
14. Connect the outlets of *makenote 100 500* to the first two inlets of *noteout*.

The *noteout* object takes a number in its third inlet to specify MIDI channel number. You can also specify a default argument for MIDI channel by supplying a number in the object box after the word *noteout*. For now, we'll use the object's default MIDI channel, channel 1.

15. Lock your patch and click the *button* to generate a random number, which will be synthesized as a MIDI pitch with a velocity of *100* and a duration of *500* milliseconds.

Because the duration of each note lasts one half of a second, it would be nice to have the patch automatically generate a new random note each half a second.

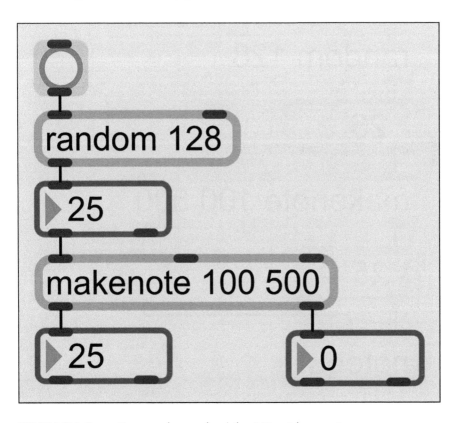

FIGURE 14.15: Generating a random number | the_RAT_patch.maxpat

## Adding Timing

The *metro* object functions like a metronome sending out bangs at a specified interval of time. The time, in milliseconds, is specified as an argument for *metro*. In the same patch, unlock your patch and:

16. Create a new object called *metro* and give it the argument *500*.
17. Create a *button*.
18. Connect the outlet of *metro 500* to the inlet of *button*.

When the *metro* object is "on," it will cause the *button* to blink (send bangs) every *500* milliseconds. To turn the *metro* on, we will use the *toggle* object.

The *toggle* object is an on/off switch for Max objects. Like a light switch, *toggle* has two states: on or off. The *toggle* is such a common object in Max that it

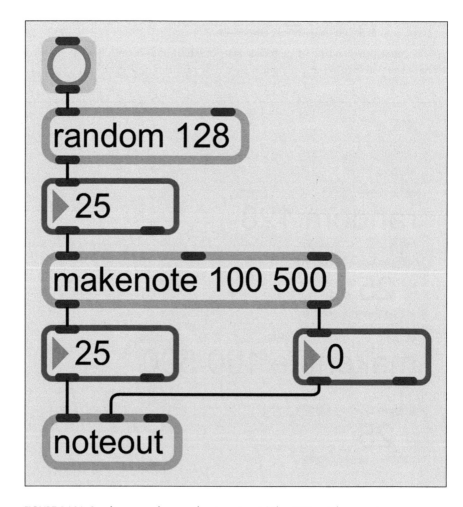

FIGURE 14.16: Sending a random number to noteout | the_RAT_patch.maxpat

has its own key command shortcut for putting the object in your patch by pressing the *t* key.

19. Create a new object called *toggle*.
20. Connect the outlet of *toggle* to the first inlet of *metro 500*.
21. Lock the patch and click on the *toggle* to turn it on.

An *X* means the *toggle* is on and that the *metro* object will begin sending out bang messages to the *button* every *500* milliseconds.

22. Click on the *toggle* again to turn it off.

The *toggle* actually only outputs the numbers *0* and *1*, where a *0* indicates that something is off and *1* indicates that something is on. We could have also sent the *metro* object a *message* box containing a *1* to turn it on, and another *message* box with a *0* in it to turn it off, but *toggle* provides a more graphical way of doing it.

Because our *metro 500* is outputting bangs, it seems we have an extra *button* in our patch. Unlock your patch and:

23. Delete the *button* connected to *metro 500*'s outlet by highlighting the *button* and pressing delete.
24. Connect the outlet of *metro 500* to the inlet of the *button* above the *random 128* object.

With the *toggle* turned on, the *metro* will trigger a random number to become synthesized every 500 milliseconds.

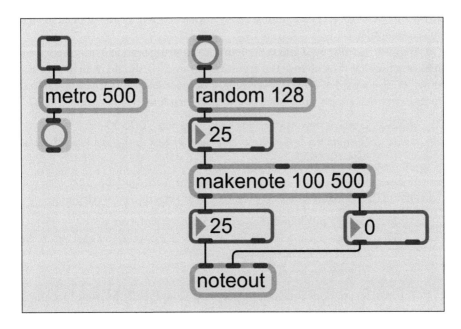

FIGURE 14.17: Trigger random notes at a set rate with metro | the_RAT_patch.maxpat

25. Lock the patch and click on the *toggle* to turn it on.
26. Click on the *toggle* again to turn it off.

This patch creates what my students and I affectionately call Random Atonal Trash, or the RAT patch.

Now that we've made our first RAT patch, we will discuss some of the ways that you can control this patch. Currently, the patch has only one control: the *toggle* to turn the patch on and off, which generates random pitches. However, there are many variables within the patch that could conceivably have controls. For instance, if you want to change the speed of the *metro*, you can send a number, either as a *message* box or a *number* box, to *metro*'s right inlet to replace *metro*'s default argument of *500*. Unlock your patch and:

27. Create a *number* box to the upper right of *metro 500*.
28. Connect the first outlet of the *number* box to *metro 500*'s second inlet.

If you change the number inside of the newly created *number* box by clicking in it (locked) and typing a new number, the number of milliseconds *metro* will wait until it sends out another bang will change from being every *500* milliseconds to whatever number you specify. (Note that the argument will actually change as soon as you click away from the object or press the return/enter key.) This is how you replace arguments for objects. Arguments don't change visually within objects just internally, so even though the *500* remains in the object box, *metro*'s argument will change to whatever you enter in the *number* box. Since we've "hard-coded" the number *500* as *metro*'s default argument, when you open the patch, the *metro* object's default time interval will be *500* milliseconds and, thus, will send out bangs every *500* milliseconds until a new number is supplied to *metro*'s second inlet.

Because *metro*'s speed and *makenote*'s duration are both 500 milliseconds, it makes sense that if we change the argument for one, we should change it for the other or else we'd have either overlapping or staccato notes. If you hold your mouse over *makenote*'s third inlet, you will see that it receives a duration value.

29. Create a new *number* box near *makenote 100 500*.
30. Connect the first outlet of this *number* box to the last inlet of *makenote 100 500*.

If you specify the same argument for both the *metro* and the *makenote*, you will ensure that generated notes are legato and not staccato or overlapping.

31. Lock the patch and click on the *toggle* to turn it on.
32. Change the arguments for *metro* and *makenote* by clicking in the newly created *number* boxes.
33. Turn the *toggle* off.

This patch functions fine as it is, but what would really be useful for those who will use this patch (your users) would be some sort of graphic object that allows you to control numbers more easily than the *number* boxes alone. One such object is the *slider* object. Unlock your patch and:

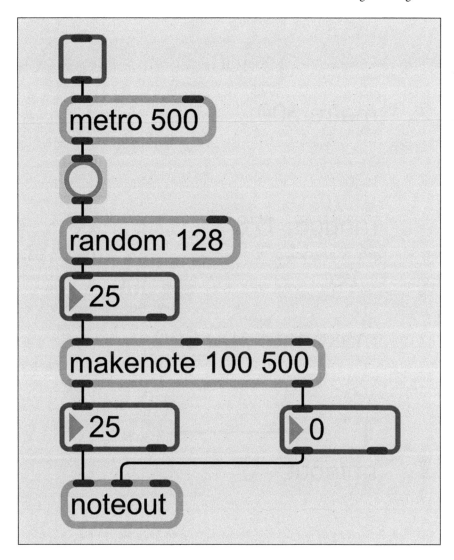

FIGURE 14.18: Creating random atonal trash | the_RAT_patch.maxpat

34. Create a new object called *slider*

When you create a new object called *slider*, the object turns into a vertical control resembling a fader on a mixing board. By default, *slider* outputs the numbers 0–127 depending on where the horizontal knob in the *slider* is positioned. If you connect the *slider* to the two number boxes that control *metro* speed and *makenote* duration, you can control both numbers simultaneously with one control.

35. Connect the outlet of *slider* to the inlet of the *number* boxes connected to the last inlet of *metro* and *makenote*.

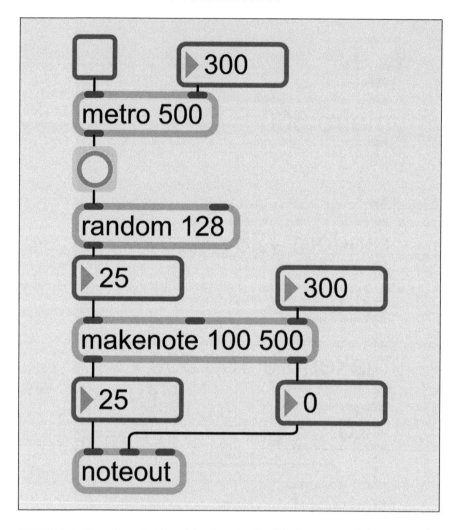

FIGURE 14.19: Control your RAT patch by changing the default arguments | the_RAT_patch .maxpat

36. Lock the patch on click on the *toggle* to turn it on.
37. Click on the *slider* and increase or decrease the horizontal knob to send the numbers 0–127 to the argument inlets of *metro* and *makenote*.
38. Turn the *toggle* off.

As I mentioned, by default, *slider* outputs numbers from 0 to 127. To increase or decrease the range of numbers *slider* outputs, open up *slider*'s *Inspector* menu. Note that the "output minimum" will offset the starting number. For example, if your *slider* range is *200* and your minimum number is 50, the *slider* will output the numbers 50–249; a range of 200 numbers. Unlock your patch and:

39. Open the Inspector for *slider* and change the range of this *slider* to *1000* and leave its output minimum at the default value 0.

You may feel that the notes come out too fast when the *slider* value is set too low. In fact, on some slower computers, if the *metro* object tries to send out bangs at a rate faster than around 20 milliseconds, it isn't always stable. To address the former concern, we can specify a minimum value for *slider* to output.

40.  In the Inspector for *slider,* set the output minimum to 20.

Because we want to make our patches foolproof, it's a good idea to put in default arguments and limits to restrict the range of numbers to known or desired values. To do this:

41.  Open the *Inspector* for the *number* box connected to *metro's* last inlet and set the *minimum* value to 20.

42.  Do the same as the previous step for the *number* box connected to *makenote's* last inlet.

Save this patch (as shown in Figure 14.20) as a "the_RAT_patch.maxpat." Before you close the RAT patch, highlight and copy the *makenote* and *noteout* objects, as we'll paste them into a new patch. This brings up a good technique: reuse working parts of patches whenever possible.

## Slider Patch

Close the old patch and create a new patch.

1.  Paste *makenote 100 500* and *noteout* into the new patch or simply create these two objects.

2.  Connect the two outlets of *makenote 100 500* to the first two inlets of *noteout.*

3.  Create a new object called *slider.*

4.  Connect the outlet of *slider* directly to *makenote 100 500's* left inlet.

5.  Lock the patch and increase or decrease the *slider* position.

In this patch, as shown in Figure 14.21, the numbers 0– 27 flow directly from *slider* to *makenote* to *noteout* without the need for any *number* boxes. Although this may save a few seconds in the creation of a new patch, it is good practice to use *number* boxes after every user interface (UI) object and other objects where the actual numbers you are working with are unclear. If something in your patch is not working right, it's much easier to locate the problem if you can see where numbers are, or are not, going. Save the patch as *the_ RAT_reused.maxpat* and close the patch.

## Rat Patch 2

Reopen the *RAT patch* you created earlier or, for good practice, rebuild the *RAT patch* from memory and select *Save As* from the *File* menu at the top. Name the file *the_RAT_patch_2.maxpat.*

As musicians, we are not used to thinking about musical time in terms of milliseconds; the *tempo* object would be more appropriate as it allows us to

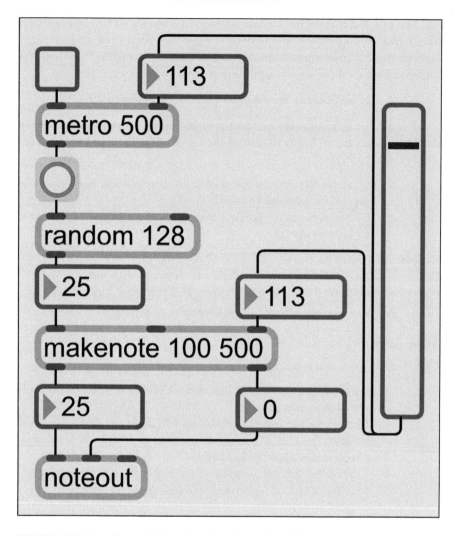

FIGURE 14.20: Control your RAT patch with UI objects like slider | the_RAT_reused.maxpat

discuss time in beats per minute, multiples of the beat, and division of the beat into notes (quarters, 8ths, 16ths, etc.). Unlock the patch and:

1. Delete the *slider* from this patch.
2. Double-click the *metro 500* object and highlight and replace the *metro 500* with the word *tempo* with the arguments *120* for initial tempo in beats per minute (BPM), *1* for beat multiplier, and *8* for beat division, in this case, the 8th note.

Our new patch with the *tempo* object, as shown in Figure 14.22, functions similarly to the original RAT patch, but we now have the ability to work with timing in terms of beat values, which musicians are typically more accustomed to working with. Currently, the *tempo* will send a bang on every 8th note at 120 beats

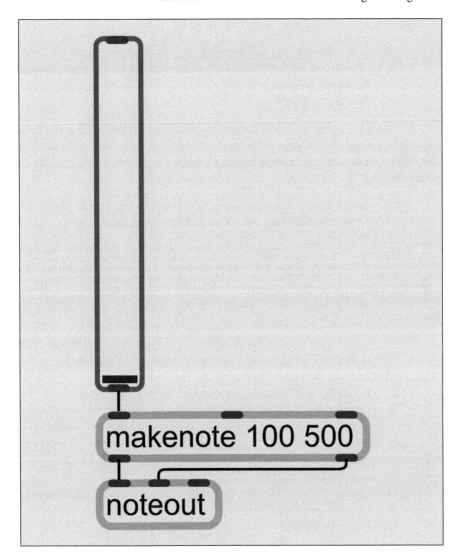

FIGURE 14.21: Slider used to generate notes | the_RAT_patch_2.maxpat

per minute. The number box that formerly controlled the *metro* time interval can now be used to control the BPM value for *tempo*. We know, from our discussion of changing default arguments, that the *8* indicating 8th notes can be changed, so let's give our patch the ability to beat whole, half, quarter, 8th, and 16th notes.

3.  Create 5 *message* boxes (press *m*) containing the number *1* for whole notes, *2* for half notes, *4* for quarter notes, *8* for 8th notes, and *16* for 16th notes, respectively.
4.  Connect the outlet of each of these 5 *message* boxes to the fourth inlet of the *tempo* object (the inlet that corresponds to the beat division value).

Other beat division values are possible, but let's start with these numbers.

> 5. Lock the patch and turn the *tempo* object on via the *toggle.*
> 6. Change the beat division of *tempo* by clicking the different *message* boxes you created.
> 7. Turn off the *toggle.*

Although we know what will happen to the tempo when you click the message 8, the average user of your patch may not understand how to use the control. Let's take a moment to make some more articulate controls to our patch. Unlock your patch and:

> 8. Create 5 new *message* boxes containing the text *Whole Note, Half Note, Quarter Note, 8th Note,* and *16th Note,* respectively.

The *tempo* object will not understand these much more descriptive *message* boxes, so we will connect these *message* boxes to the first inlet of the numerical *message* boxes you created earlier. Doing so will cause clicking on the descriptive *message* box to send a bang to the numerical *message* box that *tempo* can interpret.

> 9. Connect the outlet of the *message* box containing the text *Whole Note* to the first inlet of the *message* box containing the number *1.*
> 10. Connect the outlet of the *message* box containing the text *Half Note* to the first inlet of the *message* box containing the number *2.*
> 11. Connect the outlet of the *message* box containing the text *Quarter Note* to the first inlet of the *message* box containing the number *4.*
> 12. Connect the outlet of the *message* box containing the text *Eighth Note* to the first inlet of the *message* box containing the number *8.*
> 13. Lock the patch and turn the *toggle* on.
> 14. Change the beat division of *tempo* by clicking the descriptive *message* boxes you created.
> 15. Turn off the *toggle.*

We can create an even more descriptive *message* box that triggers both a tempo change and a beat division change by connecting its outlet to other *message* boxes containing the desired arguments (as shown in Figure 14.23). Unlock your patch and:

> 16. Create a *message* box containing the text *8th Notes at Largo.*
> 17. Create 2 *message* boxes containing the text *50* and *8,* respectively.
> 18. Connect the outlet of the *message 8th Notes at Largo* to the first inlet of the *message* boxes *50* and *8,* respectively.
> 19. Connect the outlet of *message 50* to the *number* box connected to *tempo*'s second inlet.
> 20. Connect the outlet of *message 8* to *tempo*'s last inlet.

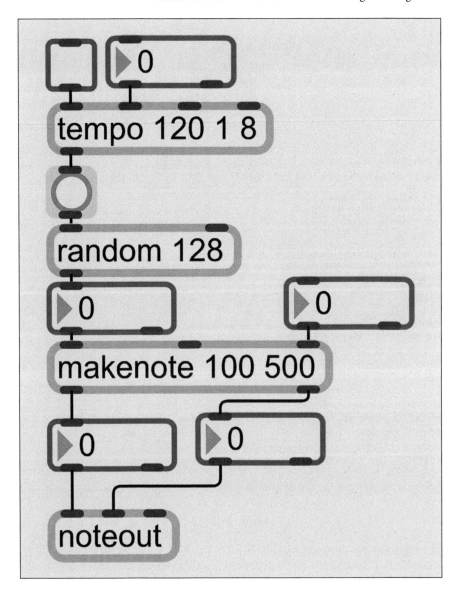

FIGURE 14.22: The RAT patch controlled in BPM instead of milliseconds | the_RAT_patch_
2.maxpat

21. Lock the patch and turn the *toggle* on.
22. Click on the *message 8th Notes at Largo* (as shown in Figure 14.24) to trigger the value *50* to be sent as an argument for the tempo and *8* to be sent as an argument for the beat division.
23. Turn off the *toggle*.

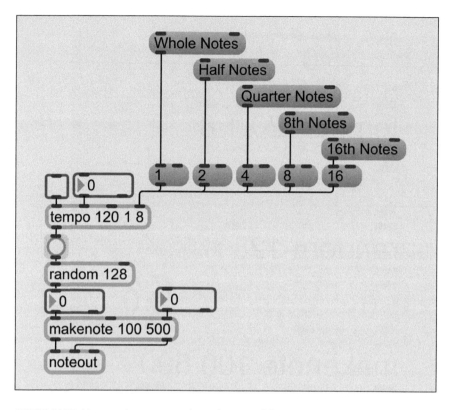

FIGURE 14.23: Message boxes trigger beat divisions of the tempo object | the_RAT_patch_2.maxpat

Note that instead of a descriptive *message* box, a single *button* could also have been used to trigger the change of multiple values. Save and close this patch.

## MIDI INPUT

The next step involves getting MIDI data into Max using a MIDI controller of some kind. If you have a MIDI keyboard or other device, take this time to connect it to your computer. You will need to close and restart Max if your device was not connected or powered up when you opened Max.

We know how to get MIDI data out of Max using the *noteout* object. We can get MIDI data into Max using the *notein* object. Create a new patch and:

1.  Create a new object called *notein*.
2.  Create 3 *number* boxes.
3.  Connect each of the three outlets of *notein* to the inlet of each *number* box, respectively.
4.  Create a new object called *noteout*.
5.  Connect the first outlet of each of the 3 *number* boxes to the three inlets of *noteout*, respectively.

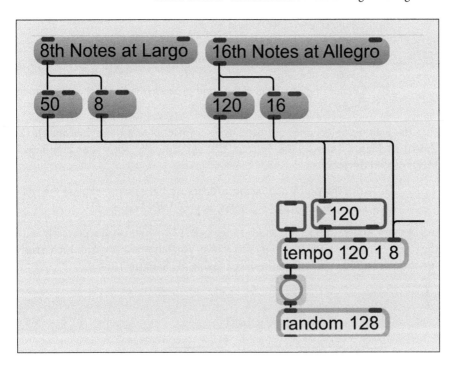

FIGURE 14.24: Message boxes trigger multiple argument changes to tempo | the_RAT_patch_2.maxpat

As you play notes on your MIDI device, you can see the numerical MIDI values for pitch, velocity, and MIDI channel displayed in the three *number* boxes (as shown in Figure 14.25). On your MIDI device, play middle C at a soft volume. The first *number* box will read *60*, and the second *number* box will read some value between 0 and 127, depending on how softly you played the note. Notice that when you take your hand off of the keyboard, you send out a velocity value of 0 for whatever pitch(es) you were playing. These velocity 0 messages are commonly referred to as note off messages. Even if you play just one key on your keyboard, multiple numbers are expressed as part of the MIDI message for that note.

The *notein* and *noteout* objects communicate with your computer's soundcard and any available MIDI devices. When the patch is locked, you can double-click on one of these objects to see a list of all MIDI devices currently connected to your computer.

MIDI data are sent on streams called channels. This allows a user to send musical data like pitches and velocity for separate instruments through a single cable without all of the separate MIDI data being merged into one instrument. Data on each MIDI channel can then be assigned to use different timbres and can even be routed to other synthesizers. Recall that, in MIDI, a program refers to the type of timbre used in the synthesis of MIDI pitches and velocities (see Chapter 5).

To change the MIDI program value in Max, use the *pgmout* object. This object allows you to send a numbers 0–127 to change the MIDI timbre.

6. Create a new object called *slider.*
7. Create a *number* box.
8. Connect the outlet of *slider* to the inlet of the *number* box.
9. Create a new object called *pgmout.*
10. Connect the first outlet of the *number* box to the first inlet of the *pgmout* object.

The *pgmout* object does not need to be connected to any further objects (as shown in Figure 14.26). Like *noteout*, it communicates with your computer's MIDI output devices.

11. Lock the patch and increase/decrease the *slider* to change the MIDI program while playing notes on your MIDI keyboard.

As you know, the default *slider* range is 0–127, which works perfectly with the range of numbers that *pgmout* can receive. You have now programmed a fully functional MIDI keyboard synthesizer capable of changing timbre.

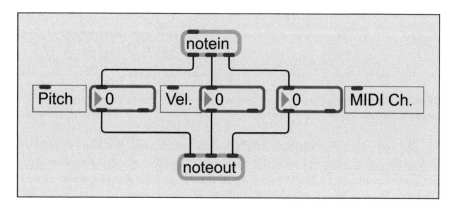

FIGURE 14.25: Basic MIDI device input | MIDI_IO.maxpat

Your MIDI keyboard sends other types of MIDI data besides pitch, velocity, program, and channel. Your controller likely has two wheels on the lefthand side: one marked modulation and one marked pitch bend. These wheels send data into Max using the *ctlin* object and the *bendin* object. (Most MIDI controllers have one wheel that is adjusted to return to its middle state and another that is freely moveable. As a result, the *bendin* object will consistently return to the same place to report a value of *64*, the middle of *128*, when the wheel is at rest.)

Let's make an instrument in which pitch is controlled by the modulation wheel and velocity is controlled by the pitch bend wheel. Unlock your patch and:

12. Create a new object called *ctlin,*
13. Create a *number* box,
14. Connect the first outlet of *ctlin* to the inlet of the *number* box,
15. Create a new object called *bendin,*
16. Create a *number* box,

17. Connect the first outlet of *bendin* to the inlet of the *number* box,
18. Create a *makenote* object with the arguments *100* and *300*,
19. Connect the first outlet of the *number* box receiving from *ctlin* to the first inlet of *makenote 100 300*,
20. Connect the first outlet of the *number* box receiving from *bendin* to the second inlet of *makenote 100 300*,
21. Create a new object called *noteout*,
22. Connect both outlets of *makenote 100 300* to the first two inlets of *noteout*,

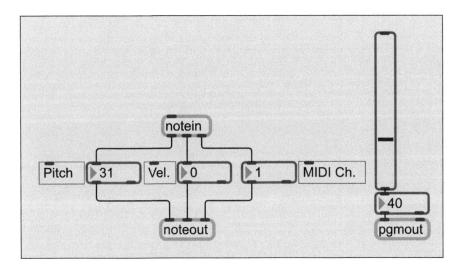

FIGURE 14.26: Send MIDI program changes through pmout | MIDI_IO.maxpat

You will now be able to control notes and velocity just by moving the two wheels. Give it a try.

Because this "wheel" synthesizer is going to exist in the same patch as the functional keyboard synthesizer we made earlier, we should specify its *noteout* object to exist on MIDI channel 2 by supplying the argument *2* to *noteout*. To be consistent, let's go back and supply an argument of *1* for our keyboard synthesizer. With your patch unlocked:

23. Double-click the *noteout* object receiving from the *ctlin* and *bendin* and type the number 2 next to it.
24. Double click the *noteout* object receiving from the *notein* and type the number 1 next to it.

Now that our MIDI data is operating on two different channels, we can change aspects of the instrument, such as timbre, on one channel without changing the other.

25. Highlight the *slider, number* box, and *pgmout* entity and copy/paste it to the right of the *ctlin* and *bendin* entity.

26. Double-click the newly copied *pgmout* object on the right and type the number 2 next to it.
27. Double-click the *pgmout* object you made earlier (Step 9) and type the number 1 next to it.

Specifying MIDI channel arguments for the *noteout* and *pgmout* objects will allow the "keyboard" synth and the "wheel" synth to use different MIDI programs simultaneously without interfering with each other because they are on separate MIDI channels, 1 and 2.

28. Lock the patch and set both *sliders* to different values, then use the MIDI keyboard and mod wheels to produce notes in some way

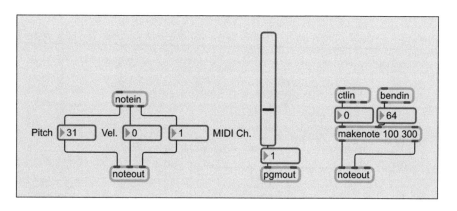

FIGURE 14.27: Mapping wheel data to pitch and velocity | MIDI_IO.maxpat

In this example, we were able to make a musical instrument by mapping numbers in a novel way. In traditional synthesizers, the wheels are not mapped to pitch and velocity, but since those controls are really just sending out numbers, we, as programmers, can map those numbers to anything we want.

In Max, mapping is everything. Furthermore, unlike other commercial music-creation software, there are no rules in Max that dictate how a program should function. If you were to try to get your favorite music notation software to interpret wheel data as pitches and velocity like we just did, the software would say, "You're crazy!" In Max, it's all just numbers, and you can use those numbers in any way you want. You can use video game controllers to play pitches, use camera tracking to trigger drum samples, and even implement Max inside of Ableton Live!

## SUMMARY

Music programming is useful for facilitating your own creative ideas for which a technological tool either does not exist or the existing programs don't meet your needs. Graphical "dataflow"-style programming languages like those used in Max are easier for nonprogrammers to work with than traditional text-based languages.

The dataflow concept from one programming object to another is similar to the way that a musician or engineer might envision the flow of an audio signal from a microphone to an audio effect to a mixer, and so on. This chapter will not turn you into an expert programmer, but as you continue to facilitate your musical ideas with technology, you may find it liberating to be able to write your own apps instead of relying on software teams to cater to your specific interests. To quote the title of Douglas Rushkoff's 2011 book: *Program or Be Programmed!* If you've enjoyed using Max/MSP/Jitter and the pace at which the concepts were presented, you may enjoy the book *Max/MSP/Jitter for Music* (Manzo, 2011).

## KEY CONCEPTS

- Max/MSP/Jitter is a dataflow, graphical programming language.
- We connect programming objects in a dataflow approach in the same way that we connect audio equipment sequentially to transform a live signal.
- In a programming language, we learn each object as if it was a new word in our language and combine it with other objects/words to make complete applications/sentences.
- In order to learn the language quickly, read the Help and Reference files for each object discussed.
- Computers facilitate randomness quite objectively and easily and can be used in the creative process.
- Creating unique apps provides a level of autonomy in terms of your creative goals.

## KEY TERMS

| | | |
|---|---|---|
| argument (Max) | inlet (Max) | patcher/patch (Max) |
| bang (Max) | outlet (Max) | programming language |
| function/object | patch cord (Max) | |

# GLOSSARY

**1/8″ TRS cables** Small mini-phone cables as would fit a headphone jack.

**A to D (analog to digital)** Process by which analog sounds, such as acoustic instruments, are converted to a representation of digits, also called a digital signal.

**acousmatic music** Variant of electroacoustic music in which works are intended to be performed by loudspeakers instead of traditional human instrumental performers. See also *electroacoustic music*.

**acoustics** Field of study related to the properties of sounds as they travel through the air or other mediums. See also *psychoacoustics*.

**additive synthesis** Type of synthesis in which waves are summed to created new timbres. When referring to audio, for example, the harmonic series can be expressed as a function by which a simple sine wave oscillating at a fundamental frequency can be multiplied by numbers to produce additional waves called *overtones*. The sum of the fundamental frequency and its overtones produces a synthetized collection of waves, which are summed at the output and perceived as a single timbre. See also *synthesis*.

**ADSR/ADSR envelope** Attack, decay, sustain, release sound profile that describes how the sound evolves or some time. See also *envelope*.

**algorithmic composition** Compositional method in which specific processes are used in the creative process. Commonly used to describe computer-based methods, though technology is not a requisite as in the case of many composers that predate digital technology.

**all pass filter** Type of audio filter in which "all" frequencies received at the input are permitted to "pass" through the output. See also *band* and *equalization*.

**amplitude** Height or "level" of a wave over a period of time. When referring to audio, for example, the amplitude of a signal is sometimes described in terms of "loudness" and "volume" when, in fact, terms like "strength" and "level" are more accurate descriptors. However, when the amplitude of a periodic sine wave is increased, the height of the wave is increased and the output is a perceived change in loudness.

**amplitude modulation (AM) synthesis** Type of synthesis by which waves are multiplied together to produce new timbres. The amplitude of one wave, known as the carrier, is determined by the amplitude of another wave, known as the modulator, which dips up and down at some rate of the modulator's frequency. The amplitude of the modulator signal is controlled differently than in the AM synthesis variant *ring modulation*. See also *ring modulation*.

**analog audio** Electrical signal captured by the microphone traveling in the signal flow, which is "analogous" to, or a representation of, the sound source originally captured by the microphone. In modern techniques, this conversion from analog signals to digital ones takes place using an analog-to-digital, or A-to-D, converter. The reverse operation from digital to analog is facilitated using a digital-to-analog converter, or DAC. See also *digital audio*.

**argument (Max)**   Value associated with an object that sets the current state for a variable.

**attack**   Initial onset of sound. See also *ADSR* and *envelope.*

**attack time**   Elapsed time it takes for the initial onset of sound to reach its peak before it begins to decay. See also *ADSR* and *envelope.*

**audio interface/sound card/recording interface**   Device for converting analog audio signals into digital streams of data such that may be used in computer recording. See also *A to D.*

**audio snake**   Bundled group of individual cables used to transmit multiple channels of audio over great distances. Usual implementation is for a junction box of female jacks to be left on a stage and for the male jacks to be connected to a mixer.

**automation**   Operation, typically in a DAW, by which effect parameters, volume, panning, and other events are sequenced to occur over time. In many DAWs, automation instructions are drawn within the timeline of the session so that automated events coincide with musical ones.

**band (frequency)**   Group of frequencies representing some part of the audible spectrum. A three-band frequency would divide the audible spectrum into three bands such as "low," "mid," and "high," or "bass," "midrange," and "treble."

**bandpass filter**   Type of audio filter in which specific groups or "bands" of frequencies received at the input are permitted to "pass" through the output. See also *band* and *equalization.*

**bang (Max)**   An event in Max.

**bank**   In MIDI devices, a bank typically holds a number of presets. See also *patch.*

**beat interference**   Sonic phenomenon resulting from the interference between two similar frequencies. The phenomenon produces an effect similar to tremolo. See also *tremolo.*

**beats per measure (BPM)**   With regard to tempo, the number of beats that occur in each measure as related to the pulse of the performance.

**bins**   Resultant samples from performing an FFT on a signal. See also *Fast Fourier Transform (FFT).*

**bit**   A binary digit.

**bit depth**   In digital audio, the number of bits used to represent an analog signal when it is converted to a digital signal.

**bleed**   In recording, the nature of unintended audio to come through a particular microphone.

**boost**   In audio, increasing the decibel level of a signal to some extent.

**breakpoint function**   Various points in a curve such as the attack, decay, sustain, and release points in an ADSR envelope. See also *ADSR.*

**carrier/carrier signal**   In modulation synthesis, the carrier is the signal that has some property changed by the modulator signal.

**carrier/modulator ratio**   In FM synthesis, the frequency value of the carrier signal as it relates to the modulator signal expressed as a ratio.

**channel**   Independent stream of audio or MIDI.

**chorus**   In audio, an effect in which the pitch of a delayed copy of a signal is altered and, optionally, combined simultaneously with the original signal. See also *delay.*

**clip** In audio, the distorted result of an increase in gain beyond what the system's "headroom" can allow; in Live, an audio file that may be played back.

**clipping** In audio, the nature of a signal to become increased beyond the level of what can be reproduced by the system. When referring to waves, for example, the amplitude of a wave may be increased to the point that the wave's height is truncated or "clipped" off, resulting in a distortion timbral change. See also *distortion*.

**comb filter** In audio, a type of filter in which signals are delayed and introduced back into the signal in order to produce feedback; a process that causes certain frequencies to resonate.

**compression** In sound propagation through air, the nature of molecules to be forced to close proximity before they expand in the rarefaction process. See also *rarefaction*.

**compression/compressor** In signal processing, an audio effect in which the high and low gain portions of the signal are adjusted toward a uniform level.

**condenser microphone** Sensitive microphone type best placed in locations where you would feel comfortable putting your ear. See also *dynamic microphone*.

**conduction** In acoustics, the transmission of sound through the air (air conduction), bone (bone conduction), or some other medium.

**control device/control interface/controller** In MIDI configurations, devices that transmit MIDI values to a synthesis module or other MIDI reception device.

**controller/continuous control (CC)** In MIDI, CC messages are reserved for transmitting performance messages like "bank select," "modulation," "volume," and "pan" changes, and so on.

**crossover** In speakers and sound systems, a crossover is the mechanism by which frequencies above and below a specified value are allocated to various speakers—typically, to a subwoofer for very low frequencies below the crossover value and to a full-range PA speaker for the remaining midrange and high-range frequencies.

**cut** In audio, a cut refers to a reduction in gain, also sometimes referred to as a "pad."

**cycle** In sound waves, a cycle is a completion of a wave from its starting point to its highest and lowest peak and the return to its point of origin.

**data-driven algorithmic composition** Type of process that is informed, in some manner, by a set of data, commonly, by analyzing a sampled set of data and using that information in the process. See also *algorithmic composition* and *rule-based algorithmic composition*.

**DC offset** In audio recording, an instance where the mean value of the amplitude is a nonzero number as a result of the recording process, commonly a positive number. The correction of removing DC offset recenters the waveform around 0.

**decay time** In an ADSR curve, the time between the point when the initial attack ends and the sustain begins. See also *ADSR*.

**decibel (dB)** Reference point used when measuring sound pressure levels (SPLs). For example, one might measure the SPL of a microphone input and determine that a person's normal speaking voice measures at 60 dB. See also *sound pressure level*.

**definite pitch/indefinite pitch**   In music, a definite pitch can be audibly recognized as a "singable" pitch with one of 12 pitch letter names. An indefinite pitch is one that is heard but that cannot be heard as having a "singable" pitch, such as a kick drum or the pitch of a door slamming shut.

**delay**   In audio, an effect in which a copy of a sound source is replayed at some specified time after the original. Many effects result from the simple *delay* effect and, in particular, additional signal processes that may be carried out on delayed copies of the original.

**diffraction**   In acoustics, the manner in which sound waves bend around an object in the space of a room or other environment. When referring to audio, for example, the way that sound waves ultimately approach your ears at a concert will vary depending upon the properties of objects in front of and around you. If you buy a ticket for a seat behind a large post, instead of hearing nothing, the sound waves will bend, to some degree, around the beam before they reach your ears.

**diffusion**   In acoustics, the manner in which sound waves spread out evenly within the space of a room or other environment. For example, sounds playing in a perfectly diffuse room would sound the same in every part of the room without the sound reverberating or becoming colored by the room's architecture and objects in the room.

**digital audio**   Conversion of an analog signal into numbers that the computer can understand. In modern techniques, this conversion from analog signals to digital ones takes place using an analog-to-digital, or A-to-D, converter. The reverse operation from digital to analog is facilitated using a digital-to-analog converter, or DAC. See also *analog audio*.

**digital audio workstation (DAW)**   In audio recording, a system in which the use of hardware like a computer is integral to the audio production process; it is common, however, for individuals to refer to the audio editing software itself, like Pro Tools, Live, or Logic, as the DAW.

**direct box/DI**   Device used for converting unbalanced instrument signals through a ¼″ input jack from guitars and basses to a balanced signal through an XLR output jack.

**distortion**   In audio, a timbral change resulting from signal clipping. In music, the effect is produced through a number of methods including increasing the signal level in amplifiers to distort speakers, tubes, and other components. Effects processors produce variant qualities of distortion such as fuzz, overdrive, and more. See also *clipping*.

**dynamic microphone**   Microphone that is best positioned close to the sound source. See also *condenser microphone*.

**effects chain**   In audio, the order of effects as they are applied to an input signal.

**effects units**   In professional audio, stand-alone hardware effects devices that may be mounted into an equipment rack or onto a musician's "stombox" pedalboard.

**electroacoustic music** Compositional method and musical genre in which sounds are, generally, created either entirely or in some part by electronic methods. Common performance practice may involve acoustic instruments that perform with electronic sounds or may exclusively involve electronic mechanisms. Composers in this genre include Mario Davidovsky and Morton Subotnick. See also *acousmatic music*.

**envelope** The "shape" of the sound as it relates to timbre. It is associated with *ADSR* curves (attack, decay, sustain, release), which determine how the sound evolves or some time. Aspects of the envelope may also be expressed in a so-called *breakpoint function* in which multiple points are used to represent aspects of the motion of a sound's properties over time.

**equal temperament** A tuning system in which, in Western art music, the 12 notes in the octave are divided equally.

**equal-loudness contours** In perception, a model in which data inform a mechanism of adjusting frequencies so that they are perceived as sounding at equal levels; this includes the famous Fletcher-Munson curve. See also *phon*.

**equalization (EQ)** the process of "tone-shaping" through the use of level controls applied to specified bands of the audible spectrum. For example, a three-band EQ would divide the audible spectrum into *low-*, *mid-*, and *high-frequency* bands and use a control to adjust the level of each group of *banded* frequencies. See also *wah-wah*.

**Fast Fourier Transform (FFT)** In audio, a process by which the *Fourier transform* is carried out on a sound or signal resulting in the discretizing of individual waves from a complex waveform. When referring to audio, for example, running an FFT on a sound can reveal information about the frequencies present in the sound, which can be plotted graphically. In general, an FFT is useful in transferring information about a signal from the *time domain* to the *frequency domain*.

**feedback** In audio, the concept of output signals from a speaker or other source returning to the microphone or other input source. In live sound, this likely produces a squealing sound also known as feedback.

**filter** In audio, a process by which some feature present in the sound is removed, be it a band of frequencies, a specific frequency, or some other quality.

**flanger** In audio, an effect in which the phase of a delayed copy of a signal is offset by a gradually changing time value and, optionally, combined simultaneously with the original signal. See also *delay*.

**frequency** The periodic vibration of a wave. When referring to audio, for example, the range of human hearing, 20 Hz to 20 kHz, comes into consideration by which a wave periodically vibrating at a rate of 440 times per second, or "cycles per second," would be said to be have a frequency of 440. A wave oscillating at 440 Hz is the frequency that is often used as a tuning reference for the note *A*.

**frequency modulation (FM) synthesis** Type of synthesis by which waves are multiplied together to produce new timbres. Specifically, the frequency of one wave, known as the carrier, is changed, or "modulated," by changing the frequency of another wave, known as the modulator. When referring to audio, the wave modulation of FM synthesis produces distorted and bell-like timbral effects that are rich in overtones. See also *synthesis*.

**function/object** In Max programming, an object is a base function by which larger programs as built such as an addition or subtraction object that, when combined with other objects, creates a larger and more sophisticated programming function.

**fundamental frequency** In a harmonic series or timbre, the bass and lowest tone frequency in the wave form. See also *harmonic series*.

**gain** Measure of the ability to increase the amplitude of a signal. When referring to audio, a gain control on a mixing board is used to increase the amplitude of a signal on a channel. Gain controls are able to boost the signal by using components within the mixer's preamplifier section.

**gain stage** Point in the signal chain, usually at the input level, where a signal is boosted by a gain control. See also *gain*.

**gate** In audio, process by which an incoming signal must exceed a set threshold in order to be passed through to the output. Devices that produce a gate are called *gates*.

**General MIDI** Formalized standard for the MIDI protocol specification.

**generative algorithmic composition** In composition, methods that use sets of rules to produce complete musical output from the stored fundamental material.

**gestalt effect** In perception, the concept of our brain forming groups, patterns, and other forms based on positioning, similarity, and other factors.

**grains** In granular synthesis, tiny slices of recorded audio that are manipulated in the synthesis process. See also *granular synthesis*.

**granular synthesis** Type of synthesis by which small slices of a recorded waveform are manipulated to produce new timbres. When referring to audio, the size of the small slices of a recorded sound, referred to as grains, are played, looped, and manipulated to produce "clouds" of sound.

**harmonic series** In music, a set of multiples of a fundamental frequency. In whole number multiples, the fundamental frequency is the first harmonic (frequency × 1), and the second harmonic is the result of the fundamental frequency × 2, referred to as the first overtone, and so on. See also *fundamental frequency* and *timbre*.

**hertz (Hz)** In audio, a unit of frequency representing one cycle per second. See also *frequency*.

**Hi-Z (high impedance)** In audio, a classification of input and output signals, like guitar, basses, and their associated accessories typically possess, sometimes referred to as instrument level. These terms, and in particular the symbol Z, refer to the concept of resistance, or impedance, which is associated with signal strength and flow. See also *microphone level signal* and *instrument level signal*.

**highpass filter** Type of audio filter in which specific groups or "bands" of frequencies received at the input are permitted to "pass" through the output. See also *band* and *equalization*.

**impulse response** In audio, a technique of observing the sound properties of a room or other system by introducing a sound or signal of known sonic properties, such as a balloon burst or a click.

**-inf/negative infinity decibels** In audio, the lowest level of gain at which no signal is transmitted.

**inlet** In Max programming, the port by which a programming object receives data from other objects. See also *outlet*.

**input** In audio, the port, or jack, by which a signal is received into a device from another source. In effects processors like reverbs, a signal received at the input port would be sent to the output port with the effected reverb. The nature of audible signals sent to a device may also be referred to as the "input" signal. See also *output*.

**installation** In music, an environment in which an individual experiences an artistic gesture often involving some level of interaction or close-up observation.

**instrument level signal** In audio, a classification of microphone level input and output signals, like guitar, basses, and their associated accessories typically possess, sometimes referred to as instrument level. See also *Hi-Z* and *microphone level signal*.

**interactive music system** In music, a hardware or software configuration that allows an individual to accomplish a musical task, typically in real time, through some interaction.

**Karplus-Strong string synthesis** In synthesis, an algorithm that produces a plucked string sound derived from modeling existing plucked string instruments. See also *physical modeling*.

**kilohertz (kHz)** In audio, a unit of frequency representing one cycle per second times 1,000. See also *frequency* and *hertz*.

**latency** In audio recording, the amount of delay a system unintentionally introduces at the recording or playback stage, usually the result of computer processing resource limitations.

**limiter** In audio, an effects device that compresses a signal as it reaches a peak level threshold to prevent clipping. See also *compression*.

**line level** Signal strength of a device like a keyboard synthesizer, a CD/DVD player, or other audio component. When referring to audio, by contrast, an electric guitar or bass guitar does not output a *line level* signal but instead outputs a much weaker signal commonly said to be at the *instrument level signal*.

**Lo-Z (low impedance)** In audio, a classification of input and output signals, like microphones and direct boxes, sometimes referred to as "microphone level," versus the other classification of microphone level, "instrument level." These terms, and in particular the symbol Z, refer to the concept of resistance, or impedance, associated with signal strength and flow. See also *microphone level signal* and *instrument level signal*.

**loop**  In audio, a prerecorded or precomposed pattern of audio or MIDI data intended to be repeated for compositional purposes, similar to ostinatos in the traditional sense.

**lossy/lossless compression**  In audio, a type of file size reduction in which the recording compromises some quality by removing some audible material in exchange for smaller file sizes. Lossless compression, by contrast, allows the "lost" material to be restored, such as in the case of ".zip" files.

**low-frequency oscillation (LFO)**  Slow-moving frequency, usually between 20 and 100 Hz, that is used to change timbral qualities of another frequency or sound source. When referring to audio, the timbral change is usually perceived as vibrato (changes to a wave's pitch) or tremolo (changes to a wave's amplitude). LFOs are particularly useful for adding expressivity to synthesized sounds.

**many-to-one mapping**  In system design, the concept of controlling many variables with a single control. See also *mapping* and *one-to-one mapping*.

**mapping**  In computer science, the term is used to describe the correspondence of one set of data with another set. See also *many-to-one-mapping* and *one-to-one mapping*.

**Markov chains**  In artificial intelligence and mathematics, a system that deals with making choices based on randomness or by memory of previous choices. See also *algorithmic composition*.

**masking**  a perception phenomenon by which one sound, or timbral aspects of that sound, are hidden or obscured by the presence of other sounds. When referring to audio, the tone of a singer's voice may be masked, or obscured, in the context of a full ensemble, requiring a sound engineer to boost the certain frequencies of the singer's voice in order to "cut through the mix" and be heard.

**mastering**  Process by which a piece of music is finalized and made ready for distribution. The process often involves mixing the project down to a stereo file and working with processes like compression, EQ, and limiting to ensure that the final mix is balanced and at a reasonable level.

**microphone level signal**  In audio, a classification of microphone level input and output signals, like microphones and direct boxes, sometimes also referred to as "microphone level," versus the other classification of microphone level, "instrument level." These terms, in particular the symbol Z, refer to the concept of resistance, or impedance, which is associated with signal strength and flow. See also *Lo-Z* and *instrument level*.

**MIDI In**  In MIDI, the input port of a MIDI device for receiving MIDI data from controllers and other MIDI devices from the MIDI output port of other MIDI devices. See also *Musical Instrument Digital Interface*.

**MIDI Out**  In MIDI, the output port of a MIDI device for sending MIDI data from controllers and other MIDI devices to the MIDI input port of other MIDI devices. See also *Musical Instrument Digital Interface*.

**MIDI Thru**  In MIDI, the thru port of a MIDI device that typically duplicates the information received at the MIDI In port and passes the information "thru" without altering it. See also *Musical Instrument Digital Interface*.

**Musical Instrument Digital Interface (MIDI)** Protocol that computers use to convey musical messages using numbers. When referring to audio, for example, the numbers 0–127 are commonly used to represent musical concepts like pitch and dynamics.

**mixer, or mixing console, or sound board** Device used for combining and balancing audio channels from a variety of inputs. For example, a mixer may have eight channels by which eight microphones are connected to its input jacks. The level of each microphone can be adjust by an engineer in order to produce a balanced or "mixed" signal sent to speakers, headphones, a recorder, or some other output destination.

**modulation** In synthesis, the nature of changing one signal's properties by way of another signal. See also *synthesis*.

**modulator/modulator signal** In synthesis, the signal that acts as an independent variable and changes the properties of a carrier signal. See also *carrier signal* and *FM synthesis*.

**mono** In audio, a single track of audio, versus stereo, two discrete tracks of audio intended to be played through a left speaker and a right speaker. See also *stereo*.

**musicing** In music, term used by philosopher David Elliot to describe the process of being musical or exemplifying musicianship.

**MusicXML** In music notation software, a type of universal protocol for conveying notated information like pitches, dynamics, and even some musical markings.

**musique concrète** Compositional method and musical genre in which recorded sounds are manipulated to produce new sounds. Composers in this genre include Pierre Schaeffer. See also *electroacoustic music*.

**note off message (MIDI)** In MIDI, messages that specify the MIDI pitch value being performed and a velocity value of 0 in order to cease a note from sounding. See also *Musical Instrument Digital Interface*.

**omnidirectional microphone** In audio, a microphone pattern that picks up sound in all directions. See also *unidirectional microphone*.

**one-to-one mapping** In system design, the concept of controlling a single variable with a single control. See also *mapping* and *many-to-one mapping*.

**Open Sound Control (OSC)** Protocol like MIDI that conveys information about musical events and more with the potential for greater bandwidth than MIDI. See also *Musical Instrument Digital Interface*.

**oscillator** Mechanism that causes a wave to vibrate at some rate. When referring to audio, for example, an oscillator may be used to generate a sine wave. A hardware or software oscillator, as in the case of synthesizers, will generally have a control knob in order to adjust the rate of oscillation, which ultimately changes the perceived pitch of the oscillating wave.

**outlet (Max)** In Max programming, the port by which a programming object receives data from other objects. See also *inlet*.

**output** In audio, the port, or jack, by which a signal is sent through a device once that device has performed its intended action. In effects processors like reverbs, a signal received at the input port would be sent to the output port with the effected reverb. The nature of audible signals from a device may also be referred to as the "output" signal. See also *input*.

**overdubbing**  In audio, process of layering recorded audio on top of previously recorded audio.

**overtones/harmonics**  In music, multiples of a fundamental frequency in which a base frequency, alone, is the first harmonic (frequency × 1) and the second harmonic is the fundamental frequency × 2, also referred to as the first overtone.

**panning**  In audio, the level of a sound signal being present in one or more speakers in stereo or multichannel speaker configurations.

**partials**  In music, short for "harmonic partial," a term used synonymously with the "harmonic." A partial may also be used to refer to any wave in a complex waveform. See also *harmonic series* and *harmonic*.

**patch cord (Max)**  In Max programming, the connection mechanism between an object's outlet and another object's inlet. See also *object, inlet,* and *outlet*.

**patch/program**  In MIDI, a sound module may organize preset instrument timbres into patches or programs within a bank of sounds. See also *bank*.

**patcher/patch (Max)**  In Max programming, the basic document by which objects are placed and programs built. See also *object*.

**phantom center**  In perception, the phenomenon in which a center audio source in stereo setups is mentally constructed despite the absence of a physically placed center speaker.

**phase**  In phase difference, the time between two identical waves. When referring to audio, the phase effect produces a jet engine sound as the amount of time between the start of two identical sounds is shifted.

**phase cancellation**  In audio, the process by which two inverse waves combine to create a 0 signal output. Such technology is used in noise-canceling headphones and other head-related transfer functions (HRTFs).

**phon**  Unit of measuring sound pressure levels with regard to loudness. As phons increase or decrease, the perceived loudness of frequencies also changes, thus equal-loudness contours change in response to the number of phons. See also *equal-loudness contours*.

**physical modeling**  In audio, a process by which a computer is used to represent aspects of a sound source by analyzing the sonic properties of the sound source and reconstructing a model to replicate the properties. The process of physical modeling involves analyzing every aspect of the sound source, such as the way sound reflects and emanates from every direction of a piano including from the lid, under the lid, off of the legs, and so on. A physical computer model can allow some aspects of the instrument, such as its playable range, to be expanded beyond the physical size of the instrument.

**piano roll editor (MIDI)**  In DAWs, a graphical representation of MIDI notes vertically according to pitch and horizontally according to duration. See also *Musical Instrument Digital Interface* and *digital audio workstation*.

**pickup**  In audio, a type of transducer used in electric instruments, like guitar and bass, that functions similarly to a microphone. See also *microphone*.

**Ping Pong Delay** In audio, a type of delay effect by which delayed sounds are sent to multichannel speakers. See also *delay*.

**pink noise** In audio, a noise source similar to white noise with different spectral qualities and a perceived low-pass filter when compared to white noise. See also *white noise*.

**plug-in** In audio software, a software application that may be used inside of a DAW or within software, often developed by a different party. For example, a company like Antares makes autotune plug-in that is intended to be used within a DAW and not as a standalone. DAWs specify the supported plug-in extensions, which often include the file formats VST, AU, or other.

**port** In audio equipment, a jack or connection input type designed to receive signals from connected cables.

**power amplifier or power amp** Component that boosts a signal to the level necessary to drive a speaker. When referring to audio, for example, a microphone signal enters the *preamp* section of a mixer's amplifier section, where the channel is mixed with other channels. The mixed channel is the sent from the master outputs of the mixer to power amplifiers that boost the level of the signal in order to cause the loudspeakers to move, reproducing the sound.

**preamplifier or preamp** Component that prepares a signal for processing or additional amplification, such as a *power amplifier*. When referring to audio, for example, a guitar signal enters the *preamp* section of the amplifier, where tone and other timbral processing occurs. The signal then travels to the power amp section, where the resulting level is boosted considerably to drive speaker movement.

**program change (MIDI)** In MIDI, the change from one General MIDI sound set timbre to another. Like other MIDI data, General MIDI program changes are numbered between 0 and 127. See also *Musical Instrument Digital Interface* and *General MIDI*.

**programming language** In computer science, a constructed mechanism for conveying information within a system. Common programming languages include C, C++, Javascript, HTML, Java, PHP, Python, and so on.

**psychoacoustics** Branch of acoustics that deals with perception. See also *acoustics*.

**Q (band shape)** In audio, the width of the band for a group of frequencies. See also *band*.

**quantization** In MIDI, process of "smoothing" MIDI data by repositioning notes to the nearest beat division. See also *digital audio workstation* and *Musical Instrument Digital Interface*.

**rarefaction** In sound propagation through air, the nature of molecules expanding after being forced into close proximity in the compression process. See also *compression*.

**RCA connection/cable** In audio, a connection type usually used in consumer-grade electrical components like DVD players and karaoke machines, though sometimes used in professional audio equipment as well.

**release time** In an ADSR curve, the amount of time a sound takes to reach silence after the sustain portion. See also *ADSR*.

**resistance/impedance**  In audio, the nature of a signal flow to be resisted, or impeded. Low impedance, or Lo-Z, means low resistance and denotes a stronger output. High impedance, or Hi-Z, means high resistance, and denotes a weaker signal flow. See also *Hi-Z* and *Lo-Z*.

**resonance**  In acoustics, the propensity of the amplitude of certain frequencies to become more prominent than others. Instruments, rooms, and objects have a frequency for which they will vibrate in sympathy when other sources produce that frequency.

**reverb**  In audio, the nature of a sound continuing to resound in a space after the original sound source has ceased. Numerous factors contribute to the process, which may be through of in terms of multiple delayed copies of an original signal. See also *delay*.

**ReWire**  Software protocol in which one program may be used as a "slave" device for another program. In many ways, the ReWire protocol can be used to treat entire applications like "plug-ins" for other applications. See also *plug-in*.

**ring modulation**  A simple implementation of amplitude modulation by which two signals are multiplied together. The amplitude of one wave, known as the carrier, is determined by the amplitude of another wave, known as the modulator, which dips up and down at some rate of the modulator's frequency. See also *amplitude modulation*.

**rule-based algorithmic composition**  Type of composition process that is informed, in some manner, by a set of rules; commonly, by rules related to voice-leading, harmony, form, and so on. See also *algorithmic composition* and *data-driven algorithmic composition*.

**sample**  In audio, the process by which a sound is recorded and used in playback. See also *sample-based synthesis* and *sampler*.

**sample-based synthesis**  In audio, the process by which recorded files, or samples, are played back to emulate the realistic sounds of acoustic instruments. See also *sample* and *sampler*.

**sampler**  Device used to play back recorded sound files known as *samples*. A sampler may also include the option to record samples. Samplers may be hardware or software based. For example, a software sampler like *Kontakt* by Native Instruments contains large libraries of prerecorded *sample* audio files. A sampler then plays these samples back when control messages are received from a DAW, a MIDI keyboard, or some other input.

**sampling rate**  In audio, the rate by which some part of the sound spectrum is recorded; by default in most DAWs, the rate is 44,100 samples per second. See also *digital audio workstation*.

**scene (Live)**  In Live, a scene represents an array of audio clips posited for playback. See also *clip*.

**sequenced algorithmic composition**  In composition, the use of prerecorded music fragments in response to some real-time input. Some aspects of these fragments may be varied in performance, such as tempo playback, dynamic shape, slight rhythmic variations, and so on.

**Shepard Tones** In psychoacoustics, the perception that a pitch appears to be infinitely rising.

**side-chain compression** In audio, a type of compression technique in which the envelope of the compressor is determined by the sonic characteristics of some other input source such as a kick drum. See also *compression*.

**side-chain effects** Type of effect parameter by which, typically, the envelope of the effect is determined by the level of another signal such as a waveform. Many types of side-chain effects exist. Side-chain compression, for example in club music, may use a steady kick drum beat to control the envelope of the compressor effect on another instrument like a synthesizer.

**sidebands** In synthesis, frequencies that occur higher and lower than a center frequency, often known as the carrier frequency. When referring to audio, for example, the nature of frequency modulation (FM) synthesis creates sideband frequencies that surround the carrier frequency as a result of multiplying waves. See also *frequency modulation*.

**signal** Function that expresses information about a system. When referring to audio, for example, an LED on the input channel of the mixer might indicate the presence of a signal traveling from a microphone to a mixer.

**signal path/signal chain/signal flow** In audio, the devices or components by a signal may travel "from" origin to destination. See also *signal* and *mixer*.

**sound** Wave of pressure oscillating at some frequency that travels through air, water, or some other medium. When referring to audio, for example, sounds are created and heard.

**sound module** In MIDI, a device by which MIDI data is synthesized into an audio signal. See also *Musical Instrument Digital Interface*.

**sound pressure level (SPL)** Measure of sound levels using a reference point such as the decibel. Measuring SPLs around a referenced value is different than measuring the perceived "loudness" of a sound source. See also *decibel*.

**speakers** In audio, devices used for transmitting audio signals. See also *mixer*, *crossover*, and *power amp*.

**spectrogram or sonogram** Visual representation of some observed range, or "spectrum," of frequencies. When referring to audio, for example, a spectrogram may be used to observe the ways that room acoustics alter the timbre of sounds by virtue of sound reflection, reverberation, and other properties.

**spectrum** In audio, the entire range of frequencies that can be perceived or analyzed.

**stage monitor** In audio, a speaker placed on a stage allowing performers to hear certain signals in the mix. See also *mixer* and *speaker*.

**stems** In audio recording, mixed and rendered individual recorded tracks of audio that represent the totality of an instrument that collectively constitute the overall performance. See also *digital audio workstation* and *track*.

**stereo** In audio, two discrete tracks of audio intended to be played through a left speaker and a right speaker, versus mono, a single track of audio. See also *mono*.

**stereo pair** In audio, two speakers used to play back stereo audio. See also *stereo* and *speaker*.

**stochastic music** Compositional method in which some aspects of the work are based on deterministic and probabilistic properties. Composers in this genre include Iannis Xenakis, who is credited with coining the term. See also *algorithmic composition*.

**subtractive synthesis** Type of synthesis by which frequencies from a sound source or complex waveform are "filtered out" or removed to produce a new timbre. When referring to audio, a subtractive synthesizer may start with a white noise clip as its initial sound source and use equalization, or EQ, techniques to change the timbral qualities of the sound. See also *equalization*.

**sustain** In audio, the level by which a sound plateaus after its decay and before its release. See also *ADSR*.

**synthesis** In audio, a process of combining, multiplying, or subtracting waves and other sounds in order to make new sounds or emulate existing ones. When referring to audio, additive synthesis is a process by which sine waves are added to create new timbres, whereas subtractive synthesis begins with all frequencies present, and filters certain frequencies to create new timbres.

**synthesizer** Device that facilitates synthesis. In most cases a synthesizer has controls like keyboard keys, knobs, and buttons to manipulate parameters in the synthesis process. See also *synthesis*.

**threshold** In audio, the level by which a process may occur; in gate effects, for example, a threshold level is set to enable the effect when an input signal reaches the established threshold level. See also *input, gate,* and *limiter*.

**timbre** Quality of a sound as related to its frequency spectrum. When referring to audio, for example, timbre is the aspect of an instrument's sound that explains how the same concert pitch, such as *middle C*, played by various instruments produces different tonal qualities. It is related to the design of the instrument and its acoustical properties. See also *harmonic series*.

**tone or tone color** In audio, terms used to described the balance of frequencies in a sound as related to its timbre. See also *timbre* and *equalization*.

**tracks** In audio recording, individual streams of audio or MIDI with a DAW. See also *digital audio workstation*.

**transformative algorithmic composition** In composition, methods that take some existing musical material and apply transformation to it to produce variants.

**tremolo** Process by which the amplitude of a wave is varied at some periodic rate. When referring to audio, a tremolo produces an effect where the volume of a sound appears to slowly duck in and out at same rate. It should not be confused with vibrato, where fluctuations in pitch occur instead of amplitude.

**TRS (tip, ring, sleeve) cable** In audio, a balanced cable by which a signal is transmitted with a ground such as might be used with a keyboard synthesizer output or a rack effect connected to a mixer. See also *XLR cable* and *Lo-Z*.

**TS (tip and sleeve) ¼" cable/instrument cable**  In audio, an unbalanced cable by which a signal is transmitted without a ground such as might be used with an electric guitar or bass. See also *Hi-Z*.

**Type 0 MIDI file**  In MIDI, files in which all instrument tracks have been merged into a single MIDI channel. See also *Musical Instrument Digital Interface*, *MusicXML*, and *Type 1 MIDI file*.

**Type 1 MIDI file**  In MIDI, files in which multiple instrument tracks are stored on different MIDI channels. See also *Musical Instrument Digital Interface*, *MusicXML*, and *Type 0 MIDI file*.

**U/unity gain**  In audio, the level by which neither an increase nor a reduction in gain is applied to an incoming signal. See also *input* and *mixer*.

**unidirectional microphone**  In audio, a microphone pattern that picks up sound in a single direction. See also *omnidirectional microphone*.

**vibrato**  In audio, an effect by which the perceived pitch of a signal is changed at some periodic rate. See also *low-frequency oscillation* and *tremolo*.

**virtual instrument software**  In audio recording, a software-based synthesizer module by which MIDI data is realized. See also *digital audio workstation*, *Musical Instrument Digital Interface*, *plug-in*, and *sound module*.

**wah-wah**  In audio, an effect that allows an individual to sweep through an EQ filter using a foot-controlled pedal or some automatic mechanism. For example, the wah-wah guitar effect operates like the filter of an EQ but adds the performance functionality of a foot-pedal. An auto-wah may use some time variant to sweep between filter settings within a performance. See also *equalization*.

**wave/soundwave**  In audio, a periodic signal of some shape, as in a sine wave, a square wave, a triangle wave, or other shaped wave; a wave may be composed of many waves creating a complex waveform. See also *frequency*, *cycle*, and *hertz*.

**wavelength**  In acoustics, the distance between two waves. Generally, the distance from the crest of one wave to that of another measures wavelength. Waves with higher frequencies have shorter wavelengths; because each cycle of the wave occurs faster than lower-frequency waves, the length of each wave is inherently shorter. Low-frequency waves, thus, have longer wavelengths.

**wavetable synthesis**  In synthesis, an approach that uses a stored set of values that represent what an instrument waveform looks like instead of combining individual sine waves. See also *synthesis* and *additive synthesis*.

**wet/dry**  In audio, the control on an effect device that determines the output balance of the input signal before the effect is applied and the signal after the effect is applied. See also *digital audio workstation*.

**white noise**  In audio, a noise source consisting of the presence of all frequencies in a spectrum. See also *pink noise* and *subtractive synthesis*.

**XLR cable**  In audio, a cable type by which balanced signals, like microphone signals, are transmitted as opposed to unbalanced signals, like instrument signals from electric guitars and basses. See also *Lo-Z* and *Hi-Z*.

**Z (symbol)**  In audio, the symbol that denotes resistance, or impedance, in a signal flow. See also *Lo-Z* and *Hi-Z*.

# REFERENCES

Ammers, R. J. (2012). Technology-Based Music Classes in High Schools in the United States. *Bulletin for the Council of Research in Music Education, 194*, 73–90.

Amos, E. (2010). *Composite cables.* [Photograph]. Retrieved August 17, 2013, from http://en.wikipedia.org/wiki/File:Composite-cables.jpg

Anderson, B. (2007). Melltroon. [Photograph]. Retrieved August 17, 2013, from http://commons.wikimedia.org/wiki/File:Mellotron.jpg

Arfib, D., Couturier, J. M., Kessous, L., & Verfaille, V. (2002). Strategies of mapping between gesture data and synthesis model parameters using perceptual spaces. *Organised Sound: Cambridge University Press, 7*(2), 127–144.

Bauer, W. (2014). *Music learning today: digital pedagogy for creating, performing, and responding to music.* New York: Oxford University Press.

Boyd, M. (2000). Bach. New York: Oxford University Press.

Broadbent, D. E. (1958). *Perception and communication.* New York: Macmillan.

Butler, D. (1989). Describing the perception of tonality in music: A critique of the tonal hierarchy theory and a proposal for a theory of intervallic rivalry. *Music Perception, 6*, 1219–1242.

Butler D. (1990a). A study of event hierarchies in tonal and post-tonal music. *Psychology of Music, 18*, 4–17.

Butler D. (1990b). Response to Carol Krumhansl. *Music Perception, 7*, 325–338.

Carterette, E. C., & Kendall, R. A. (1989). Human music perception. In R. J. Dowling & S. H. Hulse (eds.), *The comparative psychology of audition: Processing complex sounds* (pp. 131–172). Hillsdale, NJ: Lawrence Erlbaum Associates.

Chittka L., & Brockmann A. (2009). *Anatomy of the human ear.* [Photograph]. Retrieved August 17, 2013, from http://en.wikipedia.org/wiki/File:Anatomy_of_the_Human_Ear.svg

Chomsky, N. (1957). *Syntactic structures.* The Hague, the Netherlands: Mouton.

Chomsky, N. (1965). *Aspects of the theory of syntax.* Cambridge, MA: MIT Press.

Chomsky, N. (1968). *Language and mind.* New York: Harcourt Brace Jovanovitch.

Construct 2. (2014, February). Scirra Construct 2. Retrieved from http://www.scirra.com

Cope, D. (1987). "An Expert System for Computer-Assisted Music Composition." Computer Music Journal 11,4 (Winter): 30–46.

Cope, D. (1987). "Experiments in Music Intelligence." In Proceedings of the International Computer Music Conference, San Francisco: Computer Music Association.

Cope, D. (1988). "Music and LISP." AI Expert 3,3 (March): 26–34.

Cope, D. (1988). "Music: The Universal Language." In Proceedings of the First Workshop on Artificial Intelligence and Music. Minneapolis/St. Paul, MN: AAAI: 87–98.

Cope, D. (1989). "Experiments in Musical Intelligence (EMI): Non-Linear Linguistic-based Composition." Interface Vol. 18: 117–139.

Cope, D. (1990). "Pattern Matching as an Engine for the Computer Simulation of Musical Style." In Proceedings of the 1990 International Computer Music Conference. San Francisco: Computer Music Association.

Cope, D. (1990). "Recombinant Music." COMPUTER. (July).

Cope, D. (1991). "Computer Simulations of Musical Style." Computers in Music Research, The Queens University of Belfast, 7–10 (April): 15–17.

Cope, D. (1991). Computers and Musical Style. Madison, WI: A-R Editions.

Cope, D. (1992). "A Computer Model of Music Composition." In Machine Models of Music, Stephan Schwanauer and David Levitt, eds. Cambridge, Mass.: MIT Press.

Cope, D. (1992). "Computer Modeling of Musical Intelligence in Experiments in Musical Intelligence." Computer Music Journal 16,2 (Summer): 69–83.

Cope, D. (1992). "On the Algorithmic Representation of Musical Style." In Understanding Music with AI, M. Balaban, K. Ebcioglu, and O. Laske, eds. Menlo Park, Calif.: AAAI Press.

Cope, D. (1993). "Virtual Music." *Electronic Musician*, 9(5) (May), 80–85.

Cope, D. (1996). *Experiments in musical intelligence*. Madison, WI: A-R Editions.

Cope, D. (1996). "Mimesis du style et de la structure musicale." Symposium on Composition, Modelisation et Ordinateur. IRCAM, Paris: 21–3.

Cope, D. (1997). "Composer's Underscoring Environment." In *Proceedings of the International Computer Music Conference*. San Francisco: Computer Music Association.

Cope, D. (1997). "The Composer's Underscoring Environment: CUE." *Computer Music Journal* 21/3 (Fall).

Cope, D. (1999). "One Approach to Musical Intelligence." Intelligent Systems. Los Alamitos, CA: IEEE Computer Society (14/3, May/June).

Cope, D. (1998). "Signatures and earmarks: Computer recognition of patterns in music." In *Melodic similarity, concepts, procedures, and applications*. Walter B. Hewlett and Eleanor Selfridge-Field (eds.). Cambridge, MA: MIT Press.

Cope, D. (2000). "Facing the Music: Perspectives on Machine Composed Music." *Leonardo Music Journal 9*, 79–87.

Cope, D. (2000). *Techniques of the contemporary composer*. NY: Schirmer Books Press.

Cope, D. (2000). *New directions in music*. 7th ed. Prospect Heights, Illinois: Waveland Press.

Cope, D. (2000). *The algorithmic composer*. Madison, WI: A-R Editions.

Cope, D. (2001). *Virtual music*. Cambridge, MA: MIT Press.

Cope, D. (2002). "Computer Analysis and Composition Using Atonal Voice-Leading Techniques." Perspectives of New Music 40/1 (Winter): 121–146.

Cope, D. (2003). "Computer Analysis of Musical Allusions." *Computer Music Journal* 27/1: 11–28.

Cope, D. (2004)." A Musical Learning Algorithm." *Computer Music Journal* 28/3: 12–27.

Cope, D. (2005). *Computer models of musical creativity*. Cambridge, MA: MIT Press.

Cope, D. (2007). "Composing with Algorithms: An Interview with David Cope (Keith Muscutt)." *Computer Music Journal* 31/3 (Fall): 10–22.

Cope, D. (2008). "Preface: The OM Composer's Book - Vol. 2." IRCAM.

Cope, D. (2008). *Tinman: A life explored*. Bloomington: IUniverse.

Cope, D. (2009). *Hidden structure: Music analysis using computers*. Madison, WI: A-R Editions.

Crowe, B. J. (2004). Implications of technology in music therapy practice and research for music therapy education: A review of literature. *Journal of Music Therapy, 41*(4), 282–320.

Cuddy, L. L. (1982). On hearing pattern in melody. *Psychology of Music, 10*, 3–10.

Cuddy, L. L., Cohen, A. J., & Mewhort, D. J. K. (1981). Perception of structure in short melodic sequences. *Journal of Experiments in Psychology: Human Perception and Performance, 7*, 869–883.

Demorest, S. M., Morrison, S. J., Jungbluth, D., & Beken, M., (2008). Lost in translation: An enculturation effect in music memory performance. *Music Perception: An Interdisciplinary Journal, 25*(3), 213–223.

Deutsch, D., & Boulanger, R. C. (1984). Octave equivalence and the immediate recall of pitch. *Music Perception, 2*(1), 40–51.

Deutsch, D., Moore, F. R., & Dolson, M. (1984). Pitch classes differ with respect to height. *Music Perception, 2*(2), 265–271.

DiBlasio, N. (January 10, 2013). Performing arts face strikes, layoffs, bankruptcy. In USA Today. Retrieved May 21, 2014, from http://usatoday.com/story/news/nation/2013/01/10/orchestra-financial-strike-budget/1806511/.

Dowling, W., & Harwood, D. (1986). *Music cognition.* Orlando, FL: Academic Press.

Elpus, K., & Abril, C. (2011). High school music students in the United States: A demographic profile. *Journal of Research in Music Education, 59*(2), 128–145.

Elliott, D. (1995). *Music matters: A new philosophy of music education.* New York: Oxford University Press.

Elliott, D., & Silverman, M. (2014). *Music matters: A philosophy of music education.* New York: Oxford University Press.

ETS. (2010). *Music: Content knowledge (0113).* Retrieved from http://www.ets.org/Media/Tests/PRAXIS/pdf/0113.pdf

Everest, F. A. (2000). *The master handbook of acoustics.* New York: McGraw-Hill.

Farnsworth, P. R. (1969). *The social psychology of music* (2nd ed.). Ames: Iowa State University Press.

Feitscherg. (2005). *Pickups Humb 2Single.* [Photograph]. Retrieved August 17, 2013, from http://en.wikipedia.org/wiki/File:Pickups_Humb_2Single.jpg

Fergusson, I. (2006). *The Shure SM58 microphone.* [Photograph]. Retrieved August 17, 2013, from http://en.wikipedia.org/wiki/File:Shure_SM58.jpg

Fergusson, I. (2007). *X/Y or coincident pair stereo microphone technique using cardioid mics at 90°.* [Photograph]. Retrieved August 17, 2013, from http://en.wikipedia.org/wiki/File:XY_stereo.svg

Fletcher, H., & Munson, W. A. (1933). Loudness, its definition, measurement and calculation. *Journal of the Acoustical Society of America, 5*(2), 82–108.

Freedman, B. (2013). *Teaching music through technology.* New York: Oxford University Press.

Green, L. (2002). *How popular musicians learn.* Aldershot, UK: Ashgate Publishing Limited.

Green, L. (2008). *Music, informal learning and the school: A new classroom pedagogy.* Surrey, UK: Ashgate Publishing Limited.

Goudeseune, C. (2002). Interpolated mappings for musical instruments. *Organised Sound: Cambridge University Press, 7*(2), 85–96.

Grannis, E. (2012, August). Orchestras fight hard times through bankruptcy seeking new model. Retrieved March 21, 2014, from http://www.bloomberg.com/news/2012-08-21/orchestras-fight-hard-times-through-bankruptcy-seeking-new-model.html

Hicks, Michael. (2000). *Sixties rock: Garage, psychedelic, and other satisfactions.* Champaign: University of Illinois Press.

Hofmann-Engl, L. (2008). The Tristan Chord in Context. Retrieved May 12, 2015, from http://www.chameleongroup.org.uk/research/The_Tristan_Chord_in_Context.pdf

Hunt, A. & Wanderly, M. (2002). Mapping performer parameters to synthesis engines. *Organised Sound: Cambridge University Press, 7*(2), 97–108.

Iko1992. (2012). *Eboardmuseum 3b.* [Photograph]. Retrieved August 17, 2013, from http://en.wikipedia.org/wiki/File:Eboardmuseum_3b.jpg

International Organization for Standardization. (n.d.). *ISO 226:2003.* Retrieved March 10, 2009, from International Organization for Standardization: http://www.iso.org/iso/iso_catalogue/catalogue_tc/catalogue_detail.htm?csnumber=34222

Kamilbaranski. (2010). *M-Audio Firewire 410.* [Photograph]. Retrieved April 30, 2014, from http://en.wikipedia.org/wiki/File:M-Audio_Firewire_410_top.jpg

Kennicott, P. (August 25, 2013). Orchestras in Crisis: Outreach is Ruining Them. In New Republic. Retrieved May 21, 2014, from http://www.newrepublic.com/article/114221/orchestras-crisis-outreach-ruining-them.

Koehler, M. J., & Mishra, P. (2008). Introducing TPCK. In J. A. Colbert et al. (eds.), *Handbook of technological pedagogical content knowledge for educators* (pp. 1–29). New York: Routledge.

Krumhansl, C. L. (1979). The psychological representation of pitch in a musical context. *Cognitive Psychology, 11,* 364–374.

Krumhansl, C. L. (1990). *Cognitive foundations of musical pitch.* New York: Oxford University Press.

Krumhansl, C. L., Bharucha, J. J., & Kessler, E. J. (1982). Perceived harmonic structure of chords in three closely related musical keys. *Journal of Experimental Psychology: Human Perception and Performance, 8*(1), 24–36.

Krumhansl, C. L., & Kessler, E. J. (1982). Tracing the dynamic changes in perceived tonal organization. *Psychological Review, 89*(4), 334–368.

Kuhn, W. (2012). Reaching the Other 80% by Adding Music Technology to Your Curriculum. TRIAD, 96–98.

Levitin D. J., McAdams, S., & Adams, R. (2002). Control parameters for musical instruments: a foundation for new mappings of gesture to sound. *Organised Sound, 7*(2), 171–189.

Lindosland. (2005). *Equal-loudness contours.* [Photograph]. Retrieved August 17, 2013, from http://en.wikipedia.org/wiki/File:Lindos1.svg

Lipscomb, S. D. (1996). The cognitive organization of musical sound. In D. A. Hodges (ed.), *Handbook of music psychology* (2nd ed.), (pp. 133–175). San Antonio, TX: IMR Press.

Lundin, R. W. (1967). *An objective psychology of music* (2nd ed.). New York: Ronald Press.

Machover, T. (1992, January). Hyperinstruments - A Progress Report 1987–1991. Retrieved April 25, 2012, from http://opera.media.mit.edu/publications/machover_hyperinstruments_progress_report.pdf

Mann, S. (2006). Hydraulophone design considerations: absement, displacement, and velocity-sensitive music keyboard in which each key is a water jet. *Proceedings of 14th Annual ACM International Conference on Multimedia* (Santa Barbara, CA: International Multimedia Conference archive), pp. 519–528.

Manzo, V. (2005, January). *Cliché progresions.* Retrieved from http://www.clicheprogressions.com

Manzo, V. (2006, January). *The modal object library: A collection of algorithms to control and define modality.* Retrieved from http://www.vjmanzo.com/mol

Manzo, V. (2007a, Winter). *EAMIR* [The electro-acoustic musically interactive room]. Retrieved from http://www.eamir.org

Manzo, V. (2007b, January). *The EAMIR software development kit (SDK).* Retrieved from http://www.eamir.org

Manzo, V. (2010, May 5). *Computer-aided composition with high school non-music students.* Temple University, Philadelphia. Retrieved from http://www.vjmanzo.com/automata

Manzo, V. (2011a, June 14). *Polyphony as bias in determining harmony.* Temple University, Philadelphia. Retrieved from http://www.vjmanzo.com/clients/vincemanzo/scores/abstracts/Polyphony_as_Bias_in_Determining_Harmony.pdf

Manzo, V. (2011b, January). Software-assisted composition instruction for non-music students. *TI:ME News, 3*(1), 3–9. Retrieved from http://www.vjmanzo.com/clients/vincemanzo/TIMENews_Winter2011.pdf

Manzo, V. (2011c). *Max/MSP/Jitter for music*. New York: Oxford University Press.

Manzo, V. (2014). Software-assisted harmonic function discrimination. *Journal of Music, Technology & Education (JMTE), 7*(1), 23–37(15).

Manzo, V. J., & Dammers, R. (2010, August). *Interactive music technology curriculum project (IMTCP)*. Retrieved from http://www.imtcp.org

Manzo, V. J., Halper, M., & Halper, M. (2011). Multimedia-based visual programming promoting core competencies in iT education [Tools & environments]. In *Association for Computing Machinery SIGITE National Conference: Vol. 1. Proceedings of the 2011 ACM Special Interest Group for Information Technology Education Conference* (pp. 203–208). West Point, NY: Association for Computing Machinery.

Manzo, V., & Kuhn, W. (2015). *Interactive composition*. New York: Oxford University Press.

Meyer, L. B. (1956). *Emotion and meaning in music*. Chicago: University of Chicago Press.

Meyer, L. B. (1967). *Music, the arts and ideas*. Chicago: University of Chicago Press.

Meyer, L. B. (2001). Music and emotion: Distinctions and uncertainties. In P. N. Juslin & J. A. Sloboda (Eds.), *Music and emotion: Theory and research* (pp. 341–360). Oxford: Oxford University Press.

Mursell, J. L. (1937). *Psychology of music*. New York: W. W. Norton.

NASM. (2012, January 25). *Handbook 2011–2012*. Retrieved from http://nasm.arts-accredit.org/site/docs/Handbook/NASM_HANDBOOK_2011-12.pdf

Oh, J., & Wang, G. (2011). "Audience Participation Techniques Based on Social Mobile Computing." In Proceedings of the International Computer Music Conference. Huddersfield, UK.

Oteri, F. J. (Interview with Tod Machover). (1999). *Technology and the future of music*. Retrieved May 25, 2011, from NewMusicBox: http://www.newmusicbox.org

Pask, A. (Interviewer) & Oliveros, P. (Interviewee). (2007). *The adaptive use instruments project*. Retrieved July 11, 2011, from Cycling '74: http://cycling74.com/2007/12/07/the-adaptive-use-instruments-project/

Pedersen, S. (2005). *Jack Plug*. [Photograph]. Retrieved August 17, 2013, from http://en.wikipedia.org/wiki/File:Jack_plug.png

Piotrowski, M. (2005). *XLR Connectors*. [Photograph]. Retrieved August 17, 2013, from http://en.wikipedia.org/wiki/File:Xlr-connectors.jpg

Radocy, R. E., & Boyle, J. D. (2003). *Psychological foundations of musical behavior* (4th ed.). Springfield, IL: Charles C. Thomas.

Reccius, M. (2009). *Triton rack adjusted*. [Photograph]. Retrieved August 17, 2013, from http://en.wikipedia.org/wiki/File:Triton_rack_adjusted.jpg

Robinson, D. W., & Dadson, R. S. (1956). A re-determination of the equal-loudness relations for pure tones. *British Journal of Applied Physics, 7*(5), 166–181.

Rowe, R. (1993). *Interactive music systems*. Cambridge, MA: MIT Press.

Rubin, D. (2007). *Inside the Blues, 1942 to 1982*. Hal Leonard. Milwaukee, Wisconsin: Hal Leonard Corporation, p. 61.

Rudolph, T., Richmond, F., Mash, D., Webster, P., Bauer, W. I., & Walls, K. (2005). *Technology strategies for music education*. Wyncote, PA: TI:ME Publications.

Rushkoff, D. (2011). *Program or be programmed: Ten commands for a digital age*. New York: Soft Skull Press.

Scanlon, L. (October 1, 2003). *Toy symphony maestro.* In MIT Technology Review. Retrieved April 4, 2014, from http://www.technologyreview.com/news/402057/toy-symphony-maestro/.

Schenker, H. (1979). *Free composition* (E. Oster, ed. & trans.) (originally published, 1935). New York: Longman.

Schlegel, A., & Lane, J. (2013). An exploratory study of adult amateur musicians' identification of instrumental timbre. *Bulletin of the Council for Research in Music Education, 196,* 65–79.

Schogler, B. (2010). *Skoog music.* Retrieved Oct. 24, 2011, from Http://www.skoogmusic.com: Http://www.skoogmusic.com

Serafine, M. L. (1983). Cognitive processes in music: Discoveries and definitions. *Council for Research in Music Education, 73,* 1–14.

Shakespeare, W. (1992). *The tragedy of Hamlet, prince of Denmark* (B. A. Mowat & P. Werstine, eds.). New York: Washington Square-Pocket.

Sheldon, D. A. (1999, Fall). The effects of live accompaniment, intelligent digital accompaniment, and no accompaniment on musicans' performance quality. *Journal of Research in Music Education, 47*(3), 251–265.

Shepard, R. N. (1964). Circularity in judgments of relative pitch sequences. *Journal of the Acoustical Society of America, 36*(12), 2346–2353.

Shulman, L. S. (1986). Those who understand: Knowledge growth in teaching. Educational Researcher, 15(4).

Sloboda, J. A. (1985). *The musical mind.* Oxford, UK: Clarendon Press.

Sloboda, J. A. (1991, October). Music structure and emotional response: Some empirical findings. *Psychology of Music, 19*(2), 110–220.

Sloboda, J. A. (2005). *Exploring the musical mind.* New York: Oxford University Press.

Super Mario Brothers [video game]. (1985). Tokyo, Japan: Nintendo EAD.

Taylor, J. A. (1976, Winter). Perception of tonality in short melodies. *Journal of Research in Music Education, 24*(4), 197–208.

Ten, J. (2013). *Solid State Logic SL4064G.* [Photograph]. Retrieved August 17, 2013, from http://en.wikipedia.org/wiki/File:Solid_State_Logic_SL4064G%2B.jpg

Terhardt, E. (1987). Gestalt principles and music perception. In W. A. Yost & C. S. Watson (Eds.), *Auditory processing of complex sounds* (pp. 157–166). Hillsdale, NJ: Lawrence Erlbaum Associates.

Thomas, R. B. (1970). *MMCP synthesis: A structure for music education.* Bardonia, NY: Media Materials, Inc.

Tiemann, M. (2006). *Photo of Buchla 200e patched to provide asymmetric portamento rates for up and down intervals.* [Photograph]. Retrieved August 17, 2013, from http://commons.wikimedia.org/wiki/File:Buchla_200e.jpg

Timohummel. (2006). *Teleharmonium 1897.* [Photograph]. Retrieved August 17, 2013, from http://en.wikipedia.org/wiki/File:Teleharmonium1897.jpg

Unity 3D. (2014, February). *Unity.* Retrieved from http://www.unity3d.com

Vienna Symphonic Library. "VSL Studio Chat with Danny Elfman." YouTube, April 4, 2014. Accessed April 10, 2014.

VK1LW. (2012). *Audio multicore cable with XLR connectors and stage box.* [Photograph]. Retrieved August 17, 2013, from http://en.wikipedia.org/wiki/File:Audio_multicore_cable_with_XLR_connectors_and_stage_box.JPG

Watson, C. S. (1973). Psychophysics. In B. B. Wolman (Ed.), *Handbook of general psychology* (pp. 275–306). Englewood Cliffs, NJ: Prentice-Hall.

Watson, S. (2005). *Technology guide for music educators.* Boston: Artist Pro Publishing.

Watterman, M. (1996, April). Emotional responses to music: Implicit and explicit effects in listeners. *Psychology of Music, 24*(1), 53–67.

Wel, R. V. D. (2011). Retrieved July 5, 2011, from My Breath My Music Foundation: http://www.mybreathmymusic.com

West, R., Howell, P., & Cross, I. (1985). Modelling perceived musical structure. In P. Howell, I. Cross, & R. West (Eds.), *Musical structure and cognition* (pp. 21–52). London: Academic Press.

Wikipedia-ce. (2006). *File:HalberstadtBurchardiChurchOrganForOrgan2ASLSP.jpg.* [Photograph]. Retrieved April 16, 2014, from http://en.wikipedia.org/wiki/File:HalberstadtBurchardiChurchOrganForOrgan2ASLSP.jpg

Williams, D. B. (2012). The non-traditional music student in secondary schools of the United States: Engaging non-participant students in creative music activities through technology. *Journal of Music, Technology, and Education, 4* (2 & 3).

# INDEX

# BIOGRAPHY

 **V. J. Manzo** (PhD Temple University, M.M. New York University) is Assistant Professor of Music Technology and Cognition at Worcester Polytechnic Institute (WPI). He is a composer and guitarist with research interests in theory and composition, artificial intelligence, interactive music systems, and music learning. V.J. is the author of the book *MAX/MSP/Jitter for Music* on programming software-based interactive music systems for composition, performance, instruction, and research and co-author of the book *Interactive Composition* on creating and performing interactive music, both published by Oxford University Press. For more information visit vjmanzo.com.

Printed in the USA/Agawam, MA
June 9, 2022

794110.004